# BEING THERE

## OTHER BOOKS BY JOHN DILLON

*The Middle Platonists (1977/1996)*
*Salt and Olives:*
*Morality and Custom in Ancient Greece (2004)*
*The Heirs of Plato: A Study of the Old Academy (2005)*
*The Roots of Platonism (2018)*
*The Lockdown Papers (2021)*

## AS EDITOR

*The Greek Sophists (Penguin Classics, 2003)*
*The Enneads by Plotinus (Penguin Classics, 1991)*
*Tourism and Culture in Philosophical Perspective,*
*Marie-Elise Zovko & John Dillon (Springer Verlag, 2023)*

## FICTION

*The Scent of Eucalyptus (2019)*

# BEING THERE

## TRAVEL DIARIES, 1970S – 1980S

## JEAN & JOHN DILLON

KATOUNIA
PRESS

*Being There: Travel Diaries 1970s-1980s*
1st Edition
Published by Katounia Press,
Dublin, 2023

www.KatouniaPress.com

ISBN: 978-1-8383454-3-3

*This book is set in "Aviano Royale", "Mrs Eaves" and Palatino fonts, sourced from Adobe Creative Cloud, 2023.*

Photo credits:

Pages: 95, 96 (top), 97, 98, 183, 84, 185, 186 (bottom), 247 (top), 250 sourced from Dreamstime.com

p.247: *The Bay, Paros*: Athanasios K. Vionis

Pages: 86, 96 (portraits), 186 (top),248, 249, Dillon family private collection.

Cover photo: Adobestock.com/Orange Studio

*All text originates from original diary entries written as it happened by the authors.*

# TABLE OF CONTENTS:

# ℬIOGRAPHICAL 𝒩OTE

*Jean Dillon* (née Montgomery) was trained as an artist and graphic designer, studying in Rome (1961-3), and later in Dun Laoghaire, and is one of the founding members of the Leinster Print Studio. Her works are in a number of private collections. She originally painted in oils, but turned to print-making after her return to Ireland from Berkeley in 1980. After her marriage in 1965, however, she devoted herself primarily, both in Berkeley from 1966 to 1980, and back in Dublin after that, to running a household.

*John Dillon* is Regius Professor of Greek (Emeritus) at Trinity College, Dublin. Born in 1939, in Madison Wisc., U.S.A, but returned to Ireland in 1946. Educated at Oxford (B.A., M.A.), and University of California at Berkeley (Ph. D.). On faculty of Dept. of Classics, UC Berkeley,1969-80 (Chair of Dept. 1977-80); Regius Professor of Greek, Trinity College, Dublin, 1980-2006. His main focus of research has been Greek philosophy, and in particular Plato and the Platonic Tradition.

# 𝒾NTRODUCTION

My wife Jean and I have never kept narrative diaries of our daily lives in general – simply the usual notes of appointments to be kept and visits made – but we did, from the mid-1970s on, develop the habit of making detailed records of our trips abroad, and it is these that I have decided to preserve in a more permanent form, in the perhaps presumptuous hope that they may be of some interest to a wider public, and to later generations. The travels are a mixture of family holidays – initially just the two of us, but then, from the mid-1980s onwards, joined by our daughter Ruth (b. August 1982), affectionately known as 'The Mouse' – and jaunts undertaken by me in connection with academic conferences and other get-togethers. Up to the autumn of 1980, we were based in Berkeley, California, as I was still on the faculty of Classics in the University of California there, though we tended to return to Ireland for the summer months. From the summer of 1980 on, our base became Drumnigh House, Portmarnock, as I returned to take up the position of Regius Professor of Greek in Trinity College, Dublin. Only the first three journeys, in fact, belong to the former period.

It cannot be claimed that our travels were particularly ground-breaking or intrepid. While based in America, we did achieve a road-trip across the continent, and a visit to the antiquities of Yucatan. After our return to Ireland, I did manage two rather interesting trips to Israel – a country to which I also made a number of later visits, which may feature in a future volume. But otherwise our journeyings tended to take us to Greece (within which we developed a favourite destination, in the form of Katounia, near Limni, in the north of the island of Euboea, home of the noted literary scholar and theologian Philip Sherrard and his family, to which we returned again and again over the next few decades); or simply to France and Italy, though usually somewhat off the beaten track. Exceptions to this would be various conference jaunts of mine, most notably to Hawaii.

It happens that I am currently co-editing what I consider a most stimulating volume of essays on the theme of 'The Philosophy of Tourism' (due to appear in the latter half of 2023), and this has led me to reflect on the topic of why one travels, and what insights or inspiration one hopes to derive from this activity. It must be admitted that we set off on our travels with no very noble purposes – merely a quest for new experiences (of a positive nature), in new places, and hopefully to the accompaniment of pleasant weather; in our book, however, we are prompted to speculate on deeper issues: the search for beauty, the meaning of life, the nature of the human condition. It does seem to be a feature of the human condition that we are restless animals, inclined to wander, always in search of something new – but this instinct, sadly, facilitated as never before by increasing prosperity, at least in the developed world, is now putting insupportable burdens upon previously charming venues, and indeed contributing to the devastation of the planet.

These travels, from half a century or so ago, are a record of a period when this was not yet the case – much though we complain, from time to time, about the proliferation of 'turkeys'! I only hope that they may provide some entertainment to whoever may come upon them.

# 1. VISIT TO GREECE,

## APRIL–MAY, 1977

*This diary was mostly written up by Jean, so that on this occasion her contribution will be ordinary script, and my occasional interventions will be in italics. We had been back in Dublin on leave for the academic year 1976-77, and I had, sometime previously, accepted an invitation to head up the Department of Classics in Berkeley, having turned down an invitation to run, in the Fine Gael interest, in the constituency of Dublin North-East, in the General Election of that year; so we were looking for some relaxation. The diary begins somewhat abruptly: we had flown out from Dublin to Athens that morning.*

### DAY 1, MONDAY, APRIL 25<sup>TH</sup>

*Pension Home Suisse*

Our pension, where we arrived at 11.00 am, is very nice – modest, but respectable, in a convenient part of town, six blocks or so from the American School.[1] The son (or husband) of the proprietress speaks English well, and is very pleasant and helpful. We had lunch here, and it was really excellent. First, a salad consisting of beetroot, beet tops, and cucumbers, with oil and vinegar; next, potatoes, in a delicious sauce; next, Wiener schnitzel with delicious carrots; and we finished with fruit.

*6 pm:* Sitting in the square beside the church of St. Nicodemus at the edge of the Plaka. John drinking a rather large-looking bottle of Amstel beer, and I'm drinking the most

---

1    That is to say, the American School of Classical Studies, at that stage presided over by my colleague in Berkeley, Stephen Miller, who ran an excavation at Nemea, in the Peloponnese, for many years.

delicious cup of black, sweet coffee. John says there are Roman Baths by Hadrian somewhere beneath where we are sitting. I notice that many of the older Greek males carry worry beads, and the women seem to be very religious. We have visited a few little mediaeval churches (not more than about 20 ft by 20 ft) which are mostly swallowed up by the modern buildings surrounding them. One does feel like an intruder going inside, though one we just visited was packed with old ladies sitting around gossiping at the tops of their voices. We are on our way to the Acropolis, really, on a tour of mediaeval Athens at the moment by mistake.

*7.20 pm:* We have now reached a lovely little square, which we think is the square of the Church of St. Nicholas of the Rangabes, a noble family of Byzantine Athens. It has a fine small park, where some little local boys are playing football. We are now finding everybody very friendly and helpful, and most have at least a smattering of English.

– An annoying end to our evening. We stopped at what looked like a very modest café in the Plaka for dinner (we had avoided all restaurants with white tablecloths), and found to our horror that the owner had bullied us into more than twice what we could possibly eat. And charged us £5 – we had thought we could get away with about £2 for both of us. I was so furious I asked for bags and we piled in everything we could, including all the bread from the bread-basket. I was sorely tempted to 'accidentally' spill the rest of our salads onto his floor, but didn't have the nerve. We will have spent £20 today – including the pension.

## DAY 2, TUESDAY, APRIL 26<sup>TH</sup>

*10 am:* Didn't sleep very well last night, because of noise. It is really difficult to see when Greeks go to bed – they seem to be dashing around (and working) almost right through the night. At 2.30 am there was someone outside hammering, and cars rushing about. And they seem to rise quite early in the morning in spite of this.

Helena Miller[2] just phoned. We are to meet her at the American School at 11 am. I haven't done any sketching yet – it is rather difficult in the city. I hope to get going at it once we're on the islands. Neither of us sick yet!

We met Helena at 11.30, having also met Stella and Steve Miller at the gate of the School. They kindly invited us to dinner tomorrow at Piraeus (the port). They will call for us at 8.00pm.

Helena invited us back to her very nice top-floor apartment for coffee, and gave us many useful hints on where to eat, bookstores, etc. She is having a marvellous time in Greece, but seems to want to stay on here next year. I don't know how Americans can think their marriages can stand up to such long separations. Andrew is still in Pittsburgh, and seems to have a chance of a job in Stanford.

We then set off for the Benaki Byzantine Museum, and found that, it being Tuesday, it was closed. All museums are closed on Tuesdays, it seems. Next stop was the Bank of Greece to cash a traveller's cheque, but couldn't, as we had forgotten to bring John's passport. After that, we went to the Bank of America, another few blocks away, and found it closed until Wednesday. So we set off for the Agora and the Acropolis, and spent the rest of the day there.

The Agora was fascinating, the more so because tour buses don't seem to stop there, and there were only a handful of people there besides ourselves. John had a marvellous time sitting himself down where his sacred Socrates sat and looking very wise. It was difficult, for me at least, to appreciate the Acropolis as much as I would like to have because of the busloads of loud Americans and Germans about, and I had to keep reminding myself that they had as much right to be there as I had. But it is incredibly beautiful. Didn't take too many photos here because they would seem a little corny, I think. I did take quite a few in the Agora – things that were of particular interest to John, like the Altar of Zeus, the Stoa Basilikê, etc. I did take a nice one

---

2    Wife of my former graduate student Andrew Miller. He in fact stayed on in Pittsburgh, and made his career there. I do not know how well the marriage in fact lasted!

on the Acropolis, of two native cats in heraldic poses. John read in our guide book that the house of Proclus, with mosaic floors, had been uncovered near the Odeion of Herodes Atticus, and we went down to try and find that, and worship at it, but the relevant part of the excavation seemed to be locked up, despite the obstinate assertion of an old gentleman at the entrance to the Theatre of Dionysos that it wasn't. I was hoping to see a battered statue of the Hen and the *Pantelose On*[3] standing among the olive trees and weeds.

Then John decided he wanted to find the river Ilissos, which Socrates once crossed or paddled in or something.[4] In fact, the Ilissos had been paved over, so he is in disgrace. We went home in a taxi.


### DAY 3, WEDNESDAY, APRIL 27TH

We started off to the American School, getting advice from Steve Miller about the Academy, which John is determined to walk out to. Then on to the Bank (walking), to cash $100. Then a taxi to the National Museum, where we had to pay 50 dr. each as entrance fee, and a further 25 dr. each to visit the Minoan Paintings Room. We mainly saw Mycenaean things – lovely, but so numerous that we got bogged down after about two hours. We saw the Thera excavations (Prof. Marinatos), the bronze racehorse and driver, and Zeus (both of which were found in the bay), and endless other things, most of which I forget – lots of funerary monuments, which were rather gloomy.

After, it was on to Eleftheria Square, to catch a bus to Daphne. In the square, I won a battle with a fruit seller over some oranges. He tried to sell us first a kilo, then half a kilo (and even weighed the half-kilo, which came to four oranges), even though I had asked for two oranges. I insisted I only

---

3     That is to say, two key entities of Neoplatonic metaphysics, the One and the Totally Existent (pantelôs on). Jean would have met with these entities while typing out my thesis, and then *The Fragments of Iamblichus* book, some years previously.

4     Sc. at the beginning of Plato's *Phaedrus*.

wanted two oranges, and he finally gave in with a grin. They are really mean to tourists – they try to take advantage of you at every opportunity. Then we got the bus to Daphne, to see the nice little monastery there, but I was so flattened I could hardly enjoy it, and was relieved to get back to the *pension*.

At 8 pm, Stella and Steve Miller called for us and took us to dinner at the Piraeus in a super restaurant called (the unlikely name of) Zorba. They specialise in fish and a most amazing selection of hors d'oeuvres, which they carry to you on an enormous tray and you take your pick. We then all had an enormous grilled fish (a John Dory?) between us, served with a sort of oil and vinegar mixture and lemon (really delicious!). We had four bottles of white wine!

## DAY 4, THURSDAY, APRIL 28<sup>TH</sup>

John had a headache this morning. While I packed the bags, he went off to hire a car (Fiat 127). We took our suitcase to the American School (who have offered us a room at a quarter the cost of the Pension one). We then took a knapsack and drove off around the coast, first to Sounion, where there is a temple of Poseidon, where we followed the old wall (on foot), and dipped our toes in the Aegean. It was rather cold, and our ambition of taking a swim quickly faded. Our weather has not been quite up to our expectations – it has been quite windy, but if you find a sheltered spot it can be quite hot. We're getting suntans, anyhow.

Our next stop was for lunch at a delightful café, surrounded by roses, geraniums, honeysuckle and endless other gorgeous flowers. It was just beyond Sounion on the main road. John wrote down the name of it, and now can't decipher it. We had some very good shrimp and tomato salad and chips. We're finding the food here really excellent, which for me at least was quite unexpected.

Next stop was at Thorikos, where there is an old theatre and various other things of interest, like an old well, endlessly deep, and a beehive hut on the top of the hill. John climbed to the top of the hill to see what he could see, while I stayed in the theatre and drew a bit. On the top he met an enormous spider, who had spread his web between a rock and a bush, and came down again.

Then we drove on to Brauron, where there is a temple of Artemis, where little girls dressed up as bears and danced at a festival. There was a beautiful little Byzantine church too, which I sketched. From there, we drove along the coast to Loutsa and Rafina, partly on unpaved roads, past enormous constructions of hotels and flats, uninhabited and often unfinished – very weird. But this is plainly the great place for weekend and summer homes for prosperous Athenians.

Now we are in a charming restaurant in Paiania (Demosthenes' home town), *Kanakis' Gardens,* recommended by Colin Edmondson,[5] and very good. We had hors d'oeuvres, John chicken and I lamb chops, and are now having coffee. The proprietor is most friendly, and has a limp. So does his cat, who visited our table, and was most appreciative of bits of lamb and chicken. We are now having coffee and wondering where on earth we are going to spend the night. The bill came to 266 dr. (!), so we left the change out of 300 dr., as we had had such a good time.

We drove on to a town called Rafina, and booked ourselves into a hilarious hotel – rather dubious looking, with an owner who speaks with a strong Chicago accent one minute and a Lancashire one the next. He looks like a gangster, but seems a decent sort. As we parked the car, a man came up and started asking John something in German (he was Greek). It turned out that his car had run out of petrol and he wanted to siphon a litre out of our car. A large audience assembled, laughing and giving advice, as the man said he wished it was ouzo he had to suck from the hose pipe. It finally worked, and he insisted on paying John 50 drachmas, a nice incident to end the day, except there was a funnier one when we got to our room, because we found a very aged bun under the bed, at which John became

---

5    Colin Edmondson was an archaeologist, working at the American College in Athens.

frivolous and started to beat the bed, shouting "Come out now, boys, while you have the chance!" – I hope we'll find nothing worse before the evening is over.

*Well, we didn't, really, but the 'bath' was filled with cement and permanently plugged, and there is only a cold-water tap in the room, and no plug – but what does one want for 220 dr.? (although official tariff, as posted on bedroom door, is 169.50 dr., for Class D Hotel!) Still, the jax, though a bit smelly, does not have cockroaches. The name: – Xenodokheion Kymata – to be avoided!*


## DAY 4, FRIDAY, APRIL 29<sup>TH</sup>

*Woke up this morning about 9.00 to find the bloody wind (Meltemi?) blowing harder than ever – shutters banging, white horses in Marathon Bay, trees bending and dancing. Maybe we should just press on to the Sahara? No bathing at Marathon today, I think.*

We changed money at a travelling bank in the square ($40), and drove on towards Marathon, stopping on the way at a ghastly café called Monaco for our breakfast, having failed to find anywhere else inhabited along the way. We were greeted at the Monaco by a waiter in a bow tie (at 10 o'c. in the morning!). The breakfast was very ordinary, and cost us nearly £2. You live and learn. If I had seen the bow tie first, I would have fled, but John was first inside. This was, we think, in Nea Makri.

We then drove along the coast, to *Hagios Panteleimon,* and parked in the square. We gathered the bathing togs up in spite of the unpromising-looking weather (still windy) and walked along the beach about a mile, ending up at a slightly sheltered cove, where we bravely had a swim. We are convinced that we were the only people in Greece to swim that day. We also found a sweet little pension, which we hope to go back to. It has an adorable little front garden right on the beach, very simple little rooms, with balcony looking out to sea. It is run by a man with a hole in his throat, who has to use a sort of microphone to talk to you. Unlike most Greeks, he hasn't a word of English, but is extremely friendly and nice. His pension is only opening for the season on Sunday next.

He told us a story about some Germans which neither of us understood, but I gathered from his sign language and the word 'Germans' thrown in now and then, that some Germans were coming to his hotel on the 12th of May, after touring elsewhere, while John gathered from his understanding of the Greek that the Germans had assassinated his brother and given him the hole in his throat! I suppose we'll never know what he said. We had coffee at his café, and then drove on to the tomb of Marathon, where John tried to work out the battle, and I did another rotten sketch. My sketches so far have been awful, hence the new pen I bought this morning. I am making a wildflower collection – the variety is tremendous.

We then drove on through lush valleys, with vineyards, glorious fields of poppies (which they use as cattle feed) – the most lovely scenery – to Ramnous, where there is another 5th cent. B.C. ruin. It was a country town built out on a promontory, and the sort of slip where they pulled up their ships still remains. We gave a lift to two people, first an old lady loaded down with shopping, who lived in a picturesque village in the valley called Kato Souli. She talked away to us and was very pleasant. John managed to understand the gist of what she was saying. Later, on our way to the town of Marathon, we gave a lift to a young fellow who said he was from Thessaly – about 400 kilometres north. Marathon is a gorgeous little town, full of flowers. We passed over the dam on the lake (very nice), and then set off for Athens, because of a dinner engagement at 7.30 (early for Greeks, who only start to eat at about 9.00 pm).

We found our room at the American School – which is superb; and they had left us flowers – Sweet William. We had an hour to change before setting off for the bus to the Astor Hotel. We had dinner on the 8th floor, where we looked directly across at the Acropolis, an unbelievable sight. After dark, they did their *son et lumière* performance, so it was even more dramatic then. After dinner, we walked back to the School with David Romano, the new secretary of the American School.

## DAY 5, SATURDAY, APRIL 30<sup>TH</sup>

Poor John had to get up early to return the car. He set off at about a quarter to nine. I got up, had a leisurely bath, and washed my hair, before starting to repack the knapsack for our island-hopping, beginning this evening. When John got back, we set off in search of breakfast (we hadn't signed in for breakfast at the School), and found a baker round the corner, where we bought two apple pies. Then we went to the laundry with a few clothes, to be ready in a week (we said we only needed them then), and on down to Kolonaki Square (very fashionable, I believe), where we had a delicious cup of capucchino, and carried out a fruitless search for a canvas carrier bag, which we then decided we didn't need anyway. Back to the School, where John bearded Prof. Vanderpool[6] to talk to him about the Old Academy, and got great value out of him, while I wrote some cards and started to catalogue my wildflower collection. I have gathered 22 different species so far, and they look very nice stuck onto individual cards.

We set off for Piraeus at 3 pm, and had a snack there of *loukoumades* (a kind of doughnut), which were delicious, and some cheese pastries, which the Greeks make very well. Then onto the Cyclades boat at 5 pm. We sailed at six, and now – at 12.30 am – are still on our way to Paros, We are expected to arrive at 2 am Luckily we have booked our hotel (Grade D – so we tremble).

## DAY 6, SUNDAY, MAY 1<sup>ST</sup>

We checked in at our hotel, called *Kontes*, which is excellent, and we can't understand why it is graded D. Our room is *very* comfortable and pleasant, with a small balcony and a private bathroom with a shower. The poor hotel owner lost his wife recently, and that is why he looks rather sad.

---

6        Professor Eugene Vanderpool (1906-1989) was a major authority on the antiquities of Athens, and of Greece in general, and a fixture in the American School. On a later occasion, he actually walked me out to the Academy from the Plaka.

First, we went to the Museum and saw the remains of Archilochus'[7] biographical inscription. The guard spoke no English, and was surly and uninformative. John had great fun identifying words on it from his book.

Then, we took a rather unfortunate walk down the beach to the north of the harbour, since it became obvious that the beach was thick with bits of plastic and general junk. So we gave up half-way and came back to our hotel, and had a cheese pie and some baklava and coffee in the restaurant in the main square of Paros – totally surrounded by American hippies and Australians! – and then hopped on a bus to Marpissa, or in fact Kato Livadhi, where we found the local equivalent of the Hell's Angels on the beach. John had a swim anyway, and, after walking round the shore a little more, and finding a pleasanter beach, we had to leave within a half-hour or so to catch the bus back. The buses go to various towns about, but at very irregular intervals – the times are written up on a blackboard in the main square – and the afternoon runs seem not to be advertised until after the siesta (in case, they don't wake up, I suppose!).

We came back to the town and toured it on foot, and found it to be the most delightful place – all the houses spotlessly white-washed, winding narrow streets and flowers galore – bougainvillea, geraniums, orchids, honeysuckle (in full bloom, smelling divine). We came across an enormous wall of a house, whose component parts were made up bits of old temple. We were very excited at our discovery – and then found it mentioned in our guide book! It was used as a Frankish fort in the 14th cent. (Crusaders). I took a picture of two boys trying to persuade John to climb one side of the wall to see the other side. They had great fun telling him how easy it was.

We then came back to the hotel for a short rest, and at 6.30 set out on foot to the place where the stone with the Archilochus fragment on it was found – called Elitas. It is just ten minutes' walk above the port, and on the terraced slopes to the right of the road we found a little building (presumably used for

---

7    The poet Archilochus, who lived in the 6th cent. B.C., was a native of Paros, and there is a shrine to him outside the town.

storage or something) which had nine or ten pieces of marble cut as if for an old temple with grooves and holes (I wonder what you call them!). John thinks they may be fragments of an altar erected in honour of Archilochus by Mnesiepes in the 3rd century B.C., and it is probably the site where the fragment was found. I gathered some more wild flowers, and then we walked back to town and dined extremely well at a restaurant round the corner from the hotel – the best squid I have had so far; and John had a lovely fish. A little stroll around town, and then back to bed. The noisy people one floor down seem to be having a party tonight.

## DAY 7, MONDAY, MAY 2$^{ND}$

We decided to go to Antiparos, the small island next to Paros, today, to see the caves there. We got to the boat (a *large* motor boat) at 9.00 am, and there were only two other customers. We arrived at the main port of Antiparos and realised that our boatman did not intend taking us further down to the caves because there weren't enough customers (two others joined us there), but he came to an arrangement with us to take us all for 400 dr. (about £6. 10/-).

When we arrived at the cave, we realised it was not one of those caves you go into by boat, but one on top of a mountain. So we climbed for about three-quarters of an hour before we reached it. It was very dramatic (I think), the more so because the electric lights were broken, and about 40 of us (other Australian tourists had arrived meanwhile) were led down with two gas lamps. There were 400 steps down and the stalactites and stalgmites were super – some broken off, they say, by Mussolini's army! (We don't understand the story!). A river flowed through the lower part of it until 1957, when the Santorini earthquake struck. My knees knocked as we went down for quite a while – very steep steps, with nothing to hold onto most of the time, and sheer drops down in places. The other people with our group were a youngish German man called Uwe, and an elderly German couple (very pleasant), whose names we never got. The elderly German man did not make the climb down, wisely from his point of view, I think. When we got back up, we paid off the guide (10 dr. and tip was suggested by himself!), who stayed behind to wait for more customers.

Lovely hot sun all the way down the rather barren hillside – only a few donkeys and one house in sight. Back onto the boat, which dropped us at the main port of Antiparos again, where we all had a very nice lunch at a restaurant on the beach. A nice scene during lunch – mules standing in the bottom of a small boat, being taken to Paros. We saw them later in the evening on the island.

After lunch, we were ferried directly across to a little port opposite, to pick up the German gentleman's car, which he had parked there earlier in the day. There was a little church there where, if you wish a boat to come over and ferry you across, you *open* the door of the church and wait. We were driven back to Parikia *via* a monastery near the Valley of the Butterflies (*Petaloudes*), which was closed – the monastery, that is.

We took a rest, and then went out in search of dinner. We stopped at a bookstore on the way, for a new sketch-book and a copybook for John, to write his short stories! In there, we met the young German and invited him to join us for dinner, which he readily accepted. I don't know why he's on holiday alone – he has a wife and three children! We went to a very jolly place with murals on the wall in the old part of town. It was a patio covered with vines. The food was OK, but not as good as the night before. John and I went for a coffee and ice-cream on the promenade before retiring.

## DAY 8, TUESDAY, MAY 3<sup>RD</sup>

Went to Naoussa (a 20 min. bus journey round the coast), where they're supposed to have lovely beaches. Well, we stopped at the first one, which was full of the usual plastic rubbish, and had a swim anyway – you're supposed to walk further to find nice ones. While passing a field, we noticed a donkey which had its head-collar carelessly put on, resulting in its ears being pressed back, so I released his ears. He was delighted, and shook his head vigorously. Goodness knows what I've done. Perhaps it's some ingenious way of keeping them under control, or something.

Back here for a snack in the square, and then met some English people, James and Jennifer Northcote-Green, whom we had met at breakfast, and arranged to go on a donkey ride with them. We set off from near the hotel at 3.30, and had the most hilarious and enjoyable ride up the mountains. We were to visit the valley of the butterflies, where in summer flocks and flocks (if that is the right word!) of butterflies congregate. Unfortunately, it is too early in the year, and we only saw a handful. But the ride up was lovely, and well worth our while. John's donkey was called Markos and mine was called Valentino, he was a real character. Didn't like any of the others to lead, and if they tried to push past him, he would either kick or charge forward in front of them. John was very funny – sometimes he looked utterly miserable, but all in all enjoyed the ride, I think. He is complaining about his seat, though.

James and Jennie came back to our balcony for an ouzo afterwards, and then we all went to dinner at the restaurant around the corner, and after that to a bar for coffee and ice cream. At dinner we met Uwe. He drifted off before we went to coffee. James and Jennie lent us their alarm clock to wake us in the morning.

## DAY 9, WEDNESDAY, MAY 4<sup>TH</sup>

Had breakfast in the hotel. Then took the bus to Naoussa, and from there the boat for Delos-Mykonos. We had a fairly bumpy crossing, but on a comfortable boat, to Delos, where they allowed us only 1 ½ hours to inspect the numerous ruins. It wasn't half enough time for us to see what we wanted.

Mykonos was dreadful – full of blue-haired ladies and fancy gentlemen in fancy clothes. It's really a pretty town, but not worth a visit because of the company. There were *three* liners anchored in the harbour.

A very strange thing happened to us as we rounded a bend in the town onto the sea. I suddenly saw the scene of my painting in the drawing-room in Berkeley. I took a photo of it from as near the angle of the painting as possible – an extraordinary discovery, and the only positive thing about our visit to Mykonos.

When we got back, James and Jennie hadn't yet had dinner, and neither had we, so they joined us on our balcony for a drink of ouzo, before setting out to dinner. We went to a new restaurant called SOUVLAKI on the seafront, and had delicious souvlaki, and a courgette and artichoke stew, which was also delicious. They served us a dip with our bread made of yoghurt, cucumbers, garlic and onion – lovely! Later, the four J's went to our favourite coffee bar for the usuals.

## DAY 10, THURSDAY, MAY 5<sup>TH</sup>

We set off for Archilochus' 'meadows' again in the morning, and walked a good deal, but found nothing new, but John at least got an idea of the layout of the terrain. (Oh. I forgot: I went shopping in the morning, and bought a pair of canvas shoes for me, and a pair of leather sandals for John's Mum. And then when I couldn't find John again, I went along the seafront and did a sketch – still not very good; I really haven't yet got the hang of it again.) Then we had lunch, after *that* set out for the meadows.

We got back at about 5.30 pm, in time for a cake and a cup of coffee at the café round the corner. Then back to the hotel to pick up the camera, which James and Jennie had kindly stored in their room for us. We met them in the hall while waiting for the boat for Naxos, and, since it was an hour late, Jennie went upstairs and got a bottle of ouzo and glasses, and we had a jolly time until the boat arrived. They saw us off on the pier, and we were sorry to leave them – they were such a nice pair.

We found a good hotel in Naxos, but when we asked how much, he said 375 dr., and we said it was too much, and turned to go, but he called us back and told us we could have it for 300 dr. Done!

## DAY 11, FRIDAY, MAY 6<sup>TH</sup>

We're sitting now on the side of the road in the mountains

of Naxos, near the town of Kouronochori (Melanes was the place we thought we were going, thinking that was the name of a town, but it turned out that in fact it was the name of the area!). The countryside is lovely – very lush, and the farms very well organised. Agaves are used as hedges between fields here, and so far we have seen field upon field of potatoes, in addition to vines and olive groves. We have just had a very good lunch, for 39 dr., at a little café, which didn't even look like one, that we were introduced to by a girl we met on the bus. Tourists must be very unusual here, because we seem to be a great curiosity for all the children, who walk up and stare quite unabashedly. The bus had more parcels than people on it, and at each stop women piled in their breads, cheeses and vegs for the next town.

Our bus took us back at 3 pm, and because the weather was very windy, we decided to take a siesta. Our siesta lasted till about 6.30! We set off to see the remains of the temple overlooking the harbour, and had to rush across the pier leading to it because the waves were splashing over it. We made it without getting wet. John says most of it looks more like 8<sup>th</sup> century B.C. than classical.

When we walked into the restaurant on the seafront, *there was Uwe*. We laughed and he laughed, and we joined him for dinner. He is setting off for Mykonos tomorrow for a week. Our boat back to Athens leaves tomorrow morning at 11 am.


DAY 12, SATURDAY, MAY 7<sup>TH</sup>

I'm not sure if I've mentioned why we decided not to go on to Thera. The first reason is that the boat from Naxos reaches Thera at about 9 pm, and leaves for Piraeus next morning at 7.30 am. So we would have had to stay till Sunday, and we don't even know if there was a boat to Piraeus on Sunday. The second reason is that we're running out of money. The third reason is that it was very windy on Friday, and it would have been extremely cold on Thera. And John, anyhow, wanted to get back to Athens in time to walk to the Old Academy on Sunday. So here we are on the boat at 2 pm, having left Naxos at 11 am. We should be in Piraeus by 6 or 6.30 pm.

All in all, we're very happy that we chose Paros to stay in the longest. It has the nicest town, is less touristy, has good restaurants and attractive countryside. Naxos, I think, could have been a little boring for a long stay, and the food was not as good.

The boat we are on is called the *Lemnos*, and it is far superior to the *Cyclades*, which we came on. Tourist class is most luxurious, with a canteen which serves very good lunches. It seems altogether cleaner and newer than the *Cyclades*.

We arrived in Athens about 7.00 pm, and then went up to the American School, where Bob Ross[8] was waiting with some lady friend. We all went to dinner locally. She is not madly interesting, but decent enough.

### DAY 13, SUNDAY, MAY 8TH

We met Bob at breakfast. We've decided to go our different ways, as he'd like to go north, and we really want to go to the Peloponnese. I washed clothes for about an hour. Now we're in the garden for a while. The garden of the School is simply lovely – now in bloom are geraniums, Sweet William, Stock, Snapdragons, and Pansies.

In the afternoon, we went off to the Agora again, and to the Ceramicus, which was the old pottery quarter, and where Cicero started his walk to the Academy. John is going to make that walk with Prof. Vanderpool tomorrow afternoon.

We had dinner with Bob at a very nice restaurant on Dafnomili St., called *To Steki tou Mantou*. I had very good rabbit, and John had *moussaka,* and we had salads of spinach, beetroot and green peppers. Very nice. We also had a pleasant light red wine called *Kokinelli* (?).

### DAY 14, MONDAY, MAY 9TH

We went to the bank in the morning, bought some bourbon for

---

8     Robert C. Ross had been a fellow-graduate student with me at Berkeley, and was now teaching at the University of Wisconsin at Milwaukee.

the Nemea group, contemplated a nice pair of shoes, which I did *not* buy, and walked back to the School.

At 3 pm John and Professor Vanderpool set off to walk to the Academy. I stayed behind, washed my hair, and wrote some cards. I also had a tummy-ache, so I didn't feel like doing much else. They returned at 6.30. We had dinner in the School. I have met the Secretary, Miss Margaret Owen, who is very congenial, though brisk and very English.

### DAY 15, TUESDAY, MAY 10<sup>TH</sup>

We left the School at 9.30 to pick up the car. We drove first to Corinth, to see old ruins! Interesting and uneventful. After that, we set off for Nemea,[9] and were given extensive tours of the excavations by Steve Miller, Jim Wright and David Romano. In the afternoon, we dashed off to see Mycenae – a fantastic sight! John amused a bunch of high school kids by standing in a little room in the Treasury of Atreus, which was pitch-dark, and making a very eerie 'boo' sound when they approached. They came rushing out in great excitement, half-laughing and half-scared. They were on a rather staid tour with their teacher. So I think it cheered them up!

Back to Nemea for dinner with Stella and Steve, and, having eaten well and enjoyed their Nemea wine, we set off rather too late to look for a hotel for the evening. We drove first to Nauplion, a picturesque town which we couldn't see in the dark, and the Hotel Otto, which had been recommended to us, was full. The man who was at the door asked us if we would like a room in a house opposite, and we said we would look at it. I have *never* seen anything quite so grotty! The 'bedroom' was enormous, with paint peeling off the walls, lino (worn) on the floors, which were dirty anyway, and the 'bathroom' was just a scruffy little room with a grey kitchen sink. The loo was indescribable. And he wanted 200 dr.! I said 'no', and that was that. I couldn't have slept in such a filthy place.

---

9    Nemea, site of the quadrennial Nemean Games, was being excavated by a team from Berkeley, directed by my colleague, Stephen Miller.

*We then drove on to Tolon, a nice-looking resort on the sea. But it was about 11.30 when we got there. We drove to the hotel that the Millers recommended, and they wanted 700 dr. a night. Off we went again, and found another hotel, called Flisvos (the sound of the waves!) – 400 dr.! Still more than we wanted to pay, but we were desperate.*

## DAY 15, WEDNESDAY, MAY 11<sup>TH</sup>

We got up about 8.00, and went for a swim at the hotel beach. It was nice, though a little cool. Then we had our breakfast brought up to our room, and ate it on the balcony. That was very pleasant – the sun was warm, and we stayed there sunbathing until about 10.30.

Our next stop was at Tiryns, where there is another Mycenaean excavation. Not as spectacular as Mycenae, of course, but interesting. We planned to go from there to Bassae, where there is a Temple of Apollo, but we took some wrong turns, and had to give it a miss. There followed, at first, a very pleasant drive through the mountains of Arcadia, the scenery very lush, with lots of trees, but it turned fairly nightmarish in the end, because of poor signposting, and we kept ending up in impossible places.

We finally got to Olympia – an impressive sight. We decided we would drive from there to the coast and find a hotel. And that is where the *real* nightmare began. There just were *no* hotels beside the sea. The only good thing that happened to us in the last two hours or so of driving was that we found an overturned tortoise on the road, and we righted him and put him back in the undergrowth. We finally arrived at a spa resort called *Loutra Kyllinis* ('Baths of Kyllene'), on the Adriatic coast at about 8 pm. We almost drove off again in despair when we saw the enormous building in front of us, beautifully landscaped and plush-looking, and looking as dead as a doornail. We decided they would probably want 700 dr. a night. But once again we were desperate. We knew there probably would not be another hotel for 100 miles. This coast is very undeveloped – nice for the residents! So John walked tentatively through the doors and inquired of a nice English-speaking fellow (Chicago accent again! "You gonna stay one night, or two?", for example). Their hotel seems to be divided into two categories: Class A and Class C. He must have taken a good look at us before quoting their Class C price – 365 dr.! We couldn't believe our luck. Of course, it's still more (65 dr. more) than we would like to have to pay, but we were delighted. *Then,* as we started to check in, where was John's passport? Suddenly he recalled that we had not received it back from the people at the hotel in Tolon – about 200 miles back. Horrors! The man who welcomed us was very decent. He phoned the hotel *Flisvos* for us, and said at first to send it to Athens by post. Then we got nervous, thinking it might not arrive in time for our departure on Sunday, and rang back and told them we would pick it up. Now we've had to change all our plans and get to Delphi in a great rush, and try to then come back to the Peloponnese by the ferry, which will cost us a lot of time and money, because the car is costing us an extra 4 drs. a kilometer.

### DAY 16, THURSDAY, MAY 12^TH

We left for Delphi at 9.30 am or so. We drove like the hammers through Elis (very lush countryside, and very pretty farms) to Patras, which is a very large industrial city. This part of the country is unprepared for tourists. No further hotels until Patras. Then on to the ferry at Rhion, which took us across the Gulf of Corinth to Antirrhion in 15 minutes. The Turks have two castles, one at each side of the straits. We set off on their new coastal road to Itea, which is the port of Delphi, stopping on the way for a snack and a swim at a charming little settlement called Agios Spiridion, which was just off the road down on the waterfront. This road is quite new, so all the villages around are undeveloped. The schoolhouse in Agios Spiridion was absurdly small, about 12 feet by 12 feet. We stopped for lunch in a nice town called Galaxidi, because John's guide said there were old walls there, which we couldn't find. The lunch was rather expensive, and was one Greek salad too many. Our stomachs have now declared war on tomato, cucumber, olives, feta cheese and oil. We're dying for some other veg.

We arrived at Itea – an industrial town – and enquired about the ferry, which had stopped two years ago, when they completed the new road.

*We then drove up through the Sacred Plain, solidly planted with olive trees, into Delphi, and checked in to the Hotel Hermes, as recommended by the American School. They proved very friendly, and gave a 20% discount (= 350 dr.), and a room with a spectacular view of the valley back down to Itea. Then we set out to review the ruins. The French excavators have in fact laid everything out beautifully, restoring the Treasury of the Athenians in full, and significant bits of other things.*

John tried to explain what everything was, but it is too complicated, except that one came to consult the Priestess, who gave out oracles in a trance after chewing laurel leaves and inhaling fumes. We walked up to the Stadium, which is well preserved, and then down to the Castalian Fountain, out of which John insisted on drinking a few draughts. He said it tasted beautiful, and would make a creative writer out of him, but later he complained of feeling unwell, though that may have been from lunch. Then we walked down to the Tholos, the funny little round temple, and so back to the hotel.

Later, we walked out to find dinner, and tried to get ordinary, decent vegetables, but this is quite impossible, so we settled for no salad at all – after running out of one restaurant in a panic after they had served the bread. After dinner we walked out of town to the ruins and back, but the night was very dark. Then back to the hotel, and watched an American film on the television with the old mother of the hotel owner, who is a cheerful old thing, who talks away in a terrible mixture of languages. And so to bed.

## DAY 17, FRIDAY, MAY 13<sup>TH</sup>

Up very early, and left without breakfast, at 8.00, determined to get back to Tolon in good time. We did in fact do this, stopping on the way in Epidauros, where the theatre was full of school children with transistor radios, shouting and yelling, but even so it was possible for John to hear me say, "Can you hear me from there?", in an ordinary speaking voice from the centre of the theatre, while he sat right at the top. Extraordinary!

Just as we drove into Tolon, we noticed 'Rooms to Let' on the right hand side of the road. It was a very new building overlooking the sand dunes, with a lovely beach right in front of us. We took it because it cost 140 drs. less than the Hotel Flisvos who had John's passport. We then went and got the passport, came back to the rooms, and then went for a most glorious swim – the water was lukewarm. We sunbathed for a while, and then went off for a walk around the town and back along the beach. So our return visit to Tolon was *not* a disaster, but extremely pleasant. We had dinner for 200 dr. at one of the tavernas on the beach, with vines overhead.

## DAY 18, SATURDAY, MAY 14TH

Up at 7.10 am. We wanted to leave by 8 am, but in fact left by 7.45. We had to leave payment for our room in the room, because the family weren't yet up. We made a mad dash for Athens, and arrived at 10.15. John rang the car agency (Hellas Cars) and asked if we could change to the flat unlimited mileage rate at this stage, as we had had to do so much more extra driving because of the passport. They were *very* nice, and said 'of course'. That means, since it's a seven-day thing, that we can keep the car until tomorrow, which means that we can take our luggage to the airport in the morning and leave it in the 'left luggage' place until tomorrow night – we hope!

We're now sitting in the American School garden, waiting for the use of the tennis court. It is shared with The British School next door, and they have preference on Saturdays, Tuesdays and Thursdays, while we have it on Mondays, Wednesdays and Fridays. On Sundays it is a free-for-all.

*And here the diary ends. We must presume that the return to Ireland on Sunday was uneventful!*

# 2: BERKELEY TO ATLANTA & BACK

## DECEMBER, 1977 — JANUARY, 1978

*The occasion for this trip was my attendance at a conference of the American Philological Association in Atlanta, GA, but the additional purpose was to view a great swathe of the southern United States, and to visit friends in Nashville, TE. Since Jean is composing most of this, her contributions will be in ordinary print, mine in italic.*

### DAY 1, MONDAY, DEC 19ᵀᴴ

We arose at the incredible hour of 4.45 am, and were actually out of the house and on the road by 5.45. As we drove along in the dark on the freeway to Walnut Creek, we were disgusted to see commuters already rushing towards San Francisco.

We drove non-stop (except to stop for petrol) until we reached Adelanto (which took about 7 hours). In the process of driving through the San Bernardino Hills behind Los Angeles, for a distance of about eleven miles we were buffeted about by extraordinarily strong winds. Today we learned from a radio report that we were at the edge of a hurricane, which has caused a great deal of damage in Los Angeles.

In Adelanto we had our lunch (picnic) sitting on the back of our car. We noted that the petrol stations and grocery stores in the area had bars on their doors and windows, and watchdogs. A great deal of vandalism occurs here. Perhaps it has something to do with the air-force base nearby?

We crossed into Arizona feeling rather worried about three cases of wine we had in the back of the car (intended for consumption at John's convention in Atlanta), but the customs men only asked had we any fruit or plants, inspected a tangerine, and waved us on. We drove for a total of almost 13 hours (800 miles) until we reached Phoenix, where luckily we had booked a room at the Motel 6. We arrived there at about 8 pm, and then went in search of a restaurant. Our hotel was situated east of the city, near Tempe. In Tempe we found a really delightful old restaurant (reasonably priced), called La Casa Vieja. We could have had a Mexican meal, but were in the mood for something more digestible, so I settled for half a chicken (deliciously cooked) and John settled for a steak – very middlebrow of us! It was a delightful building, with all sorts of interesting relics. Senator Carl Hayden was a native son of Tempe, and his cavalry sword was on view at the Casa.

## DAY 2, TUESDAY, DECEMBER 20TH

We rose at 6.30, and drove to see the Casa Grande – an old Indian four-story dwelling which has been excavated in recent times. It was discovered by the Spanish in 1594, but at that time was partly covered. We stopped at Coolidge nearby (an ordinary town named after Pres. Coolidge, founded in 1925) and bought some groceries (we are picnicking for both breakfast and lunch, to try and save some money; we find that, including petrol, we cannot get by on less than $40 a day).

Next we drove to Saguaro National Park, to see the marvellous cacti. The Saguaro cactus can reach a height of 50 feet or so, and some of them are 250 years old. One takes a nine-mile drive around the park. We got out (illegally, we think!) and picnicked beneath one of the largest plants. There are mountain lions, among other wild things, around here, but unfortunately we didn't encounter one.

Our journey continued on to Santa Fe, New Mexico, and towards El Paso, but we stopped en route for dinner at an adorable little old town called La Messilla. It has a lovely little old square, and we had dinner at an old restaurant there called La Posta – a stagecoach stop! It was a very interesting house, with endless rooms leading off in all directions and large cages with several very colourful parrots in the front entrance. They also had a mynah bird, which 'miaowed' – his name was Joe! We had a good Mexican meal. I had *frijoles* (rolled up taco-type things with meat inside and cheese and sour cream on top). John had a specialty of the Mexican Indians of this locality called something like Red Enchiladas (had a sauce made of red peppers – very tasty!).

We stayed at the Motel 6 in El Paso – where I am now disgusted to find we left the electric coffee pot lent to us by Mrs. O.[10]

## DAY 3, WEDNESDAY, DECEMBER 21ST

We got up at 4.30 am, because we miscalculated the time, forgetting we had passed through the time zone, so we set off very blearily to the bridge in El Paso which leads into Mexico. We had intended walking over the bridge into Mexico, but the weather was so cold we decided against it. The temperature during the night had dropped to about 24°.

Our next destination was the Carlsbad Caverns in New Mexico, and the journey there was the longest and most deserted of our trip so far. We passed through an area of salt flats just before the Guadalupe Mountains, where we took a photograph. Even though this journey was the longest and the landscape the least varied, we found it fascinating because it gave us a terrific sense of the vastness of Texas.

The Carlsbad Caverns were well worth the journey. We could have gone on the three-hour walk through all of them, but settled for the one-and-a-quarter hour one, which took us to the main one. As it turned out, it was quite enough for us, as we had still a long journey ahead of us before the day was over.

From Carlsbad we headed for Midland, where we stayed the night – and hardly slept a wink, because of some noisy, beer-drinking neighbours in our motel. We had our supper at the Dairy Queen, where they offered a 'Beltbuster Hamburger', and advertised that only a true Texan could finish it! I demolished mine in nothing flat – to my own surprise! It really was enormous.

---

10    That is to say, Mrs. Mildred Osmer, our Berkeley 'mother'.

We are a little disappointed, by the way, to find that all the wildlife that is supposed to be around – mountain lions, deer, armadillos (though they're hibernating), etc. – are not showing themselves. We *did* see a coyote, though, a lovely fellow, who crossed the road in front of us. We have been picnicking *every* lunchtime, so they've had plenty of opportunity to present themselves.

DAY 4, THURSDAY, DECEMBER 22ND

We got up at about 8.45, trying to make up for our lack of sleep last night, and set out for Austin, via San Angelo-Llano (very close to where Katharine's[11] Camp Longhorn was – though we didn't know it until the Lehmanns told us. We arrived at the Lehmann's gorgeous place at about 4.30 pm and Prof. Lehmann[12] took us for a walk down to the lake beside the house. They live on 13 acres of juniper- and willow-covered land, and they entertain a great variety of wildlife, including thirteen or so raccoons, birds galore (including those lovely cardinals), domestic ducks, seven parrots, and two dogs. Mrs. Lehmann is a scream – she has marvellous stories about all her orphans. They used to entertain a fierce old billy-goat, who adopted them because they were the only ones who did not attempt to tame him or fence him in. He was with them for four or five years, and even to his dying day could not be trusted not to butt even

11    My sister Katharine had spent a summer at this camp some years before, as guests of Prof. Lehmann (a former student of my father's in Madison, now a professor in the University of Texas at Austin), and his wife, whom we were on our way to visit.

12    Winfred Philip Lehmann (1916 – 2007) was an American linguist who specialized in historical, Germanic, and Indo-European linguistics. He was for many years a professor and head of departments for linguistics at the University of Texas at Austin, and served as president of both the Linguistic Society of America and the Modern Language Association. Lehmann was also a pioneer in machine translation. He lectured a large number of future scholars at Austin, and was the author of several influential works on linguistics.

the Lehmanns from behind when they were least expecting it. One day he drove Mrs L. up a tree, and in his fury at failing to butt her, he bit her foot instead. They have the skeleton of his head, and fabulous horns, hanging on their living-room wall.

Their son Terry and his wife (with a peculiar name!) and daughter were visiting for Christmas. We had a delicious dinner of roast pork, and retired to bed by 10.30, and caught up on our sleep.

## DAY 5, FRIDAY, DECEMBER 23RD

Mrs. Marinatos invited us over to visit the riding school where she teaches dressage. We had a lovely time talking to all the horses. She is a very charming person. Mrs. Lehman mentioned a Mr. Sprague who breeds horses nearby and who was visited by a distant cousin of John's (a Dillon) last summer.[13] But we didn't meet Mr. Sprague, so we'll never get to the bottom of that (Mrs. L. feels they may have gone away for Christmas). His father used to be head of the New York Stock Exchange at one time. Mr. Sprague once visited Mr. D. in Dublin, and he (Mr. D.) described him as "an eeenormous man, who *filled* my office". We're very sorry not to have met him.

We left Austin at 1 o'clock, after the normal lunchtime picnic at one of the rest areas by the side of the road. We drove on Route 71, which goes along the Colorado river. All of this countryside is very pretty, with lovely farms and oak woods. The cow population changed as we drove east. First, we encountered Aberdeen Angus, then Red Brangus (a mix of Angus and Brahma), then Brahmas, and finally Charollais. We also saw lots of pig families loose in fields – the piglets were gorgeous. We had no time to stop and see the Space Centre, unfortunately!

We stopped for the night in Uncle Johnny's old town of Beaumont[14] – where oil was first discovered. We sent him a postcard from there with a picture of our motel – we couldn't find a shop that sold any nice cards.

---

13      Presumably one of our American cousins (from Chicago).

14      My Uncle John La Touche, who had been an oil engineer all his life, spent most of his career in Texas.

We left Beaumont at about 9 am, and decided to take a rather winding route to New Orleans, through the Delta on Highway L14. We thought it would be nice to see the little old French (Cajun) towns along the way. Wildlife abounds in the marshy areas, but most of the ones we saw were dead on the roadside – possums, foxes, skunks – though we did encounter a dear little turtle rumbling across the  road, and an *enormous* flock of thousands of wild geese, and a large hawk feasting on some smaller unfortunate. I managed to get a picture of him which I hope will come out. We found him in a field near the entrance to an old estate and gardens called Live Oak Gardens – it's supposed to be beautiful in spring, with masses of azaleas and rhododendrons and a sunken garden. Luckily for us, it was closed, because it would have cost us $2.25 each to go in. So instead we picnicked under an enormous oak tree.

The landscape of Louisiana is rather beautiful, with its winding *Bayou* (or streams), swamplands, sugar cane crops, and gorgeous oak trees. But the villages so far we have found rather disappointing – very plastic American – though with the odd pocket of really pretty Southern-style houses, with those nice porches, and some attractive vegetable gardens. We had expected a little more. The population is meant to be Cajun, descended from French and Spanish settlers, and the names are all French, but they have not much else to show for it. We have yet to hear anyone speaking French.

This evening we are checked in to a *really* plastic motel, the Ramada Inn, in an uninteresting town called Houma, and are at present eating at one of those typical stodge food chains, because, being Christmas Eve, nowhere else is open. It's very depressing to be here on Christmas Eve. But now we'll go back to the motel and open a few presents we have brought. The worst of it is that this is one of our most expensive restaurants so far, and we have *not* been extravagant. We only eat our dinner out, and we are still finding it difficult to spent less than $40 a day. And it's going to be much worse in New Orleans and Atlanta.

We went back to our motel, and, for lack of anything else to do, spent the evening goggling at the TV, opened our presents, ate a bar of lovely Swiss chocolate that John had bought me, and had a gin and tonic.

## DAY 7, SUNDAY, DECEMBER 25<sup>TH</sup> (CHRISTMAS DAY)

Arose at 7.00 am, meaning to leave, to get to New Orleans in time for Mass at about 10.00, but having talked to a very nice lady at the motel desk, we were persuaded to stay in Houma for High Mass at St. Francis Cathedral at 10:00 am. She was a friendly lady who liked to talk about her area. She is of Cajun descent, and speaks French haltingly, she says. But contrary to what we have found so far, she says there are many communities along the Bayou who speak only French. Their children learn English, but only when they get to school.

We are now having breakfast at one of the few cafés open in town – and I am staring disconsolately at a plate of *grits* and eggs. I asked for just eggs and toast, but grits come with everything. I'm not quite sure if I can manage to eat even the eggs with the distraction of the grits, which look like a large pile of semolina.

They have a nice habit around here of saying, when you're leaving a restaurant or shop, "Y'all come back now!"

*There is also an adjectival form of 'y'all'. The old lady at dinner last night said "What kinda dressin y'all want on y'all salad?"*

We arrived in New Orleans at about 12 – 1 pm It is a simply gorgeous town – very continental feel to it, with wrought-iron balconies, courtyards with banana trees, bougainvilleas, palms, and fountains – and it even *smells* different. Our hotel is right in the centre of the Old Quarter (called Château Motor Hotel), with its own courtyard and fountain. The management is rather surly, unfortunately, but we are comfortable. The cost is $28.50 a night, which is well above what we would normally pay, but it is one of the cheapest in town. The average hotel charges about $50 a night. Eating out is extremely expensive, and as a result we have been unable to dine at a lot of the restaurants recommended to us – though I suppose we would be tempted to do so if they happened to be open. Almost *all* of them are closed for the Christmas holidays, and will reopen tomorrow, by which time we will have departed! Brennan's, one of the famous ones, will be open tonight, but eating dinner there would destroy our budget for a couple of days, so we have decided that tonight we will eat at one of the seafood restaurants on the waterfront.

Yesterday at lunch time we ate at Desire Seafood Restaurant. John had fried oysters and I had a poor-boy sandwich – OK, but nothing spectacular. Then in the evening – still Christmas, mind you! – we had a supposedly Christmas dinner at Mollie's Irish Pub – but they had run out of turkey. How disappointing to come to New Orleans and eat that kind of food! But nowhere else was open, so we had no choice. Christmas is not the time to come to New Orleans!

After dinner, we went to hear some jazz at a club called the Maison Bourbon, which was a bit of a fraud, as they used microphones, and apart from the performance of an old guy called Thomas Jefferson, was not too 'genuine'. They charged us $2.75 for a beer and $3.98 for a hurricane, which John had.

We noticed, on our way back to the hotel, that Preservation Hall was open (we thought it wouldn't be open that evening), so we went in – only $1.00 each – and heard some really good jazz. Sweet Emma was there, but mostly only in spirit, as her left hand is now paralyzed, and her voice is non-existent. She plays the piano with her right hand.

## DAY 8, MONDAY, DECEMBER 26TH

We went and had the most *delicious* beignets at the French Market. The coffee is supposed to be good here, but was disappointing – the flavour was not too bad, chicory added, but too weak. We spent the morning walking round the streets, and at lunch-time had a delicious muffuletta sandwich at Frank's Delicatessen in the Square. It is made with ham, swiss cheese, and a chopped olive salad.

In the afternoon, we drove out to see the beautiful garden

district, with its large, pretty houses and beautiful gardens. We then drove out to view a restaurant up the river at a plantation called Elmwood. Their menu looked very good, and the house was one of the oldest in New Orleans (1732). We even made a reservation for dinner, because pheasant was on the menu, but when we got back to the hotel and reflected on what the dinner would cost us, we decided not to go. So instead we went to an old and well-recommended restaurant at the French Market called Tujagues. We had a moderate dinner, starting with shrimp remoulade (good); next, their speciality, served with every meal, beef brisket with a tomato/horseradish etc. sauce (good); next, beef (again!) with a kind of risotto (moderate), a salad (OK); and lastly, some poor coffee, and a very stale brownie. Altogether, a fairly unsuccessful dinner, but at least it cost about half what the other one would have.

After dinner, we went to hear some more jazz at Preservation Hall, but it was so jammed with people that we didn't stay very long – we were right at the back of that small room, and couldn't see a thing, and I was afraid of being stepped on.

## DAY 9, TUESDAY, DECEMBER 27<sup>TH</sup>

*We got ourselves woken at 7.00 am, in order to leave early, denying ourselves another go at the beignets, but we got bogged down, first waiting for the hotel café to open (which it never actually did), and then for our car to be got out of the garage – which we finally had to do ourselves. We left not much before 8.30, without breakfast, and headed across Lake Pontchartrain along Hwy 10, in the direction of Mississippi.*

*After driving for some time along Hwy 10, we realised that, if we did not take desperate measures, we would leave the area without actually setting eyes on the Gulf of Mexico, so we deviated down to the coast, and drove along the front for a while, through Biloxi (passing the home of Jefferson Davis, among other things), and turned into MacDonald's for breakfast, feasting on an Egg MacMuffin, which was actually not at all bad. Then we ran across the road and stuck a cautious finger into the Gulf of Mexico – which was quite cold!*

We arrived in Atlanta about 7.30 pm, and checked into our Travelodge Motel, which turned out to be right beside the Hilton, and which costs $11.00 less per night. We got a very comfortable room, with telephone and colour TV – luxuries missing in Motel 6! After bringing in our luggage and cleaning up a bit, we sauntered over to the Hilton to see who was there. We found Jay,[15] Cliff,[16] and Ivars,[17] and had supper in the snack bar there with them. It was very good to see them all. Ivars and Cliff are looking very well, but poor old Jay is rather miserable, Susan having gone off and left him.

### DAY 10, WEDNESDAY, DECEMBER 28TH

John got up fairly early, and went over to the Hilton to hear some of the talks, and I stayed in bed until nearly 11.00! Went downstairs and availed myself of the motel's free coffee and sandwiches from machines, and ate them in my room. Then I took off and drove to the main shopping centre, which was miles out, called Peachtree Square. They had some very nice stores there, including Neiman Marcus, Rich's, Davison's, and lots of others. I bought a fur-lined raincoat which was on sale at Neiman Marcus. I also saw a pair of shoes for John on sale at Zachary's, and waited for half-an-hour to be served, and finally gave up, deciding to persuade him to come out with me to get them the following day.

I drove back to the hotel and met John in the Hilton at 5 pm We went out to dinner with Cliff and Jay to an awful restaurant called Émile's, which we thought Fred and Melitta

---

15     Jay Bregman, who had taught with me in the Division of Interdisciplinary and General Studies (DIGS) in Berkeley, and subsequently made his career at the University of Maine at Orono. He was (and is) a great jazzman, a master of the tenor sax. He subsequently married the singer Nancy Ogle.

16     Clifford Weber, former fellow-graduate student with me in Berkeley, and now on faculty of Kenyon College, Ohio, where he remained for the rest of his career.

17     Ivars Avotins had taught for a number of years in the Classics Department in Berkeley earlier in the decade, and was now in the University of Western Ontario, where he remained for the rest of his career.

had recommended. It was a dreadful dinner. We started with a fairly good onion soup, next a really ghastly salad (a bowl of lettuce with a really vinegary dressing with red pepper), next grilled flounder (not *too* bad) – but no vegetables (all they had to offer were frozen beans); lastly, dreadful coffee.

We went back to the hotel to hear Bill Anderson's[18] Presidential Address, which was read by someone else because he had to leave the meeting that morning, as poor Lorna had died the night before.

## DAY 11, THURSDAY, DECEMBER 29TH

John got up early to try and hear some papers. I collected him at 11 am, and we drove off to buy the shoes. I also tried to contact Cliff, who had expressed an interest in coming, but I phoned him and paged him, and failed to find him.

After our shopping, we drove back to the old part of the city, which is now underground.[19] It is rather nice, but not much goes on there during the day. We unfortunately had no time to go back at night. It has mostly bars and sort of nightclubs. John went back to the Hilton, and I returned for him at 4 pm and drove him, Leslie,[20] Robert and Barbara,[21] and Jay to a party at Agnes Scott College. Since it is a ladies' college, *someone* (we suspect Leslie) started the rumour that the reception was to be dry. This proved to be false, and it was a most jolly party.

---

18     William S. Anderson, my senior colleague in Classics at Berkeley, an authority on Latin Literature, particularly Horace and Vergil. Lorna was his wife.

19     *Underground Atlanta* is a shopping and entertainment district in the Five Points neighbourhood of downtown Atlanta, Georgia, near the Five Points MARTA station. First opened in 1969, it takes advantage of the viaducts built over the city's many railroad tracks to accommodate later automobile traffic.

20     My colleague in Berkeley Leslie Threatte (1943-2021), an authority on Greek inscriptions, and a person of some eccentricity.

21     Robert Rodgers and his wife Barbara Saylor Rodgers, at this time my colleagues in Berkeley, but subsequently in the University of Vermont, where they remained for the rest of their careers.

We came back to the hotel (Hilton) and had our dinner there, because we were to have the Berkeley party at 9.00, and we wanted to be on the premises. We had really quite a good dinner. The party (in a special suite on the 20th floor) was a great success. Not much was drunk, so we had to load one-and-a-half cases of wine back into the car next morning.

*Good party – Arthur Adkins affable, Sterling Dow in fine form, Peter Marshall also, but – great faux pas! – we forgot to invite Ernst Badian![22]*


## DAY 12, FRIDAY, DECEMBER 30TH

John got up early to deliver, at 9 am, an obituary on Prof. Ivan Linforth.[23] The secretary had asked him to do it. It wasn't easy, because John never knew the man, but I think it went off OK. We had lunch with Prof. Westerink.[24] John had not known he was at the meeting, and was delighted when he ran into him.

We set off after lunch for Bill and Diane's[25] in Nashville,

---

22    All these distinguished Classicists. Badian, a very sensitive figure, had just been our Sather Professor for the previous year (as had Sterling Dow, in 1963/4).

23    Ivan Mortimer Linforth (15 September 1879, San Francisco – 15 December 1976, Berkeley) was an American scholar, Professor of Greek at University of California, Berkeley. According to the *Biographical Dictionary of North American Classicists* he was "one of the great Hellenists of his time". He is best known for his book *The Arts of Orpheus* (1941). In it he analysed the body of texts dealing with Orpheus and the Orphics. He concluded that there was no exclusively 'Orphic' system of belief in Ancient Greece. He had retired long before my time.

24    Leendert Westerink, Professor of Greek at the University of New York at Buffalo, was a major authority on Neoplatonic philosophy, and was of great help to me both in my assembling of the fragments of Iamblichus and in my translation of Proclus' *Commentary on the Parmenides*.

25    William Race, who had also served with me in DIGS (see above), and who now had joined the Classics faculty at Vanderbilt University in Nashville. He was (and is) a great authority on Greek poetry, especially Pindar. After a distinguished career at Vanderbilt, he joined the faculty of Classics at the University of North Carolina at Chapel Hill, where he remained until his retirement.

Tennessee. it was a beautiful drive through mountains, with frozen waterfalls along the roadway. We arrived at their house at about 6 pm It is a really lovely house on about two acres in a most attractive suburb. The furniture was very tasteful – mostly mahogany (which is my favourite). Their two children are marvellous – Mary Katharine, who is 2 ½, and Nori (short for Eleanor), who is 5 months. Mary K is like a little cartoon character – speaks extremely well, and goes about the house singing songs, such as 'Oh dear, what can the matter be?', and is not one bit shy. She let me put on her pyjamas the first night we were there.

## DAY 13, SATURDAY, DECEMBER 31ST

We were woken in the morning by the song 'Oh dear...' sung by Miss M.K., and then I heard her say, "Where are John and Jean?" By then I was in the bath, and I heard the door knob rattle and her mumbling, "I can't open it." Then she trotted off in to John. She asked to be helped up onto his bed, and then sat cross-legged in front of him and mumbled to herself, as she decided how to open the conversation. Then she said, "We feed the birds in the winter...". Then she bounced on the bed and nearly fell off.

*After a long conversation at the breakfast table, Bill took us off to visit Vanderbilt University, and the 'Parthenon'. The University is spaciously laid out, and of a respectable age. Bill showed us his office in the Classics Department, which is very pleasantly situated. Then we drove to a park to visit the Parthenon. This is an exact replica of the Athenian Parthenon, constructed originally in some temporary material for an exhibition, which the citizens later decided to make permanent, when it was about to fall to pieces. They got the archaeologist Dinsmoor to advise them, and made a very exact copy of the original, frieze and all, in concrete made to look like weathered Pentelic marble. It is actually a most impressive sight, inside and out. They are now saving up for a 40-foot high chyselephantine statue of Athena to go inside it. Good luck to them![26]*

We drove back to the house and had a sandwich for lunch.

---

26    The statue of Athena was duly installed in 1990, so it took a bit of time!

Later in the afternoon, Diane and I took off to do some antique shop browsing, and I found a chair at the Antique Mall – a nice mahogany one. I saw another just like it, but couldn't decide whether to get it or not. When we got back to the house John and Bill decided for me, and we went back and got the second one – $20 each – really a good buy!

Because it was New Year's Eve, they invited some people over for drinks at about 5.30. They were Nancy and Emerson Brown and their son and daughter, and the chairman of their Classics Department, called Bob Drews, a native of Wisconsin (like John).

*The boyfriend of the Brown daughter was a young Englishman who had been to Marlborough, the same school as Mark Griffith[27]. Emerson Brown brought over some home-made mead, which we consumed gladly. The party broke up about 7.00, and Diane served a simple but excellent meal of steak and salad.*

Then Bill proposed that we go to see if we could find some good Bluegrass music to see in the New Year, and we jumped at this (Diane had to stay home and babysit). The first bar we went to charged rather a lot to get in, and didn't have Bill's favourite fiddler, so we went on to another, the Bluegrass Inn, where we found what we wanted – Hubert Davis and his group (consisting of his wife, daughter, and we think son-in-law), and Bill's favourite fiddler, who is indeed superb, and said to be the best Bluegrass fiddler in Nashville, Mr. Richard Hoffman. The music was wild and brilliant, and very well received. We bought their record (and a second copy for John and Trice), and found ourselves at midnight on our feet roaring with the crowd to the strains of the Confederate anthem, 'Dixie'. A great evening.[28]


## DAY 14, SUNDAY, JANUARY 1ST (1978)

Having asked M.K. to call us when she got up in the morning, she duly came trotting down about 8 am, looking

---

27    My colleague in Classics in Berkeley.

28    We still possess the record of the band we bought that night – signed by them all: 'It's Bluegrass Time Again'.

extremely bleary, holding her blankie, and sat in our room on the floor while we got dressed and packed. By the time we were dressed, all the family was up, and we had a nice, leisurely breakfast with them.

We left Nashville (quite regretfully) at 8.45, and headed off to Oklahoma City, *via* Memphis. The countryside around is pretty, though after a while one wishes it would change now and then. It is identical for miles and miles. We arrived in Oklahoma City at about 8.30 pm We had booked at our Motel 6, so our room was waiting for us. We went out to have a ghastly dinner at ghastly Denny's[29] – there seems to be very little choice in Oklahoma.

## DAY 15, MONDAY, JAN 2ND (OUR ANNIVERSARY)

We got up about 8 am, and set off for New Mexico. As we were driving through Oklahoma, I noticed, as we passed a car, *a man with earphones and a walkie-talkie*, which he spoke into as we passed. This happened a few times, as he would pass me, then slow down, etc. I had the weirdest feeling that we were being spied on, but I thought that if he was in contact with the police about speeding, we would have been stopped ages ago. This went on for at least half-an-hour. At one point, we left the road to fill up with petrol, and when we got back onto the freeway, *another* man (in a car with a *Kansas* registration) started the same act. I wondered if I was just being paranoid – we *were* driving rather fast – but drove on at the same rate. It was not till we were sailing through *Texas* at 80 mph that a Highway Patrol man pounced. Luckily, his radar only registered us at 72 mph. But it just shows how organised they are, and how long they are willing to follow you before pouncing.

We arrived in Santa Fé about 5.30 pm, and checked into our hotel (Motel 6 again!). It was quite far out of town, so before dinner we drove into town, which is really charming. Once again, the fact that we were in town on a *Monday* night meant that most of the restaurants were closed. We went to a

---

29      One of America's most popular fast-food outlets.

Mexican one called Rosita's, which was only moderately good, though they did serve *soparpillas*.

## DAY 16, TUESDAY, JANUARY 3<sup>RD</sup>

We decided to spend the morning pottering about the old town, which turned out to be quite fascinating. We heard both Navajo and Spanish being spoken in the main square, where the Indians sit and sell their jewelry. We visited the cathedral, which has been reconstructed to a point where one can only imagine what it must have originally been.

The Mission San Miguel was a great disappointment, for the simple reason that, as we walked in the door, a 'priest' came out and in a monotone said something about "the tour begins here", and promptly switched on a loud and blaring tape-recorder. I think it was disgraceful – there was no question of kneeling down to say a prayer. I just left, I was so furious, but John remained, and they got a dollar off him. A little house stands across the way, which they say is the oldest house in America, dating from about 1200! I suppose the Indian ones don't count. This one was actually originally Indian, and the lower walls are supposed to be the original ones.

We had a sort of breakfast at a very nice patisserie in the square. John had a croissant, and I had a delicious apple slice. John very much wanted to see a multi-story pueblo at a place called Taos, but it turned out to be about 50 miles away, and I couldn't face the extra drive there, so we decided to visit one a little closer. It was a nice little town, but all the houses were single-story, so we decided to drive on and try to find another one. Well, we had a very futile time, because we drove about thirty miles without seeing what we wanted. But the countryside was lovely, anyhow, with a background of those majestic snow-capped mountains.

By 3.30 we were on the road again, heading for Acoma, which has an attractive pueblo up on a high mesa. We were rather late arriving (they close one hour before dusk), and so we just drove up to the entrance and turned around again. We were also too mean to pay the $4.00 they wanted for entry.

We drove on to Gallup then, to spend the night, this time staying at the Colonial Motel, which was no more expensive than a Motel 6, and a lot nicer. Gallup is a dreadful town, with one neon-lit main street.

## DAY 17, WEDNESDAY, JANUARY 4TH

We were on the road by 8.45 am. Had an uneventful drive, stopping for breakfast at Stuckey's somewhere along the way. We ran into signs of snow around Flagstaff, but missed it. Everything looked pretty, with its thin white film of snow. We stayed overnight in Barstow, where it was raining hard.

## DAY 18, THURSDAY, JANUARY 5TH

When we rose, it had stopped raining, but there were signs of storms not far off. The rain did not catch us up until we got about half way up Hwy 5. Then it came down in buckets. We were horrified once again to see that dreadful cattle-fattening farm at Kettleman City, where thousands of unfortunate animals are jammed together in a small muddy area. It's a terrible sight.

*And here the diary ends. We were back in Berkeley by the evening, presumably, and that much more appreciative of our immediate environment after having surveyed a wide swathe of the southern United States!!*

# 3: THE TRIP TO YUCATAN,

## DECEMBER, 1979

*This trip was proposed to us by our old friends (and former landlords in Berkeley) Ron and Sally Fremlin, and undertaken, with them, in the foreboding that this might be our last real chance to visit Mexico, if I returned to Ireland to take up the position of Regius Professor of Greek in Trinity College Dublin – as in fact proved to be the case. Once again, Jean is the chief narrator, and her contributions are consequently in ordinary print.*

### DAY 1, SATURDAY, DECEMBER 8<sup>TH</sup>

A pleasant flight from San Francisco to Mexico City, on Mexicana Airlines. They served us a delicious breakfast of egg tortilla (omelette) with hot sauce, refried beans, roll, sweet roll, orange juice *and champagne.* Then they came around with a trayful of assorted meats, including sausages, liver and bacon, ham, etc. And of course coffee to finish.

We had a few minutes to wander around outside the airport before catching our plane to Merida. It is easy to imagine how the dense smog which hangs over the city comes to be. The population of Mexico City is now 12 million, and they seem to have no notion of smog controls. Dirty old buses and ancient cars abound. But we have yet to see the real city.

Our flight to Merida was a hair-raiser. The pilot, having decided that he was 15 minutes behind schedule, tried to make it up on our *descent* into Merida. He went like a madman for about ten minutes with the plane at a fearful downturned angle, and we all felt as if we were leaving our insides behind. It reminded John of Allegheny Airlines, but I fear it was even worse. It was raining when we arrived, but it cheered up after a short time, although the humidity is tremendous. The temperature is in the 80's, and will probably go higher tomorrow.

Our hotel is fabulous (the Panamericana). It has wonderful downstairs courtyards with gorgeous plants – palms and other tropical ferns, etc. – enormous high carved doorways, a swimming pool, with dining room overlooking it, and large rooms, with marble floors everywhere.

We had dinner at a little restaurant across the road, which is called 'Los Almendros', offering Yucatan specialities. It was truly delicious. Ron, Sally, and I had their 'speciality', 'Poc-Chuc', which we first thought must be a version of 'pork chop', but which turned out to be a genuine Yucatan dish, grilled pork with marinated onions, and excellent. John was a devil, and went for a concoction called 'Pavo con relleno negro', which was turkey in a villainous-looking black sauce, but which turned out to be delicious (he is now – 12.30 am – lying quietly, waiting to die). This was all washed down with XXX beers and limes.

After dinner, we walked round a little neighbouring square, admiring the architecture, and then down to Calle 69 towards the centre of town. In front of the hotel we found a little horse and trap. The old man who owned the horse said that he was six years old, and would live to be 35 or 40! He worked him only every second day, and he was beautifully cared for. The old man obviously loved him dearly, judging by the way he spoke about him. He was only about 12 hands, but looked like a miniature horse rather than a pony, as I believe he was – one of those South American breeds!

We went and sat beside the swimming pool in our hotel for another hour or so, and had some coffee and listened to the small orchestra, which (disappointingly) played 1930s American music. (I forgot to mention that during the afternoon a group of Spanish dancers performed on a stage beside the pool – they were very good.)

We were rudely awakened at 8.30 am, and were *told* that we were to be taken on a tour of Merida city by car, with our own guide, called Benjamin. He is a very pleasant man, and, like all the people in the villages round about, speaks both Mayan and Spanish. It was fascinating to hear him speak Mayan – John says that the glottal stops and plosive consonants are very similar to Amharic.[30]

Our tour of the city (pop. 300,000) was interesting. Besides taking us to the main square (Independenzia), he drove us along the Avenida Montejo, named after the founder of the city, and whicht is the posh residential area. The houses are very grand, and many of them are built with Carrara marble, which the merchants of the 18th and 19th centuries, who exported sisal to Europe, brought (along with a good deal of fine gilt furniture) back as ballast.

*Most of the old sisal barons have had to abandon their palaces because of high taxes, and many of them look pretty tatty (the humidity is such that one has to repaint one's house every year or so, if one wants to keep it presentable – otherwise black mould grows). These families had more contact with Europe and the U.S. than with the rest of Mexico, because surface connexions between the rest of the country and Yucatan were virtually non-existent – indeed, until a highway was completed in 1960. Intensive tourism has only begun in the last few years or so.*

*At the end of the Avenida, there is an imposing monument, built by a Colombian sculptor called Romolo Rozo, depicting the various stages of Mexican history. It is covered with narrative bas-relief, in a rather decadent Mayan style. The avenue itself is lined with flame-trees, which were unfortunately not in bloom.*

We were then driven to Uxmal (pronounced 'Ushmal'), through countryside which from a distance looks very fertile, but which in fact is poor (and because of the amount of rock which covers the soil). There is no lack of moisture here – the water table is only 25 feet below the surface, and what does grow looks extremely lush. Sisal fields are all along the road to Uxmal – each yucca plant from which the sisal is taken lasts about 25 years.

---

30      I had spent two years in Ethiopia (1961-63), which enabled me to make this observation.

An interesting thing about present-day Yucatan is the lack of horses or mules. They are not used at all here. The people walk everywhere, carrying their loads on their backs or on their heads – unless they can afford a motorbike! And the funny thing about the ancient Mayans is that they built twelve-foot wide roads even though they didn't use carts. Apparently they were built so wide to accommodate their religious processions.

*The ruins are astonishing. It is annoying to feel that there is another whole civilisation here that one has to reckon with, but exciting when one looks out over the jungle landscape and sees that there is as much more again that hasn't been dug up yet. Ben took us off, after a leisurely lunch, to the ruins of Uxmal. After admiring the artificial well, we approached the first pyramid, the Magician's Palace. The steps are remarkably narrow and steep. How the priests climbed them with any semblance of dignity is beyond us. I scrambled up in a most undignified manner, and was then most unwilling to come down, when I saw where I was. But, helped by two charming co-eds I found at the top, I came down the other side, where the façade is broken up a bit. One diversion, in fact, is the Rain-God Chaac's mouth, which one can go into, to find a small vaulted room, which has bad breath – presumably bats or swallows!*

*Ben, our guide, is most voluble and learned about all the ruins. He was particularly anxious that we should understand how the temples were built. Two peculiar things about the Mayans: they kept building on top of old buildings, and not when the old ones were worn out, but for some other reason. Ben maintains that that it is when, in their view, the old building's natural life has come to an end – perhaps after five periods of 52 years = 260 years. We don't know where he got that idea. Anyhow, if you take off one layer of Mayan temple, you find another underneath, and then another, and another… In some cases, archaeologists have done this. The other thing is that their basic pattern for constructing a room is the same as that used to build their huts, then and now – a high, vaulted ceiling on a rectangular base. He showed us patiently how this was constructed. One can see it in various places.*

*So we viewed the 'Nunnery', the 'Governor's Palace', the 'Turtle Temple', the 'Great Pyramid' – all names given either by ignorant Spaniards or desperate archaeologists. We don't know what any of them were for, but the great 'Nunnery' quadrangle may have been a residence for student* priests. Lots of individual rooms, anyhow. The friezes are magnificent, but tend to get repetitive – rain-god masks and serpents, all individually carved, but looking as if they had rolled off an assembly line.

After dinner, we were to go to a Son et Lumière show up at the Nunnery, but decided to postpone it till tomorrow, and just play cards instead. We are feeling a bit superior and begrudging at the busloads of tourists who appear from time to time, but who in some mysterious way don't cross paths with us except tangentially. The latest group that blew in are called The Funsters – average age 65, and rarin' to go! Old gents in white shoes, old hens in stretch pants – real swingers!

But the Hotel is lovely – marble floors, high ceilings, lots of space, a beautiful courtyard round the pool, and all about us the jungle. One wishes one could explore the jungle more – perhaps surprise a wild turkey or an armadillo – but it is well-nigh impenetrable, in spite of the lack of soil that Ben complains of. "If only", he says, "we had some soil, this would be a paradise. Three crops a year, anything you want to grow!" Ron and I, of course, are full of suggestions as to how soil is to be made, but private enterprise is not, it seems, encouraged in Socialist Mexico!

## DAY 3, MONDAY, DECEMBER 10<sup>TH</sup>

*Ben got us going about 9.30, for an expedition to K'abah, another site not far from Uxmal (there are more again back in the hills, but not so easily reachable). K'abah (which means 'hand of water' – k'ab, 'hand', ah 'water') is not nearly as developed as Uxmal, and in that way more fascinating. We first went to see a large arch, which marked one end of a ceremonial road from Uxmal to K'abah, of which only the beginning, at K'abah, has been uncovered. The gate was presumably also the entrance to the city. The Mayans used no wheeled vehicle or beast of burden. They walked (or jogged) everywhere. But yet they built a number of elaborate paved roads, as good as Roman roads. This one runs for about ten miles, but there is another one discovered which goes for twenty-seven. An interesting feature of the gate, pointed out by Ben, is that you can still see the red hands imprinted on it (k'ab again!).*

*Other than the gate, there are three buildings uncovered, the chief one being the Temple of the Masks, the façade of which is covered in more rain-*

*god masks than one would ever wish to see. It is an impressive sight, though. I climbed up to the top of it, and, with binoculars, could pick out numerous unexplored mounds rising up from the surrounding jungle.*

We came back in the afternoon – bathed, snoozed, and watched the Funsters. In the evening it rained, so we didn't go to the Son et Lumière as we had planned, but stayed in the hotel and played cards. The lights kept failing because a thunderstorm came up. The hotel has an auxiliary electrical system, so they kept revving it up, and we never suffered for more than ten minutes at a time. We found out later that the whole of Yucatan was without electricity for three hours.

### DAY 4, TUESDAY, DECEMBER 11<sup>TH</sup>

We drove to Chichen Itza, where we found the most impressive monuments of all – first stopping at our hotel, called La Hacienda. Also a beautiful place, with gorgeous antique furniture at every turn, fountains, and the usual lush growth.

*I had unfortunately been very ill last night. Montezuma's Revenge had finally struck. I reached a plateau of exhaustion at about eight in the morning, though, and, after one of Sally's pills, was well enough to attempt the drive, leaving at about 10.00. At first we thought we were stuck in Uxmal, or should try just to get to Merida, which would have been tragic, but I just about made it to Chichen Itza, and retired to bed to contemplate my folly (which is still obscure to us, since everybody has been eating about the same things), while the others went to the ruins.*

Ben gave us a great tour, which I can't remember much of. I think he makes most of it up, but it really brings things to life. And he has obviously studied Mayan civilisation, and loves it. We saw first a large pyramid, the Castillo, which has another pyramid inside (naturally!), but which has been laid open by archaeologists. Here they found a splendid jaguar throne, red and inlaid with jade. Other remarkable features are the great Ball Court, with a frieze round it depicting something of how they played, though we still don't know the rules. One rule seems to have been, though, that the captain of the losing side lost his head. There is a representation of the winning captain (?)

cutting off the kneeling losing captain's (?) head – or it may have been the other way round, Ben thinks. Maybe the winner had the special honour and privilege of losing his head! Anyhow, there is a weird platform adjacent to the ball court with a frieze of skulls on it. Presumably the losers, whose heads were no doubt mounted on the platform. Charming!

Another charming habit the Mayans – or Toltecs, rather – had was throwing maidens, and small children, into a large cistern or *cenote*, a little way from the main plaza. It is an awesome sight – an enormous hole in the ground, carved out of the limestone, with a platform above it, whence the unfortunate maiden was pushed into the water far below. Apparently she was so doped up by this time that she didn't really mind, but still... Ben has a story that if she managed to survive from dawn to noon (clinging on to something, perhaps?), the priests hauled her out, presuming that the gods had sent her back, and made her a priestess, but insisted that she tell them what the gods wanted them to do next, or what they had done wrong. So she had to have her story ready. Not too many survived, though, because when this man Edward Thompson dredged the well early in the century, he came up with some 40 skeletons of maidens, and a good many children – and he only dredged a portion of it. He also recovered a lot of jade and gold ornaments.

Thompson was an interesting man. When American Consul here early in the century, he bought Chichen Itza from a local farmer (who thought he was crazy!) for $150, and began to excavate it. He lived in a beautiful old colonial hacienda nearby, which Ben showed us. Later, the Carnegie Institute took over the job.

But back to the ruins. They are divided in half by the road, and one goes across this and down a forest path to other fascinating sites, such as the Observatory, where very sophisticated astronomical observations were made, and (once again) a bogus Nunnery, plus 'Church' – a little richly-ornamented building on its own. The Nunnery had a nice façade, covered in good old rain-god masks. And there are lots of other goodies in the bushes, when anyone ever gets around to digging them out.

It doesn't seem possible that all this was just a religious, or 'ceremonial', centre. It looks in fact just like 'downtown Chichen', with all the government offices, theatres, opera house and so on – maybe a university! Until they decipher the hieroglyphs, we won't know, and possibly not even then.

While we were gone, John got cautiously up, wandered round the hotel, and even up to the ruins, where he tottered in and sat on a mound for a while. Then it began to rain, and he got a lift back from a young American couple in a car who took pity on him. It rained pretty hard for a while. Ron stood Ben a beer, and then invited him to eat John's dinner, which he seemed glad to do. John remains fairly well, having not eaten today. He was well enough for a game of rummy after dinner. As usual, our wild card game, with Ron cursing his cards in colourful language, and winning most of the time, is the last thing to stop in the hotel – all the funsters go to beddybyes about 9.30 or 10.00 pm, and it's just the crickets, the bats and us.

## DAY 5, WEDNESDAY, DECEMBER 12<sup>TH</sup>

*Feast of Our Lady of Guadalupe.*

John felt better, so we decided to go to the ruins early. We got down to the dining-room at 7.30 am and had coffee and rolls. This time they couldn't have been more attentive, with their endless refills of coffee.

Then off to the ruins. We were admiring the bas-relief at the entrance to the ball-court when we heard a whining noise behind us. John hoped it might be a jaguar, but it turned out to be friendly little dog. She then followed us for the rest of our tour, sitting down occasionally to wait patiently while we poked at this and that. I took a photograph of John scratching her tummy.

We got back to the hotel at 10 am, had a swim, and then Ben drove us down to the 'Castello' (the biggest pyramid) again, because it hadn't been open in the morning and John wanted to see the Jaguar Throne. This is one of the few objects found inside the pyramids. It is made of limestone, painted red, and has jades for eyes. Quite beautiful! It was found inside the second pyramid of the 'Castello' and, instead of removing it and putting it in a museum, they decided to leave it *in situ*, so they have cleared out a narrow section of the stairway, so one can walk up 62 steps inside to view it. We then asked Ben to take us to the old hacienda of Eric Thompson, which borders the old city of Chichen Itza. A nice old house, which is now a hotel and has been changed little.

Then the drive back to Merida, which was long and hot. On the way, we passed many schoolchildren piled on top of lorries, with one kid running in front and one behind, each carrying a torch. Apparently these were representatives of all the villages for miles around who were to converge on Merida for a celebration of the feast of Our Lady of Guadalupe. The kids took turns at the running.

We were given much more modest rooms this time at the Hotel Panamerican. Perhaps we didn't tip enough the last time around! It is interesting, but these people have really got the idea of tipping embedded in their minds, and one is expected to tip at the *American* rates, which is not really fair, considering the service isn't that great. One doesn't mind in the small restaurants and public places, but in these fancy hotels they are very casual  and unfriendly, which is not in the nature of the local population round about, who respond very quickly to a smile, and seem to have a good sense of humour – especially the pure Mayans, who apparently are very even-tempered and mild people. Perhaps the American habit of not using the word "please" had turned them off. "Please" always gets a smile in response.

We went to lunch at a café which had been recommended to us by a man from Martinique whom we had met on the steps of the hotel the day before we left for Chichen Itza. It was a couple of blocks from the hotel and was called an Arab name, 'La Califa'. Ron and Sally didn't want to eat, but John and I had an *excellent* shrimp cocktail. The shrimps were floating in a sauce of fresh lime juice and tomato. And with our beers we were brought a plate of delicious hors d'oeuvres, a fish in mayonnaise sauce, a savoury rice (very good), tacos, chips and peppers. The bill for 4 beers, a coke, the shrimps and hors d'oeuvres was 84 pesos, which is about four dollars. The boy was very pleased with our generous tip – especially, I think, because it is not a place where tourists go. It was crowded with locals.

We then wandered off in the direction of the market-place, which had nothing to excite us. Either the usual tourist stuff, or fairly shoddy (and expensive) local stuff. It's hard to imagine how the people themselves can afford to shop here. Ron and Sally continued on, while John and I went off to see the Cathedral, which is unremarkable, but dates from 1598, and is partly built with stones from Mayan buildings! It is apparently the first cathedral in continental America. There is a beautiful park in the Square (Independenzia, or Zocalo) with usual trees, and benches to rest on. Next we went across the square to the Palace of the Governor, the walls of which are decorated with murals by the Yucatan artist Paceco (painted in 1978). They depict the birth of civilisation from the Mayan point of view. The building is very pretty, with a large tiled courtyard and wide staircase, leading to a balcony which covers all the sides of the courtyard.

We decided to have dinner in the hotel and watch the Spanish dancing, which was excellent. One of the cleverest efforts was when the men balanced a wine bottle on their heads, and the girls a tray with filled glasses and a bottle, and they did a long dance like this (with no accidents!). The dinner was OK, but unremarkable, as in all these hotels – tourist food.

P.S. I forgot to mention that, in the afternoon, we visited the Montejo House, the oldest house in Yucatan (1542?), which the descendants of the original Montejo (the founder of the city) have lived in ever since. It is a nice old house, full of ill-assorted furniture and family portraits. We were shown round by a preposterous old retainer, who spoke in a rapid-fire mixture of Spanish and English, which came out like Esperanto. His main phrase was "Very bad taste – all very bad taste." When John tried to tip him, he proudly returned the tip, so we feel he was probably the last of the Montejos himself.

## DAY 6, THURSDAY, DECEMBER 13<sup>TH</sup>

We were taken to Merida airport at 7.30 am, where we had a cup of coffee and some of the Swedish biscuits I had packed. Our flight to the island of Cozumel took only 25 minutes, and then a short drive took us to our hotel, the Cozumel Caribe, which is right on the beach at the west side of the island. It is truly a paradise. We got (at our request) a room on the bottom floor, with a patio built right out onto the beach, which is planted with lots of coconut palms, and the beach is beautiful soft white sand. The water is that beautiful clear greenish colour of the Mediterranean, turning to a kind of purplish colour further out from the shore. It is like swimming in a warm bath, and you can stay in for ages without chilling. The coconut trees are laden with fruit, which falls continually. We haven't yet found out how to open them – we suspect we'd need a machete!

We spent most of the day just swimming and sunbathing, and John and I played tennis in the afternoon. They seem to have four courts here! We went to lunch in the town at a restaurant called Las Palmeras, had a very good beef taco and beer. The town is rather swinging with lots of 'beautiful' American people about, so there are lots of souvenir shops (some of high quality) and nightclubs. We wandered around the town after dinner and bought a large blanket from a boy who was selling them on the street. It is woven with the central theme from a Mayan design – very standard, we later found out, but very attractive nevertheless. Paid $20 U.S. for it.

## DAY 7, FRIDAY, DECEMBER 14<sup>TH</sup>

We decided not to take the hotel up on its offer of breakfast on the patio, because they add a service charge and we're feeling too mean to pay it. Anyhow, by breakfast time we're usually up and ready to go. The continental breakfast here is anything but continental – just a few slices of soggy toast; no decent rolls, even though the breads and pastries here are delicious. But the fruit juices and coffee are good.

John and I took a walk up the road a mile or so, where it ends, and saw an iguana, a large lizard, and a tree decorated with turkey vultures. Also numerous gorgeous brightly-coloured birds. I wish I had a bird book to look them up!

John then rented a snorkelling outfit, and ever since has been like a turtle – happily pottering about looking at the gorgeous fish. We have the beach in front of our room practically to ourselves, so we potter in and out when we feel like it, without bumping into other bathers. The beach on either side of us, down a hundred yards or so, is really quite crowded, so we are very lucky. The coconut palms keep us cool when we don't want to sunbathe.

We all swam on and off through the afternoon (we decided to skip lunch, and nibble on the bits of bread and cheese we had picked up). Then at about 4.30 John and I had a feeble bash at a game of tennis, but it proved to be too hot, so we only played 5 minutes or so. Before dinner, we found the most fabulous bakery. We bought lots of rolls, doughnuts, pastries with fruit, and one small cake – all for 22 pesos (around $1.00 or so), and they're delicious.

Into town for dinner (one gets a taxi from here) to the Restaurant Platera. We had a very good dinner – first of all, nachos (tacos with beans, tomato sauce, grated cheese), very good; then J and I had seafood soup (kind of bouillabaisse), and he finished with conch, and I had red snapper. Then we all went off browsing in the shops. J excused himself at one point, and went to sit on a park bench, but when we went to find him a while later he was nowhere to be seen. So we phoned the hotel, and found that he was ill again, and had had to rush back.

## DAY 8, SATURDAY, DECEMBER 15<sup>TH</sup>

We hired a car (a VW Safari) and drove around the island, which took us all of two and a half hours. We stopped first at the Chancanab Lagoon, where we saw the most gorgeous fish, some enormous, with lovely rock formations. John had brought along his hired snorkelling outfit, and had great fun. The parrot fish was the most impressive – very large bluish-green colour, with gorgeous markings. We were disappointed to find a lot of junk – bottles, plastic, etc. – on the beaches on the south and east sides of the island. We wondered where it all came from.

We had a picnic of cheese, rolls, and beer on a piece of beach on our journey. Then we drove on round the island, until we came to a turning onto a dirt road, down which John was convinced we would find a Mayan ruin. We drove on for miles, Ron cursing all the way, and finally arrived in the square of a little village, where there was no one to be seen but a flock of turkeys and one old woman. She seemed a nice old thing, but we suspected the turkeys were actually the previous tourists, and that we would be next! Anyhow, we asked was there a *ruina,* and she pointed to an overgrown edifice beside the little church, which turned out to be a small Mayan temple – just one room, no rain-god masks visible! I took a picture of her, and bought a warm coke from her, and have not turned into a turkey yet!

We arrived back at our hotel at about 2.30, and spent the rest of the afternoon swimming and lounging about. Then we went into the town for dinner at the same restaurant as last night, and then viewed some black coral. Ron had found a very nice piece some days ago at the *supermarket*! He had paid 80 pesos for it, and everyone he shows it to says it is a great bargain. Certainly our comparative shopping around has proved this to be so. We saw a lovely carved lizard for the equivalent of $33. John is tempted.

## DAY 10, SUNDAY, DECEMBER 16<sup>TH</sup>

J and I arose at 7.30 and had a swim before breakfast. We had breakfast as usual at around 8.30. We arranged to take a trip on a glass-bottomed boat at 11.30, but first John decided he *had* to have that lizard, so we dashed off to town to get it. We got into the shop, and didn't see the boy who had served us yesterday, but there was an older man there. We pointed to the lizard and offered him U.S. $30. He looked at us aghast, and said it was $50. We argued, and said that we had been quoted by the boy (his son) $32. He said "Impossible". We left the shop, and just as we got outside, John said "But there was a sticker price on it yesterday!", and it was gone today. So we went back in, and the man was fair. He said he would find his son, and we could come back in ten minutes. When we returned, the son confirmed his price, and we got it for $32. So at least the old man was honourable. He obviously felt, if it had been offered at that price, then he had to sell it for that.

We rushed back to the hotel, just in time to see the glass-bottomed boat leave the pier, but they saw us and waited for us. It cost approximately $2.50 each for three-quarters of an hour, and was not terribly exciting. We expected to see coral reefs, but they were further out than these people went, but we did see lots of fish life – lancers (bright blue!), parrot fish, two sharks, black-faced angel fish, and many others whose names I can't remember.

We had a quick swim when we got back, and then packed our bags. We had to check out by 2.30 pm, but we got an extension of one hour. We weren't to leave for the airport until 4.30, so we had a rather long time to hang around. But by the time we had had a cup of coffee and sat by the swimming pool (which we hadn't really noticed before), it didn't seem any time before we were off. We were very sorry to leave, and wished we had arranged to stay longer in lovely Cozumel.

We arrived in Mexico City at 7.30 pm, and, after a day there, during which we were able to pay a visit to the old Aztec capital of Tenochtitlan, we had an uneventful flight home to San Francisco

# 4. TRIP TO ISRAEL: MAY – JUNE 1981

*The purpose of this expedition was to attend a conference in Tel Aviv, organised by John Glucker, of the University of Tel Aviv, himself a noted authority on the Platonic Tradition, as well as on Cicero, and a great character, on the great German-Jewish classical philologist and philosopher Jacob Bernays (1824-1881). I also took the opportunity, at the invitation of Samuel Scolnicov, of the Hebrew University, to pay a brief visit to Jerusalem.*

## DAY 1, THURSDAY, MAY 28TH

Straightway in London airport, one begins to feel the aura of emergency and 'security' that surrounds Israel. The bags had to be unloaded, identified and searched. We were frisked, as well as passing through the usual appliances, and frisked again further on, before we boarded the plane, in case we should in some mysterious way have picked up something in the interval. I met up with a group of Irish travel agents, including three from Easy Travel, Gerry – and two girls, and Andy McKenna from Atlas, and they were all very friendly. On the plane, I was beside an Israeli diamond merchant, who had just flown in from Miami (where he has an office), in his shirt-sleeves, and who was, temporarily, miserably cold. He wrapped himself in a blanket, and we talked for a bit. He was born in Egypt – and he looked quite Arabic – but moved to Israel at the age of six, in 1948. The family came originally from Spain, but fled during the Inquisition to Holland. It is a common enough pattern, I suppose. He went to sleep soon, after giving me some information on prices: 140% inflation, exchange rate changes all the time, so don't change much money at a time! A good hotel would cost around $50 a night, which alarms me – I hope John Glucker has been moderate! (I learned from the girl from Easy Travel, in fact, that the Ramat Aviv is a nice old hotel on the north side of town, near the University, and probably *not* expensive.)

We had an unremarkable meal, and by 5.00 pm were over Salonika (one hour time change), then over Samos, which I gazed down on reverently, in memory of Pythagoras; and then, at about 6.20, the coast of Israel came in sight, just before sunset, looking very prosperous and well-developed. The airport – Lod – is on the south-east of town. The sun was just going down, a blood-red ball, as we landed. It sets early, and suddenly, down here, as one would expect. The travel agents introduced me to their local agent here, David Steenberg (late of Harold's Cross, but a very orthodox Jew – with a skull-cap) – very friendly, and urged me to call on him in his office if help was needed, and then gave me a ride into town in their bus. A frightful asshole from Limerick was the only black spot, making compulsive anti-Semitic jokes and singing loudly – probably got pissed on the plane. Thank God I am not stuck with him!

They found me a taxi, and I got out to the Ramat Aviv Hotel at about 8.00. It cost 40 shekels, not bad, at 10.5 to the $. I settled in – a nice rustic cabin in a grove of trees – swimming pool in centre – and then rang John Glucker, who urged me to come round for a drink. I had dinner, which was OK – kebabs and salad – and went round in a taxi – having just missed the 25 bus. Glucker met me on the corner, and we walked up to his flat. He doesn't have a car.

A young German scholar, Hermann Funke, of Mannheim, had just arrived, a little after me, and is staying with them for the conference. I'm rather glad I'm not – it's really a very small flat, nice though they are. The hotel actually quoted a price of $38.50 for bed and breakfast (though $33.00 is on the room door!), which is not too bad. I brought a bottle of Irish Mist, which John attacked, while we drank beer. A student of his, Ivor Ludlum, was also present, and helping with arrangements. I stayed till about 11.30, and then found a 25 bus back to the hotel.

And so to bed. The temperature was about 85° when I arrived, slightly cooler in the evening. Very pleasant, though – a slight breeze.

DAY 2, FRIDAY, MAY 29<sup>TH</sup>

Up at 8.00 or so. On the way to breakfast, I met a very strange bird on the lawn – a crest and a long beak – and learned later it was a hoopoe. The hotel breakfast was an elaborate spread, with tahini, hummus, cucumbers, smoked fish, tomatoes, etc. Then eggs, and rolls and jam. I will have to be more cautious about it in future.

I had agreed last night to go with Hermann Funke first to the museum across the road – Ha'aretz – on the site of a Phoenician settlement with a temple, Tell Qasile. The museum is well laid out, but on a popular level – pottery, glass, coins, alphabet – a basic biblical house. Good stuff, but no indication of where it came from. The Phoenician temple is just a ground plan – it was demolished by King David, it seems, shortly after 1000 B.C.

Then, at about 1.00, after a beer at the hotel, we went off on the 25 bus to Jaffa, at the other end of the line. Hot, but a stiff breeze from the sea, which is welcome. We got off near the Clock Tower in Jaffa, and began to wander. Hermann has been before, the last time he was in Israel (these Germans have been everywhere!), so he knows his way around a bit. We stopped at a little café, where a fierce-looking lady was grilling a fish for two customers, out on the pavement. She looked at us venomously, as if we were trespassing in her kitchen, but we were undeterred. One learns not to expect people to be polite to you in Israel – it is like New York, I suppose; people are not trying to be rude, but they have no time to waste being polite (I asked an Israeli colleague, Shimon Appelbaum, later, to tell me the words for 'Please' and 'Thank you' in Hebrew, which he did, but added, "Well, you'll find people don't actually use them very often."). Anyhow, we settled down, and were asked what we wanted. "Lunch," we said. She looked at us with contempt. "What you like?" We liked the look of the fish, but were afraid of it, so we asked for kebabs, and were in due course served excellent kebabs, with hummus and salad. I ate it in fear and trembling, knowing that, if this were Lebanon, I would be ruined.[31] However, a day later, I am still standing.

We walked up a winding road to what must have been the acropolis of Old Jaffa. There is in fact an excavation at the top, revealing remains going back to Hasmonean times. We had a coffee overlooking the sea, with a fine view up the coast. There was a strong wind, but a brave or foolish fellow was windsurfing in the little harbour below. As we watched, he turned over three or four times. We then walked round 'Old Jaffa' proper, which is a fossilized complex of little streets preserved for the tourists, and allegedly inhabited by 'artists'. If there were any artists, they were asleep, it being siesta time. We met only a single dog. 'The House of Simon the Tanner' was firmly closed.

We also walked round what must have been a Turkish fort, now a complex of shops, mainly selling 'antiques' – all closed, fortunately. I must try to buy something, but so far have seen basic junk only. I don't know how reliable the gold or silver would be. I should have bought a diamond from my companion on the plane!

We went back down the hill to get a bus before the Sabbath, as all public transport then stops – about 5 pm. The rest of Old Jaffa is pretty squalid, but at least real. The people look Arab, but I believe are mainly Jews from Arab countries. I seemed to hear mainly Hebrew, though pretty guttural. There is still an active mosque, though, so a few brave Arabs may survive.

Back without incident, parted from Hermann, and had a bathe – very pleasant. I sat at the pool for a while, and read. I decided *not* to eat dinner, but went out instead and found a café open in Judah ha-Maccabee St., and had an espresso and ice-cream, at the cost of 20 shekels. And so to bed.

---

31    The reason for this remark was that, on my last visit to the Middle East, which had occurred back in August 1969, touring Lebanon, Syria, Iraq and Iran, in the company of my father and brother Peter (accompanying my father on his way to India), I had been poisoned by a kebab, presented to me by a taxi-driver in Tripoli. Only a minimal diary, unfortunately, survives from that trip.

The Sabbath is a bit tedious. If one has no car, there is simply nothing to do, for a poor tourist. I had a pleasant bathe, and read. But the pool began to fill up with citizens (very few actual *guests* in the hotel – rumoured by JG to be closing down!), and by noon it was roaring with families and kids.

I was invited to lunch at Gluckers, so set out at 12.15 to walk to their flat. It took about half-an-hour, and the sun was beginning to get to me by the end of it. A splendid lunch was served, cooked by John, called *chollent,* which is a spicy stew of chicken, almonds, vegetables, and raisins – cooked very slowly, since before the Sabbath, i.e. before dusk on Friday. Their two little daughters were there today, very charming. The younger one, Ilanna, made the fruit salad. We drank good Carmel hock, and had a large cup of excellent Turkish coffee to follow.

Then John proposed a walk to the seaside, and we set out. I had an interesting talk with him on the way. They are about to move out of their flat into the country – it has become too noisy (building is booming all round) and too expensive (now costs about two-thirds of his salary to rent). One lives pretty badly here as a professor. They are looking forward to retiring out of town.

He is inclined to be gloomy about the deal with Sadat that brought them peace with Egypt – this arising from a remark of mine that surely Israel had a guaranteed source of oil from the Sinai, even after handing the oil-wells back – feeling that Sadat is a far smarter politician than Begin, and outmanoeuvred him. This surprised me, but I see it echoed in articles in the *Jerusalem Post.* John is no admirer of Begin – he even criticises his flat Polish way of pronouncing Latin! John himself is in fact a *sabra,*[32] which I hadn't realised. His parents came from Austria at the beginning of the '30s, and settled in Haifa. He came to England only to university – I think to Oxford. It must be longer than that, in fact, as he has only a slight accent. His wife is English, was a student of his in Exeter, and a Classicist. She is

---

32      That is to say, a Jew born in Israel.

now starting up again, to do an M.A. in Classical Archaeology here. I don't know if she is even Jewish.

The seashore was very dirty and oil-polluted, but it is not yet scheduled as a beach. In spite of that, it was full of people. Looking back inland, one can see the inexorable growth of building in Ramat Aviv – apartment block after apartment block. Grim!

I asked if the younger generation of Israelis preserved the idealism of their ancestors. Would they, for example, clean up the beach if called upon? John doubted it. He feels they just want a good job and a quiet life, like anyone else. But I doubt that that is the whole story. There are certainly still idealists left – but then so there are in Ireland, after all. One tends to regard the religious extremists as rather quaint, in their funny hats and funny hair-styles, but how are they different from, say, rampant Legion of Mary members at their worst? I'm afraid they are just boring and nasty.

We slogged back and had a cup of tea, and then I took my leave. Both Hermann and the Gluckers are going to feel pretty cramped by the end of his stay, I should think! After John's excellent *chollent,* I didn't need any dinner, and, after an evening swim, I went out on the town, to take a walk on Dizenkoff.

The bus took me most of the way, but a bit inland. I walked a few blocks, and then was on the thoroughfare. In true Mediterranean manner, everyone is out for a promenade, from very young to very old, the pavement cafés are packed, and the pavements themselves thronged. I stopped for an American-style ice-cream at an American-style ice-cream parlour, served by a young Englishman who was plainly rather high on something, giggling loudly and dropping ice-cream all over the place – unable to understand what various elderly oriental customers wanted, and very pleased to meet me. I walked then to a very bogus place called Namir Square, laid out on the sea-front, between the Plaza and Marine Hotels, to give the tourists the feeling that they're in a real old *sûq* – which they seem to love. Finally had a *very* rich blintz further north on Dizengoff, got a taxi home, and so to bed.

I am feeling slightly pointless so far, despite the Gluckers' hospitality. Tel Aviv is about as romantic as Chicago, and I look forward to escaping from it in some direction. It is annoying not knowing the language – my Hebrew is useful only for deciphering the Book of Genesis – though everyone *does* speak English, I must say.


## DAY 4, SUNDAY, MAY 31ST

Sunday is really Monday for Israelis, and so it feels. At last we get down to business. With great effort, I get up and get through the massive breakfast in time to be up at the University for 9.00, when the conference was to open with a musical recital – a setting to music of the beginning of Lucretius' *De Rerum Natura* by a man (Braun) who is head of the School of Music and also a Classicist. I must say it was beautifully performed by a young lady and a male flautist from the Department of Music, and formed a good start to the proceedings. We should consider that for our F.I.E.C.[33] meeting in 1984.

The emphasis of the day's talks was on Bernays himself, whom I was glad to learn more about. Prof. Urbach, President of the Academy of Sciences, kicked off, with a description of Bernays' Hebraic researches. Then the preposterous Jean Bollack ('Bollocks'),[34] on some metaphysical reflections connected with Bernays. Then a good young scholar, Berndt Effe (who has done a monograph on Aristotle's *On Philosophy*, and now works on Hellenistic poetry), on Bernays and the dialogues of Aristotle (Bernays vindicated their genuineness against Valentine Rose, but tried to prove them consistent with the esoteric works, which is misguided).

After a welcoming luncheon, during which I communed with a jolly man originally from Liverpool, Shimon Appelbaum

---

33    The Fédération Internationale des Études Classiques

34    Jean Bollack (1923 – 2012) was a reasonably distinguished French philosopher, philologist and literary critic. I can no longer remember quite why I am so rude about him here, but I think he was a bit of a bore.

(now retired from Tel Aviv) and Bernhard Kyteler of Berlin, whom I had met in Berkeley – a rather smooth man, it must be said (e.g. he couldn't be sure where he'd met me – could it perhaps have been at a conference in Dakar?). Appelbaum guided me after lunch to the school shop, where I bought this notebook.

After lunch, Mrs. Bollocks (totally incomprehensible); then, a rather good lit-crit. effusion from Jeffrey Duban of Georgia State (who does come on a bit strong, though – as if he was trying to get a job, or a promotion), then Kyteler, on an ephemeral talk of Bernays' which should have been left unpublished, as he has intended; then a fellow called Toury on German Jewry in Bernays' time.

After the session, I had fixed up with Hermann F. to go out to dinner. Went back and had a shower, he met me at about 7.45, and we set off to find a Russian restaurant called Piroshki. The bus got us near enough, and the restaurant was small and unpretentious, and we had borscht and piroshki and beer, and it was good. Then we walked along Dizenkoff, and finally settled down for a cappuchino. Hermann actually got elected to the city council of Heidelberg last year as a 'Green' or ecological candidate, and has been learning a great deal about practical politics as a result. He lives quite near to Herwig Görgemanns,[35] in fact. We talked a great deal about politics and elections.

Finally got a taxi back (27 shekels), and so to bed.


DAY 5, MONDAY, JUNE 1ST

I was fearing that I might be ill this morning, but am holding out well. Was welcomed by a 'dawn chorus' of unusual intensity, and looked out the window to find a regiment of about half a dozen different kinds of birds hounding a very embarrassed cat. The cat was climbing around in a small bush, and the birds were dive-bombing it, or sitting on adjacent branches and roaring their heads off. Finally, the cat retreated round the side of the

---

35    A German classicist whom I had met long ago, in Calgary, Alberta, and had stayed in touch with.

cottage, with great 'unconcern', sniffing the bushes and pausing frequently for meditation.

Back at the conference, we had a good talk from Hermann Funke, on Bernays' theory of *katharsis*,[36] which he seems to have been the first to interpret correctly. A mad woman from Bar-Ilan University then spoke, followed by nice old Yehoshua Amir of Jerusalem, on Theophrastus' doctrine of *eusebeia*.[37]

Unfortunately, at the end of Amir's talk, the preposterous Bollocks got up to make four or five points, so I decided I felt rather faint, and retired to the hotel (it was already 1.00), missing a talk by Samuel Scolnicov, on Heraclitus. This rather embarrassed me later, because he kindly approached me after my talk and offered to fix me up in Jerusalem, if I would come up. So I will go up on Thursday, by *sherut,* as they call their communal taxis.

My talk took place at 3.00[38] – the lady who was to have talked before me, Jenny Morris, on Philo's *Hypothetica,* had fallen ill and backed out, which was a pity, since the subject was of interest, and had concerned Bernays. I got some good comments – including an exhortation to look again at the techniques of commentary of the Dead Sea Scrolls – but I don't expect to find real antecedents to Philo there, except the general idea, which he may well have got from Therapeutae and/or Essenes.

After the meeting, I came back and decided to go out to dinner at a sea-food restaurant, Danis, that we had looked at the previous night. I did that, and had a good meal – *tahini* and 'loup-de-mer', in a mushroom-cream sauce, with a bottle of Carmel white, and Crème Bavaria to follow. Cost me about $19, though. When I saw the air-conditioning and the Americans, I knew I was in for it – but even so, cheaper than Dublin!

---

36    That is to say, Aristotle's theory, in his *Poetics,* of the sort of 'purging' or 'purification' of the spirit induced by hearing, or reading, a well-composed tragedy.

37    That is to say, 'piety'.

38    This was entitled 'The Formal Structure of Philo's Allegorical Exegesis', and was not actually published till 1996, in the volume of conference proceedings.

Then I decided to go to the movies, in a cinema just opposite, where *Private Benjamin* was playing, starring Goldie Hawn – subtitled. It is actually very good, though a rather facile feminist tract – but the idea of Goldie joining the army must have seemed much less fantastic to the young Israeli audience, all of whom, male and female, must have served their three years in the armed forces!

## DAY 6, TUESDAY, MAY 2<sup>ND</sup>

I had intended today to skip lectures, and take an Egged tour to Caesarea and Akko. I was duly booked, but the fools failed to pick me up. I was left sitting in the lobby like an eejit till after 9.00.

So I fulminated, fixed another one for Galilee for tomorrow, and resolved to do today what I had planned to do tomorrow – go downtown to shop, and visit the Museum of the Diaspora – Beit Hatfutsot – on the campus. I headed off on the No. 25 bus and reached Allenby, in the older quarter. With the help of a nice old lady who saw me studying the map, I found myself in the Carmel Market, where I bought what *seem* an excellent pair of sandals for 130 shekels (= $13) – I had seen similar ones on Dizengoff for 190. I just paid – didn't even haggle – and then said to the girl selling them that I knew I should bargain, but I was too ignorant. She smiled indulgently.

I then pottered down Allenby, searching for stamp shops. I found one which looked promising, and it was good, but only had a few early Palestine. I bought one pair, at what seems a very good price, and some early Austrian P.O. postmarks, just for fun. Then I found a second-hand bookstore, just in an alleyway, and picked up an ill-printed book which turned out to be fascinating – *A Village by the Jordan,* an account of his life by Joseph Baratz, who founded the kibbutz of Degania (the first to be founded). It gives me lots of ideas for what we might do in Ireland.

Then back to Ramat-Aviv, had a swim, and went up to the campus to see the museum. I decided not to go to the afternoon talks, because I couldn't go to *all* of them, and would offend *someone*, and this was my only chance to see the museum. It is indeed an impressive display – a panorama of the Diaspora, with particular exhibits on the Jews of India and of the Caribbean, but also multi-media shows about communal life in Europe and North Africa down the ages. I spared myself yet another wallowing in the Holocaust, and came back for another swim. This time I went to the store and bought some provisions for dinner – salami, cheese, rolls, pressed meat, nectarines, arak – and had a good feast on my front doorstep.

Then went off to the conference party, at 8.00 – joined at the bus-stop by Kyteler and his wife. The party was a curious affair, and hadn't quite got going (though I had good talk with Katzoff of Bar-Ilan, who is an American, graduate of Columbia), when John beckoned me and young Ivor into his den, and revealed a plan to publish a collection of his students' howlers in Greek philosophy. I said I'd help to recommend it to publishers (if it turned out to be worth recommending), but it would have to be really good, which it didn't sound yet. But we kept on at this for ages, and when we came out, the party was dissolved. Presumably, the lack of a host depressed them, or perhaps they were depressed already. So the Gluckers, Ivor, Hermann and I settled down to drink Bar Mitzvah wine and do a post-mortem on the conference. I am glad that everyone finds Bollocks preposterous. I suppose I should read his Empedocles book, though.

Anyhow, I staggered out slightly before midnight, rather the worse for wear, hoping that I won't be too delicate in the morning. I had been drinking Maccabi beer all evening, and it may not mix with Bar Mitzvah wine.

## DAY 7, WEDNESDAY, JUNE 3<sup>RD</sup>

I felt tolerable this morning, though I scrounged some aspirin from the desk. This time the tour *did* arrive to collect me, so I got to see Galilee.

*Excursion to Galilee*

We drove through Ramat Aviv, then out onto the Haifa Road.

The guide remarked on new buildings as we went, e.g. a new vocational school for girls, built by ladies of the Mizrachi[39] of France and Canada. Apartment blocks are spreading out north, as far as Hertzliya, founded fifty years ago by American Jews – private villas for millionaires – obviously a very rare thing in Israel to have a private house; most land is communal or government-owned.

We passed a village, Kfar, founded by German Jews in 1933-38. Then a *kibbutz* (Shefayim), which was most impressive – a bit like an army camp, but cheerful enough. It has a guest-house, where we picked up some people, large farm buildings, fruit orchards, a school, and so on. Certainly it would be unreasonable to hand this over to the Arabs.

We drove then through the Plain of Sharon – very fertile and pleasant. There is sufficient rainfall, it seems. It is mentioned in the *Song of Songs*. We viewed the Wingate Institute for Physical Culture. Then Netanya, founded in 1930, originally sand-dunes up to eight miles inland, but gradually being reclaimed. It is mainly a vacation town, but with over 100,000 inhabitants. It has a diamond industry. Again, vast blocks of flats.

Out of Netanya, then, through orange groves – end of season now. Further on, what had been a malarial swamp is now drained and developed. No more malaria in Israel! (I saw some U.N. vehicles parked on the side of the road – had they fled from Lebanon?). Our guide described a plan to use the Dead Sea as a vast reservoir of solar energy.

We passed Caesarea, and headed away from the coast to Afula. Great problems with controlling sands, it seems and keeping out salt water. There are fish-hatcheries and a nature reserve just at the turn off from the Haifa road. Eucalyptus widely planted – good for drainage. We passed a *Communist* kibbutz, called after a famous rabbi! They raise chickens.

Then we entered the valley of Hiron, on the first road to go from Egypt to Mesopotamia. There is the Jewish town of Hiron (ancient), and the new town of Avah, mainly Arab. About 10%

---

39      That is to say, Jews of Middle Eastern descent.

of the representatives in parliament are Arab, it seems. Arabs, claim our guide, have a better deal in Israel than Jews – they don't have to serve in the army! The Hotel Galilee in Nazareth is a Jewish-Arab combine. And he told us a joke: Arabs in Israel can only have one wife – but they can keep four secretaries, if they like!

We climbed into the hills – dry and rocky, but cultivated in places. Olive groves. This route was the Roman Via Maris. Thutmoses III came this way, to fight at Megiddo. Megiddo guards the pass through the Carmel ridge, near the springs of the river Tishon. Kléber beat the Turks at Megiddo because he read the *Song of Deborah*. Now in a plain again – mountains of Gilboa in a haze on the right. On the left, the mountains of Nazareth. We arrived at Afula at 10.10. Intensive cultivation of sunflowers. A characterless modern town, with the usual apartment blocks – some older houses in ruins. We turned left for Nazareth and Tiberias. Said to be 36° Celsius in Afula today. Our bus is air-conditioned, fortunately. There is also more Afula in the mountains. We passed the Afula Medical Centre, for workers – a good view back over the plain. I note the Jewish National Fund tree nursery.

The Christian village of Naim on the right, under a hill. Mt. Tabor ahead. Stopped for coffee at 10.15. 'Tabor' it seems, means 'centre' (of the body), or 'navel'. It is the presumed site of the transfiguration of Christ. The present Franciscan monastery is built on a fortress constructed by Josephus in the war against Rome.

We went round Mt. Tabor, and into another plain, that of lower Galilee. Here there is solid cultivation – many almond groves. Under Mt. Tabor, at Sejera, there took place the first gathering of 'Hashomer', the Jewish defence organisation founded to protect the early settlers. Under the Turks, there were only 65,000 inhabitants in Palestine altogether – it was almost uninhabited. We passed a village of Circassians, Kfar Kama. The Circassians, it seems, wanted to go home to the Caucasus in 1948, but came back after six months, saying that it was better in Israel! They are mainly Sunni Muslims.

We drove through the Valley of Yavniel, beautifully cultivated. It is one of the oldest Jewish communities in the country, founded in 1901. Private houses flourish in Yavniel – much cheaper to live than down in Tel Aviv (50,000 shekels for a house and garden). We passed the site of Yeno'av, an ancient Hebrew town. Cypresses and pines as windbreaks.

Over a last ridge, and we see the Sea of Galilee – rather like Tahoe from Hwy 50, though less spectacular. There is quite a haze. The Golan Heights beyond. The Jordan Valley stretches down to the south. One can see right across to the Yarmuk Valley, stretching down to the south – an ancient settlement, of the same period as Jericho. We viewed Degania, in Kinnereth, the first *kibbutz,* where the Jordan leaves the lake. We crossed the Jordan – clusters of date palms, and bananas – a Syrian tank! We stopped by the exit of the Jordan for a few minutes. Tiberias was founded by Herod Antipas, and named after the Emperor Tiberius, with whom he wished to curry favour. Before that, there had been just the village of Rakkat, where there were hot springs. It was destroyed in the 4th cent., but re-founded in the 16th cent. by a Spanish Jew, Don Joseph, and that lasted about forty years. Re-established under the British Mandate. Now a population of about 30,000. The Baths of Herod on the left of the road. Tomb of Rabbi Meir above the springs. Palace of Princess Berenice, sister of Herod Agrippa, on the mountain. The old walls of Tiberias still visible. Again, though, a modern resort town, with some archaeological remains, and a Turkish mosque. On then to the Valley of Gennesereth, where the hills come close to the water. There is a refuge of zealots in the caves on the hills. We passed the new village of Magdala, and the Kibbutz Gilosar, where Yigal Allon[40] lived. Passed the ancient town of Kinnereth again. The Sermon on the Mount

---

40      Yigal Allon (1918 –1980) was an Israeli politician, commander of the Palmach, and general in the IDF. He served as one of the leaders of Ahdut HaAvoda party and the Israeli Labour Party, and briefly as acting Prime Minister of Israel in 1969 - the first native born prime minister. He was a Knesset member and government minister from the third Knesset to the ninth inclusive. Allon died unexpectedly in 1980 after he suffered a cardiac arrest.

was delivered here! There is a German Benedictine church at its base, and an Italian church at the top of the Mount of Beatitudes – also a hostel for Christian pilgrims. We toured the ancient synagogue at Capernaum, guarded jealously by the Franciscans, though, as our guide claimed, it is all Jewish. The Franciscans have done quite a good job of lay-out. The synagogue is right on the lake front, but there is a block of houses between it and the lake, where Peter must have had a place. I heard a series of dull booms as we were pottering about. I hope war hasn't started!

Then back to Tiberias for lunch. We marched into a restaurant which was waiting for us. Prices were in dollars (but not too bad: $10 all in, including a coke!). I had a pleasant trout-like fish. There was a nice British couple and a Brazilian couple (rather older) at the table. The girl in front of me on the bus was more sensible, though. She went swimming. We were cheated of our swim.

A steep climb from Tiberias into the hills – a fine view of the lake, looking back. Groves of eucalyptus everywhere, making things less bleak. There is intensive cultivation wherever possible. We passed the Horns of Hattin, where, in 1187, the Crusaders fought Saladin, and were heavily beaten, losing 10,000 men, largely from heat and thirst. There is much clearing of rocks from fields, as in the west of Ireland. We turned off the main road to Haifa, towards Nazareth. First came to Cana, now a modern village – funny old red-domed church, where the marriage feast miracle is meant to have taken place. It is mainly a Christian village, it seems, but there are some Muslims. The next village, Rama, is Arab.

Nazareth is really two towns, the old and the new. The Israelis built here the administrative headquarters for Galilee, and it is now a vast, sprawling metropolis. The old town, in the valley, is Arab, and almost like entering an Indian reservation, after the new Jewish town. Suddenly one seems to be in the Middle East – everything dirty and inconsequential. Perhaps the black ghetto of an American city would be a better comparison. We parked the bus, and our guide told us, contemptuously, that he would have to hand us over to an Arab guide, to see the

Holy Places here. "We have to keep them employed somehow," he said. He duly then handed us over to an old Arab (perhaps a Christian?) called Abu Abdullah, who was actually a very competent and humorous old boy, spoke English, French and German, and had lots to say.

The Church of the Annunciation is a quite new erection (1960-69), but impressive as a piece of modern architecture. It replaces a small church the Franciscans had here, which was of no architectural value, and incorporates bits of all the previous churches, from the 2nd cent. A.D. to the Crusades. There are absurd items, like 'Mary's Grotto', in the *exact* spot where the Annunciation took place, and then further up the hill another new church, enclosing the residence of the Holy Family, and Joseph's workshop! These things *may* go back to Constantine, or Helena, but still... The visit of Pope Paul was obviously a great occasion, and celebrated in mosaics. Also wall-panels from all over the world in honour of the Virgin. The Irish contribution came a bit late, and had to be accommodated in a porch outside!

There was no chance to visit a mosque (though the muezzin called while we were there), or the old market. One could sense a tension and hostility on the part of the inhabitants. A girl in front of me on the bus had an interesting experience in the souvenir shop we were ushered into (as usual) in Nazareth. She is by origin Greek-Jewish, and grew up in Lebanon, though she now lives in London. She spoke to the man in Arabic, asking him how much something was. His attitude immediately changed. He said, "Pay no attention to those prices. I give you a different price." And he refused to take payment for the beer she had bought. She was so confused that she couldn't think of anything to buy. In fact, the prices were preposterous – very much like that place outside Mexico City that we were shoved into. I bought nothing, but made mental notes, for when I get to a real market.

After that, our progress home was fairly unremarkable – the same intensive cultivation and functional modern towns, with occasional older Arab villages in the distance. We got back at dusk, about 6.30. All in all, a rather basic tour, but offering insights, mainly into what the Jews have done to the land, and what they have done to the Arabs. Our guide had ill-concealed contempt for the Arabs, but also a slight guilt complex – a compulsion to explain how well off they are, compared to what they were. The explanation of the apartheid in Nazareth was peculiar – that the Jews wanted better services and were prepared to pay for them, so they founded their own separate community. On the other hand, it was great to see Degania, after reading Joseph Baratz's autobiography, as I have been doing (I found it in a second-hand bookstore on Allenby).

## To Jerusalem

On my return, I found a message from Samuel Scolnicov and, on calling, found that he has booked me into the University Hotel on Mt. Scopus, and has arranged a little party for Saturday evening – so I won't come back to Tel Aviv after all, and must give Caesarea a miss. But I gather there is not much there of consequence to Origen,[41] anyhow, and I will probably be glad to spend more time in and around Jerusalem. I can, it seems, go straight to the airport from there.

Since I had taken the lunch at Tiberias, I used my rolls to make another humble home-made dinner on the front step, washed down by *arak*. There is some sort of 'function' going on on the lawn by the pool – presentation of awards, everyone middle-aged and prosperous, then a cabaret, with lively singing! I went to the café across the road for a coffee and beer, and watched Israel being demolished by the USSR at basketball.

And so to bed.

## DAY 8, THURSDAY, JUNE 4TH

I have more or less given up on the full breakfast – just had an egg (fried), a roll, and coffee this morning. I bought the

---

41      My favourite Church Father, who spent time there in the mid-third cent. A.D., where he founded a catechetic school.

*Jerusalem Post,* and absorbed it over breakfast. Israeli politics is lively and amusing. Still no war. The booms yesterday must have been 'normal' shelling. Certainly no one seemed too bothered.

I met a nice old crone who does the rooms, and conversed with her in German. I decided I should leave her something, and accordingly left 50 shekels. I saw an interesting little brown bird as I sat on my front step – like a humming-bird, with a long beak, only a bit larger, fussing around the flowers.

On checking out, I found that I had managed to spend $276.82 for my week in the Ramat Aviv Hotel. Hope I can get some of it back. I always have this experience on travels – everything ends up costing rather more than the maximum I had conceived possible.[42] And yet I have survived for almost 42 years, and am not bankrupt yet. But this whole trip is going to cost something over $1000 if I'm not careful – though at least some of that should be repayable.

I staggered out onto the Haifa Road with my bags. They are just too bulky to be hauled around in this heat, but I had gallantly resolved to take a 27 bus to the Central Bus Station, then a bus to Jerusalem, and a taxi to Mt. Scopus. However, I decided on a taxi to the bus station. I got a rather nice, weather-beaten man, and when he heard where I ultimately wanted to go, he said, "I don't want to *press* you, but I can take you to Jerusalem for 200 shekels (less than $20), and you will spend *almost* that on two taxis and a bus." So I thought about that for a bit and then reckoned "What the hell, I'm the Regius Professor of Greek, and this is only the price of a good dinner" – so I said "OK, you win. Drive on, James!"

So we headed off out of Tel Aviv (which I am glad to see the back of, I must say!), and into the countryside. Once again, highly developed agriculture, the reverse of quaint, and a modern freeway. My driver is pleasant but taciturn, with not much English. Born in Jerusalem, he now lives in Rishon, south of Tel Aviv, as Tel Aviv is too expensive. He fought in the '48 and '67 wars, and showed me, as we passed through a narrow

---

42    It is indeed sobering to reflect on the fairly trivial sums, from a contemporary perspective, that I am fussing about here!

pass in the mountains, a place (Sha'or haGay) where he had fought through to get food to Jerusalem in '48. An old truck was still left by the side of the road, and he pointed to it with pride.

The approach to Jerusalem is like the ascent from the Central Valley of California to Lake Tahoe – the same sort of scenery, but a few more villages, perhaps, and all is compressed into a smaller compass. We passed Emmaus on a hill, with a monastery. Up to the Ayalon Valley, with the Arab village of Abu Ghosh, and a new town on the hilltop, Mevasseret Tsion. The hills are all ridged, as if evidence of ancient cultivation, but it may be just the way the rock is structured.

One's first view of Jerusalem is impressive. One comes over one ridge, then a steep descent into a valley, and there it is on the next ridge. There is the usual dull approach to modern cities, but then we come gradually into an older quarter, and then into an Arab quarter (suddenly there was a loud explosion not far away, and we accelerated!), heading for Mt. Scopus on the north of the city. My driver said "This is all Arab part. But they live the same. We all same people, really." There was a no-man's land between it and the gleaming fortress of the Mt. Scopus campus on its hill. My driver hadn't heard of Maiersdorf House, and was baffled when we got there (I actually gave him an extra 50 shekels for his trouble, which pleased him). It is all quite new, and still being built, The Faculty Club is certainly splendid, but I haven't had a chance to explore it yet. It is poised looking out over the valley to Arab Jerusalem. It was cut off from the rest of Israel until 1967, and it is the measure of Israeli determination never to surrender Jerusalem that they are indulging in this vast building programme here. One sees again and again what World Jewry have contributed to Israel – every building here is donated by (or at least called after) some foreign benefactor. The Maiersdorfs were Belgian, it seems.

*Later, 6 pm:* What a dreadful thing it is to be a tourist! A tourist is an illiterate mental defective, open to being preyed upon by everyone. Modern mass tourism is a disgusting phenomenon, debasing everyone involved in it. I am now back safely in the thoroughly respectable Faculty Club, and can reflect calmly on these matters – but I have had some bad moments!

Impatient as always, I set out almost immediately, about 1.00pm, to walk around. The idea grew on me, and I set out to walk to the adjacent Mount of Olives. It wasn't quite so adjacent as it looked, and I found myself suddenly in an Arab area, which is rather like crossing to the wrong side of the tracks in an American town. A sort of ill-suppressed hostility and predatoriness became apparent. One is followed by small boys – 'Hey, Mister, where you from? Give me money!", and so on. I got to the Mount of Olives, however, viewed the Chapel of the Ascension – and indeed the very Footprint that Jesus made as he Ascended into Heaven! Then I wandered down an alleyway, just avoided being invited by an old gentleman to have a drink with him, but was collared by a boy, who appointed himself my guide. Everything was closed, of course, till 3 pm – Gethsemane, Mary's Tomb, everything. Another boy joined us, and they quarrelled for a while over my hide, and then plainly decided to divide me. We paraded down a little path into the Valley of Hinnom, they feeding me with information on various topics, until we reached Mary's Tomb, and the beginning of the road up to the Old City – the Via Dolorosa, in fact. No other tourist was about – sensibly enough; I was alone in my idiocy. I managed to dispose of them for 50 shekels, which they affected to regard as a derisory pittance. Probably more than they'd seen in years!

I battled up to the walls of Jerusalem, and then turned south along them till I came to St. Stephen's, or the Lion's Gate, where I turned into the Old City. Still not a solitary tourist about – just Arabs going about their business. Immediately one is in the old East – little passage-ways leading off into stinking mysterious recesses, massive walls, archways, little shops tucked away in holes in the wall. With the first tourists, half way along the Via Dolorosa, as it turned out to be – at the first Station of the Cross, very suitably – the first urchin appeared, determined to guide me. I brushed him off. A single tourist is freed from the sheep-like processioning of the group, but is much more vulnerable to pestering. One dare not stop anywhere near a shop to look, because the proprietor will come charging out, waving special offers, and urging you to come inside.

I won a few battles, but finally I succumbed to a young salesman (whose name was Sami). I was feeling a little groggy, and allowed myself to be ushered into his shop, and served a coffee. As soon as he heard that I was Irish, he was all over me. "You know, we sympathise very much with your troubles, because they are the same as ours. When Bobby Sands die, you know, there was trouble here. The police had to come. We understand our struggles are the same." He warmed to his theme. "You know, always the police are beating us. Once, a few years ago, they shot a friend of mine – he was the champion of Jerusalem (at what I didn't ask). We came out and made some trouble, and they beat us. Look!" He turned, took off his shirt, and showed me his back, where there was a noticeable weal. "They went on beating me and kicking me on the ground, until I was almost unconscious. I just got home, all bloody, and my mother put me to bed. I couldn't go to the hospital or I would have been arrested, so a doctor who was a friend came. For many weeks I could not walk or move my arms. They beat my girl-friend too, and now she is lost to me, because, you know, they beat her on the head, and she lose her mind. We are still trying to cure her. The doctors think maybe electric shock will help, but I don't know." So I sympathised, and agreed that we had similar problems, and finally bought a blouse and a small brass vase, for far too much ($20), though this was a 'special price', since I was Irish. What I paid for, perhaps, was an insight into a young Palestinian's state of mind. There, at least, I think, he was talking straight – not trying to fool any tourists. In fact, I suppose he was taking a bit of a risk. How did he know who I was, after all?

I wandered on through the *suq,* being pestered most of the way, but bought nothing more – I suddenly find that I have only 12 shekels left – I must find a bank! I found my way to the great square containing the Dome of the Rock and the El-Aqsa mosque. One can't get in to either, of course, but they are spectacular from the outside, especially the Dome, with its lovely ornamental tiles. Then down to the Wailing Wall, where those silly old fellows are bowing and muttering vigorously. I find these fundamentalists profoundly depressing, I must say, but they are partly what Israel is about, I suppose. I was even approached by one character outside a *yeshiva,* asking me for a contribution. No way! They are doing quite well enough. Most of the old Jewish Quarter is being rebuilt in spectacular style. Once again, this was in the Arab zone. No way are they going to give this up! And fair enough, I suppose, in this case.

I worked my way round the walls – which are intact, and magnificent – till I reached the Jaffa Gate, feeling by now pretty groggy. There I found a Bank Leumi, and the man changed $50 on my Visa card, even without my passport, which was decent. Then I decided to head for home, just stopping at a nice old Armenian store, where *no one bothered me,* to buy a string of wooden camels for 12 shekels.

*Later again:* I was so exhausted that I took a taxi back, which cost me 35 shekels (final bit of swindling!), had a shower, to ease my poor feet (I am also lame in my right leg), and snoozed until about 6.30, when I had a little salami and fruit – and went out again, this time *with a purpose* – to the Hilton Hotel and H. Stern, to buy a diamond! I took the 28 bus to the terminal, and walked to the Hilton. I get foolish after being separated from Jean for even a short time, and think how much I love her and value her, and then go out and do something to celebrate that. Now I have it in my head to see what I can get by way of a diamond for about $500, as I am informed that this is the world centre for cutting and marketing them. Of course, it is idiotic to go to a Hilton Hotel for this, but I can't risk buying something of such magnitude from a fellow in a side-street ("Hey, Mister, how are you? You want diamond? I have very good diamond. Come look! Only hundred dollar – special price for you!"), where I would end up, in all probability, with a broken glass bead. Stern's were exemplary, I must say – most professional. They explained all the intricacies of diamond grading. If I have been swindled, it has been done with great style. What I have in mind is to place this diamond between the paws of my previous bit of foolishness (the product of J.'s previous absence), instead of the stone there now. But I must consult the beloved recipient, who will probably half-kill me!

I thought there was a reading of Sholem Aleichem's works tonight in the Hilton, but that is tomorrow. So I came home, again on the 28 bus. An eventful, if not entirely pleasant, day!

## DAY 9, FRIDAY, JUNE 5<sup>TH</sup>

Rose betimes, and rushed out about 7.10, to catch a bus to the terminal, and get an EGGED tour to Qumran and Jericho. I just made it, with time for a hasty cup of coffee in the bus station café.

*Visit to Qumran and Jericho*

Leaving Jerusalem, we passed developments initiated by Levi Eshkol – the Prophet Samuel Project. Aha! We passed Ammunition Hill, where the Jordanians stored their ammunition. Now crossing into 'Jordanian' territory – on the border, a very strategic area. Eshkol had houses built very cheaply, to get people to live here. Mt. Scopus came into view. For years it was cut off.

Drove through the Wadi el-Joz, then Kidron. Then through Bethany – home of Lazarus, etc., (House of the Poor). Then into the desert – two to four inches of rainfall a year; just Bedouin, tending their goats and camels – *and new Jewish settlements* (we saw three of them).

Half way to Jericho, we came upon an old *khan* (ruined) – the Inn of the Good Samaritan! The old road to Jericho runs beside us. We passed below sea-level, and, through a pass, into the Jordan Valley – a view appeared of the Jericho Oasis. We passed a military settlement (Nekhal), growing vegetables in the desert – part of military service! In an hour, we are in Qumran, just slightly up from the Dead Sea, backed by abrupt hills. The settlement is on a slight rise, bounded by deep gullies caused by erosion (though these appear to be later developments).

They got water from winter floods which came down from the mountains.

Only a few miles up the Jordan is the traditional place where John the Baptist baptized (a church there was sealed off for military reasons), so it makes the hypothesis that he and Jesus were dissident Essenes[43] more plausible geographically.

From Qumran (failing to stop at the Dead Sea, unfortunately), we headed for Jericho, noting new *kibbutzim* on the way. How the hell they explain to themselves what they are going to do with these if they ever hand the area back to the Palestinians I quite fail to see. I don't believe they ever intend to.

Jericho is a pleasant little town – all Arab, it seems – adorned by flame trees and date palms, owing its existence to a well created by the prophet Elisha (!). We headed first for the magnificent remains of an Umayyad palace, built for the caliph Hisham (who died before occupying it), c. 740 A.D. It was destroyed by an earthquake shortly after being built, and excavated by Kathleen Kenyon (daughter of Sir Frederick!),[44] who also dug ancient Jericho. She did a good job here – bath-house particularly interesting – splendid mosaic floor, and some plasterwork preserved in a guest room.

Then on to the 6th cent. Jewish synagogue, discovered only in 1917, when a shell destroyed a cowshed. On repairing the cowshed, a mosaic floor with Jewish symbols was discovered. It

---

43    That is to say, members of the sect which composed the Dead Sea Scrolls.

44    Sir Frederic George Kenyon (1863 – 1952) was a British palaeographer and biblical and classical scholar. He held a series of posts at the British Museum from 1889 to 1931. He was also the president of the British Academy from 1917 to 1921. Dame Kathleen Mary Kenyon (1906 – 1978) was a British archaeologist of Neolithic culture in the Fertile Crescent. She led excavations of Tell-el-Sultan, the site of ancient Jericho, from 1952 to 1958, and has been called one of the most influential archaeologists of the 20th century. She was Principal of St. Hugh's College, Oxford, from 1962 to 1973 and studied herself at Somerville College, Oxford.

is still in private – Arab – hands. The Israelis are anxious to get hold of it, as it is not being looked after very well. As I say, no Jews are settled in Jericho now. The Israeli government has prevented it, presumably fearing aggravation.

We went next to the Tell, and viewed the ancient tower and wall of Jericho, way below the present surface – 70 ft. down. The remains go back to Mesolithic times – up to 10,000 B.C., it was stated. Then we had a pleasant glass of orange juice in a small café, and I bought some dates. (The periodic bangs, by the way, are just some booms from military aircraft passing over – nothing more serious. There are no more developments in the crisis:[45] Begin and Sadat have just been, happily, in Ophira, but the Israelis are very sceptical: they think it is just an election gimmick. There is much indignation at Begin for 'giving away' the Sinai. Only the Communists – Hadash – are interested in a real settlement with the Palestinians – all others are obviously determined to brush them under the carpet.)

And so back to Jerusalem, noting on the way a spectacular new housing development in the desert outside the city, called Ma'aleh Adumim, condominiums costing from $45,000 to $60,000 – all sold already! And this in Palestinian territory! Our guide is outraged at the escalation of real estate prices – 4000%, he says, since 1978.

On our return, the bus left me down at King George and Ben Jehuda, on the No. 9 bus-route. Feeling groggy again – the sun on the Tell of Jericho really got to me – but I decided to potter around this area before going back. As it is coming up to the Sabbath, I won't really be able to get out in the evening. I had a coffee, and then committed another extravagance. I found an antique shop full of Persian things. I was attracted by silver, engraved cigarette boxes – beautiful, but $800 and $1200! This fellow was not fooling around. Then I looked at some pages of

---

45    I am no lontger sure what this 'crisis' may have been, but these negotiations are in the wake of the Camp David treaty, signed back in March 1979 by Begin and Sadat, at the prompting of President Jimmy Carter.

manuscripts – also vast prices, but I rather fell for one at $180. I hope I haven't been totally swindled, but this was all very respectable. He is probably a refugee from Khomeini's Iran. I also bought a nice tray ($30). No little bargains hereabouts, but I am fed up with the oceans of junk that one is confronted with. I will have the page framed.[46] It is tragic to cut these things up, but the damage has been done, after all, so I'm not making it worse.

*A page from a manuscript*

Having thus completely ruined myself, I retired to Mt. Scopus on the No. 9 bus, took a shower, and tried to snooze. I have a slight headache, which I hope is not a sign of something worse. I also bought a baklava from a roadside stand. Very good it was, but it may prove fatal!

It is amusing, by the way, to see the unconcerned way that citizens accept the phenomenon of young soldiers with machine-guns (I *hope* unloaded!) slung over their shoulders, boarding buses and strolling around the town. Such a thing in Dublin would send citizens scurrying for cover. Also girls, some very attractive, going about in khaki with revolvers on their hips. It is a nation under arms!

I lay about till around 6.00, waiting to see if I was ill or not, and was then served a good dinner (*chollent*, I assume – chicken stew) in my room. After dinner, I went down and demanded to get out on the balcony to watch the sun go down over Jerusalem. The balcony was locked, which was crazy, so I climbed through a window, and took a chair out after me. It must be the best view in the city – the Dome of the Rock gleaming at me across the valley, the lights gradually coming on, the great wall suddenly

---

46    I did, and it still hangs on the wall of our drawing-room.

illuminated – a young crescent moon looking down on Jerusalem. Then the muezzin starts up, just at nightfall, from the Arab quarter. It is a most stirring sight.

I am getting rather pissed off with the Sabbath, though. What this town needs is a heavy influx of atheists! The lack of public transport, or any real services, for a day and a half, is a total curse for an innocent visitor; and between Arabs, Jews and Christians in this town, Friday, Saturday and Sunday are wholly or partly holidays! The Jews are really *kakotheoi* – Bernays' emendation of Theophrastus applies admirably to them.[47] If Jahweh were offended by the various things they imagine to offend him, he would long since have blown his stack, and dissolved into something like a black hole, taking the universe with him. But these are the rantings of a trapped and frustrated tourist. Perhaps tomorrow will be better. However, Shavuot[48] on Monday is probably going to mean a king's ransom to get to the airport.

## DAY 10, SATURDAY, JUNE 6TH

Awoke betimes, for some reason – about 5.30 – and read for a while. I have been getting some reading done, actually. I finished William Trevor's curious novella, *The Old Boys*. It is good, but the dialogue is excessively stilted – almost a sort of blank verse. I can't decide whether he intends that effect or not. As regards the action, a Waugh-like ingenuity. I have read also a good many stories of Michael McLaverty. He is superb. If one can be as good as that and still remain obscure, what hope is there for

---

47      Theophrastus, quoted by Porphyry, *De Abstinentia*, 2. 7. The word is extremely rare, and means, broadly, 'unfortunate is relation to one's gods, or God'. Bernays is also on record, as I recall, as describing his fellow-Jews as 'ein gottbestrafende Volk', 'a god-smitten people'.

48      Shavuot, commonly known in English as the Feast of Weeks, is a Jewish holiday that occurs on the sixth day of the Hebrew month of Sivan (in the 21st century, it may fall between May 15 and June 14 on the Gregorian calendar.

*me* as a writer? He is marvellous on animals, for one thing. I have read also the Degania book of Baratz, which is fascinating. Otherwise, I am working away at my Hebrew, and have finished Tcherikover's *Hellenistic Civilisation and the Jews*.

Down to breakfast. All laid out without a soul in sight, like some sort of enchanted castle. I found some boiling water for the Nescafé, and set to. Not bad. Finally, another few guests arrived, just as I was retiring.

At 9.00 exactly, Samuel Scolnicov appeared, and drove me off to the Old City. We parked near the Jaffa Gate, and started out, after casting a glance at David's Tower. Retracing the Via Dolorosa, we came first to the Church of the Holy Sepulchre. It is a glorious hotch-potch of styles and periods, much disrupted at the moment, unfortunately, by reconstruction. We viewed the tomb itself, and the actual rock which was rolled away and/ or where the angel was standing (an old lady tried to explain to us in Greek, and was not entirely perspicuous). Anyhow, it is a *very* small rock now – perhaps worn down by the kisses and embraces of the faithful over the ages! The whole place is battled over by Catholics, Greek Orthodox, Armenians and Copts, who all occupy bits of the structure – the Armenians being quite prominent.

We then passed on to the old Antonia fortress of Herod, adjacent to the wall of the Temple compound, now in the hands of nuns (Church of the Flagellation). We viewed the pavement of the courtyard where Christ was played with by the soldiers. Apparently he was made part of a game of some sort, as we have markings on the paving stones of a wheel of fortune, crown of thorns, and places marked '*basileus*'.[49] But I would like to see a fuller explanation of this. (It is amusing being shown around by Scolnicov, who is Jewish, but a great enthusiast for all aspects of the Old City.)[50]

---

49    That is, 'king'.

50    In fact, Samuel (or Shmuel), whom I later got to know pretty well, was highly amused by the antics of Christians, as he was also by Jewish fundamentalists, and was very good company as a guide. He himself had been born and grown up in Brazil, but had now made his career in Jerusa-

Then to the Pool of Bethesda, which is, again, an extraordinary complex of buildings – originally a pool, going far down below the present surface, at least, but then a complex of buildings on top of that; firstly, a temple to Asclepius, of the third century B.C., then Sarapis was added, then an early Christian church, then a Crusader church. The present Crusader church is good, but austere, Norman architecture.

After this, we had a glass of freshly-squeezed orange juice, and, thus revived, headed off for the Dome of the Rock and El-Aqsa. We had a bit of a wait when we got there, since mid-day prayers went on till 2.15, so we sat on a wall and talked. Samuel did his doctorate in Cambridge under Bernard Williams and Geoffrey Lloyd, on Dialectic in Plato's Middle Dialogues (I think). I have seen his name in some connection, but can't remember what.[51]

The Dome of the Rock is breath-taking in its decoration, but the Muslims are good at that. The decoration is really *too* elaborate and fussy to be taken in properly, but the general effect is dazzling. What is enclosed is the Rock (probably originally the `Holy of Holies' of the Temple), from which Mohammad ascended into heaven (of course, there's a footprint!), and a shrine beside it contains three hairs of his beard. What a citadel of concentrated idiocy this old town is, after all! And the battles and massacres it has seen because of it! It really displays man at his nastiest and most irrational. El Aqsa is less elaborate, but has a marvellous display of carpets on the floor. Worth a visit for that alone.

After this, Samuel revealed that I was invited back for lunch, which was very kind. I tried to persuade him to let me buy a bottle, but he claimed that nowhere would be open. The family had decided to go to another museum. His wife, Hanna,

---

lem, where he held a position in the Philosophy Department in the Hebrew University, with a special interest in the philosophy of education. He died in 2014.

51     He was later author of various books on aspects of Platonic philosophy, and my predecessor as President of the International Plato Society (from 1998 to 2001).

two sons and one daughter are all very pleasant. They live in quite a nice, if cramped, flat overlooking a wadi. He's been here since 1957, having been born in Brazil – presumably of Russian parents, though I didn't ask.

We had a good lunch, and then sat and talked about Israeli and Irish politics for a while, especially their similarities. They can't see what Israel is really intending to do about the Occupied Territories, because these settlements keep going on, and certainly Jerusalem will never be allowed to be divided. There is some attempt at the moment by extremists to re-occupy Hebron. They too feel that Begin was crazy to hand back the Sinai.

Then Samuel nobly proposed that he drive me to Bethlehem, since it is really only about half-an-hour away, and would save me taking a tour there tomorrow. I jumped at the offer, and we set off. The Church of the Nativity is the only item worth viewing, so we parked in the main square, and viewed it. Down in the crypt is the *actual* cave where JC was born. It is a wonder they don't have the actual manger! The church is interesting, but either they have neglected to uncover most of the mosaics, or they have been badly destroyed. There is a good mosaic floor, and painted pillars (much in need of restoration). A quick visit to the Church of Mary's Milk – another total absurdity! Bethlehem is perched interestingly on a hill on the edge of the Judaean Desert, but these days it is almost becoming a suburb of Jerusalem.

We drove back to Mt. Scopus (he really *has* put himself out for me remarkably!), and I had a frugal cold meal. Then a call from Samuel to say that his colleague Gedaliahu Stroumsa would pick me up for the party. I was glad that he didn't have to trail over here again. Stroumsa duly picked me up. He is a very pleasant young man – studied in Harvard, is interested in Gnostics and Church Fathers, and teaching Patristic Theology (!) at the University.[52] He had actually been at the Yale conference, in the

---

52    Gedaliahu (Guy) Stroumsa (b. 1948) is now a senior and respected scholar of religion. He is Martin Buber Professor Emeritus of Comparative Religion at the Hebrew University of Jerusalem, and Emeritus Professor of the Study of Abrahamic Religions at the University of Oxford, where he is an Emeritus Fellow of Lady Margaret Hall.

seminar on Sethians, so we didn't meet. He was very sorry he didn't know I was in Dublin, or he would have asked me out to their conference on Philosophy and Religion in March (which would have been delightful!).

The party was at the residence of the Chairman, Fr. Maurice Dubois, O.P. (in the Lazarist College on Arnon St.). He is a very pleasant Frenchman, full of interesting ideas, and wanted me to come out for a term sometime soon, and teach some seminars.[53] I must pursue that possibility. We sat around, in a pleasant old room off a courtyard, and were served gin and orange, coffee, ice-cream and cake. I was taken home by Stroumsa, rather tiddly, around midnight.

By the way, the climate of Jerusalem is near-perfect. There is always a slight breeze to let things cool, and it is dry as well. It is on top of a mountain, after all!

## DAY 11, SUNDAY, JUNE 7TH

The first job after breakfast was to get some money. There is a bank down the road, and they did it for me on the Visa (another $100!), but they were quite slow this time – *almost* oriental, in some ways, I note. There is a tendency in bank officials in the Third World to do the oriental trick of studying closely the document you present to them, as if it were perhaps forged or fishy in some way – a quick glance at the back, just to make sure the key for its interpretation doesn't lie there – then perhaps a quick dive into a back room to consult some shadowy superior, with much gesticulating and shrugging of shoulders; and *then* they come back and pay up! And that is if your document is in perfect order; if it *isn't* ... Still, compared to Arabs or Ethiopians, or even Greeks, they're fine!

I paid my bill, put aside 200 shekels for tomorrow (airport taxi 95, sherut 60, plus emergencies – necessarily small ones!), and headed off on the 28 bus for the Israel Museum, near the Givat Ram campus. In fact I had a bit of a walk, and could have

---

53    That proposal never came to anything, sadly.

got much nearer on the 9 bus, but still... The Museum is a beautiful piece of architecture, perched on a hill opposite the Knesset, in a fine garden, full of sculptures ancient and modern. I stopped first at the House of the Book, which holds both the Dead Sea Scrolls material (or most of it), and a fascinating cache of documents relating to Bar Kochba's revolt, including many letters in his handwriting. It was good to salute the Scrolls. The exhibit is admirably presented. We could learn from it.

The rest of the Museum is also excellent, though I got bogged down half way through the enormous archaeology section. There is a good exhibition of finds at Arad, though – a Canaanite site (exhibit of pot-repairing a very good idea!). A fine mosaic (Byzantine) found recently at a church in the Negev – in Sinai.

After this, I took the no. 9 bus to King George and Jaffa, had a coffee and cake, and then took a 20 bus to the Jaffa Gate, to renew my wanderings in the Old City.

This afternoon things are rather quiet, in fact, which is pleasant. Only a few tours. I had only about 130 shekels with me, which made me curiously reckless. I was looking at Bedouin rugs, when a fellow rushed me into his shop, sat me down, called for coffee and lemonade, and began to bargain – $180 for a smallish rug (actually not bad by Navajo standards, but still ridiculous!). I proposed $100. He didn't have a VISA sign, so I felt pretty safe. He made a great speech about how it *cost* him $140. We finally settled on $140, but then I revealed that I had no means of paying. I would have to come back on Tuesday.

This tormented him – he wanted to take the VISA card, and see what he could do with it, but I wouldn't let it out of my sight. So finally I got away unscathed, vowing to come back to collect it (I now learn that $150 or $160 would have been a reasonable price for such a rug. It would be nice, I reflect, to have a secret list of 'reasonable prices' circulated for tourists, which would give one a basis for negotiation – but the Arabs would be furious!).

Then I stopped to examine some leather bags, and was

ambushed by an old boy – 300 shekels was the marked price on the bag. He said, 'Special price of 150!' No, I said, sorry, no money. "OK, how much you want to pay?" So I said 100. Quite impossible! So I walked away slowly. He bawled after me, "OK, 100... 90... 80." I stopped, and turned: "80?" "OK, you say 100?" "Nope, 80!" "100." "90". And it was a deal. But that is still almost $9. Now what was it *really* worth, I wonder.

After this, I veered off into the Christian Quarter – mainly Armenian and Greek Orthodox. A great relief, quite non-commercial, beautiful old streets and alleyways. I found my way eventually to Sion Gate (through a re-built Jewish quarter), and got to the Church of the Dormition (where a group of German tourists were singing foolishly), and then to David's Tomb (including the Chamber of the Last Supper and, to all appearances, a quondam mosque – again, an example of the chaotic history of this place.) Reading the little historical work I have bought on Jerusalem gives me a comprehensive picture of man's beastliness to man (mainly, Christian and Moslem beastliness to the Jews). I poked around there a while, and then returned to the Jaffa Gate (buying a falafel to sustain me), and took the 20 and 9 buses back to Mt. Scopus. I had a bath, read a bit, ate some of tomorrow's breakfast (supplied in advance), and then took a final walk round Mt. Scopus.

I am fascinated, I must say, by the spectacle of old Arab herdsmen still tending their flocks of goats quite unconcernedly in the shadow of these ultra-modern developments – though I must say that the Mt. Scopus campus is beautifully adapted to its surroundings. This particular herdsman was toiling home with about 100 goats, to all appearances in a quite different world to the modern one. Where is he going? Where are all those goats going? There are bits of primitive Arab village clinging to the lower slopes of Scopus, admittedly. An extraordinary juxtaposition of two worlds!

Once again, the muezzin raises his voice in the twilight, to add the right touch of the East to the panorama. The campus itself seems deserted. No doubt everyone is off for the weekend camping in Galilee or somewhere – as the Scolnicovs had planned to do, but some friends stood them up.

Back then, read some more, and so to bed.


## DAY 12, MONDAY, JUNE 8ᵀᴴ

Up in good time, the *sherut* duly arrived – only 60 shekels, actually. There was an interesting English girl from Oxford sitting beside me, with her Israeli boyfriend. She is working here now. We chatted pleasantly on the way to the airport.

I collected my diamond without fuss, and am now on the plane (half-empty, again) somewhere over the Balkans. It has been a most stimulating ten days, I must say!

*The Temple of Poseidon, Sounion*

*The Theatre of Dionysus, Athens*

The University of California, Berkeley, where John taught from 1969 to 1980.

*Jean and John Dillon in the California years*

*The Carlsblad Caverns, New Mexico*

*Chechen-itza Pyramid, Mexico*

*The Basilica, Nazareth*

*Old Jaffa, Tel-Aviv*

# 5: To Greece

## SEPTEMBER — OCTOBER, 1982

*[The basic purpose of this expedition was to attend a conference on Greek Philosophy, with special reference to the Sophists, organised by the Academy of Athens, and featuring many of the leading lights in the field, many of whom were old friends; but we took the opportunity also for some exploring of the islands, notably Tenos, Santorini (Thera), and – on the return journey - Paros. As I write most of this, Jean's contributions are in italics.]*

### DAY 1, MONDAY, SEPTEMBER 27TH

We started off from Dublin airport in high wind and squally rain, rather wintry, driven there by George and Grania Allport,[54] who had come to stay the night. George thought it would be a good idea to check out the route.

We found ourselves on a 747, two-thirds empty – surely a bad piece of management! We left at 11.40 pm, and flew uneventfully for about 3 ½ hours, getting to Athens (with a one-hour time difference where we expected two!) at the ungodly hour of 4.30 am Even then, though, it was warm and rather muggy – 70 % – and the characteristic smell of dust and olives met one as one stepped off the plane.

We changed $100 (at 69 dr. to the $), and passed through customs with no problem. A very competent young man from Club Travel (Australian, we thought) took us in hand, and sent us away in a bus to Athens, just as dawn was breaking, in pale pink, over Mt. Hymettos. We drove into the centre of town (Hotel

---

54     Grania is a second 2nd cousin of mine from the U.S., George her husband.

Euripides, at the junction of Euripides and Epicurus Sts.!), and thence took a taxi (for 92 dr.) to our hotel, the Ilissos, off on the east side of town, on Kallirhoe St., near the Ilissos.[55]

We were cheerfully received there, by a man who had actually spent a holiday in Northern Ireland (a *holiday*?), and flopped into bed for an hour or so, rousing ourselves at 8.45. Had a shower, and came down to the lobby, to find George Kerferd[56] and various distinguished Greeks in occupation, ready to leave shortly. We rushed in to breakfast, found Tony Long,[57] who joined us as we gulped a bit of bun and cake with coffee. Then up to change further, and off to the lecture, in procession. It was quite an affair. Not many foreign delegates, but Alex Mourelatos, Joachim Classen and Jacques Brunschwig[58] were there, and others doubtless will emerge. Richard McKirahan joined us on the journey! He is here for the year, directing, or teaching in, a Year Abroad Program, and enjoying himself greatly.

Melina Merkouri welcomed us, in her capacity as Minister of Culture, breathing into the microphone, in dark glasses, in her most alluring manner. Richard muttered that she is being very tough on foreign excavations, but I, considering how Ireland would welcome these hordes of alien excavators, thought 'Good for her!' She sloped off then, to some other urgent business, and the Mayor of Athens welcomed us. It is plainly a substantial operation – simultaneous translation set up between Greek and other languages, and all documents printed up. It is just as well we came, after all this build-up.

The papers of the first day have been extremely windy, in

---

55     A little stream flowing through Athens (now largely underground), made famous – for Greek philosophers – by its featuring at the beginning of Plato's *Phaedrus*.

56     George Kerferd (1915-1998), distinguished British classicist and ancient philosopher, then Professor of Greek in the University of Manchester.

57     A.A. Long, another distinguished British ancient philosopher, who had just succeeded me as Professor of Classics in Berkeley – where he still remains, as Emeritus!

58     All distinguished ancient philosophers, Greek-American, German and French respectively.

a distinctively Greek manner – though one was by a German sociologist from Tübingen called Tenbruck, who failed to turn up (on the nature of Aufklärung)! We think that perhaps there was a hidden aspect to all this. Greece now has, for the first time, really, an avowedly Socialist government. The Sophists are seen, plainly, as a progressive and democratic force by the younger generation of scholars, while the old men regard them in the same way at Plato did, and remain loyal to Plato and Aristotle. Against this background, many of the extraordinary discussions and arguments that have taken place would make some sense.

There are many preposterous personages. The President of the Greek Philosophical Society, Konstantinos Despotopoulos, is a grand old man who talks interminably about very general topics – no one having dared to interrupt him since the War, no doubt! Prof. Boudouris, of the Philosophy Department of the University of Athens, gave the worst speech of the day, having to do with the correct Platonic way of relating to pupils, and not charging fees!

We took a siesta, and in the evening there were two good papers, from Paul Woodruff of Texas, on a fragment of Protagoras in Didymus, and from Fernanda Decleva-Caizzi of Milan, on Antiphon – 'The Unity of all the Antiphons'![59] She is an authority on Antisthenes and Pyrrho. Questions went on rather too long, but we escaped about 9.00, with Richard and Megan, and went off to the *Steki tou Mantou,* the excellent restaurant on the other side of Lycabettus. A slap-up feed – great vegetables, rabbit stew, and flagons of the house red wine, for 700 dr. for the two of us. And so home, in a taxi, about midnight. I sent Jean to sleep by reading my speech to her. It runs a fraction over 20 minutes – should do!

## DAY 2, TUESDAY, SEPTEMBER 28TH

Up betimes, and joined Tony (Long) and Jacques Brunschwig[60]

---

59     There were two or three possible Antiphons in fifth-century Athens, only one of whom was a sophist.

60     Jacques Brunschwig (1929-2010) was a French historian of ancient

for breakfast. Brunschwig is most pleasant – based in Nanterre. A cousin of Vidal-Naquet's. He says he is much concerned at the moment with the 'trouble in the Middle East', but didn't elaborate!

I delivered my talk successfully enough, it seems.[61] No one seriously demurred, though Fernanda D-C asked some penetrating questions. Old Despotopoulos came up to afterwards and thanked me warmly in French, commending me on my command (*maîtrise*) of the subject! A young psychologist at the break made some good observations on Truth, as a psychiatric tool! Antiphon did after all, invent psychiatry!

The questions went on rather long, till about 2.00. Jean had gone up the town to see some museums, but returned frustrated. The Benaki was closed on Tuesdays, and the Folk Museum is being remodelled. Lunch in the hotel was straightforward and copious. Then we went up-town with Tony to try to book a passage to an island. After elaborate debate, we picked on Tenos, as being easy for him to get back from. Santorini we could fly to, but the plane back was full! We briefly considered, and rejected, hiring a car and going to Zakynthos. Then we had a beer and ice-cream in Syntagma Square, and returned, missing the first half of the afternoon session. Our absence was *noticed,* so we are a bit chastened, but it was *solid* Greek, and really very difficult to follow, even with the 'translation'.

A dinner expedition gradually formed during the day, and finally amounted to *nine:* Richard and Megan, Tony, Fernanda Caizzi, Myrto Dragona-Monachou (entertained by Tony),[62] Joachim Classen, and George Kerferd. We went off to a fish restaurant called *Hepta Karavakia* ('Seven Little Boats'), on the way

---

philosophy, who was at this time at the University of Nanterre, though he had taught also in Paris. His mother, Isabelle, was the aunt of Pierre Vidal-Naquet (1930-2006), the distinguished historian of Ancient Greece. His worries about the Middle East may relate to the Israeli invasion of Lebanon earlier in the summer.

61    My talk was entitled 'Euripides and Antiphon on Nomos and Physis', and was duly published in *The Sophistic Movement: Proc. of First Int. Symp. of Greek Philos. Soc.*, 1983, Athens, pp. 127-136.

62    She had been a student of his in London.

to the Piraeus. It was indeed jolly – excellent hors-d'oeuvres, good, if rather strange, white wine, and a well-grilled fish – *lithinia* (red snapper). But it was certainly expensive – worked out at 1300 dr. each – and we were standing Richard and Megan, by arrangement. So we were cleaned out, and need to visit the bank in the morning (big fish, we learn, is very expensive now).

We ended the day with a metaxa and ouzo (for Jean) in the lobby, with Tony.


## DAY 3, WEDNESDAY, SEPTEMBER 29TH

Rose late-ish, Jean being rather crapulous by reason of the ouzo. Again, we did not seem to suffer from the wine. We joined Tony and Jacques Brunschwig once again for breakfast, and then went searching for a bank, to get some money. (I should say that, earlier, we had received consecutive phone calls from Garth Fowden and Steve Miller, asking us to lunch and dinner respectively!) We found a bank some way up Syngrou and changed $100 @ 70 dr. to the $, which is not bad. Then got a taxi back to the hotel and to Panteios, arriving rather late!

The taxi-driver was an amusing case (which I related to Costas Yialoucas,[63] who turned up at the conference, and now has a temporary job in the University of Crete!). After some preliminary, staggering attempts on my part at conversation in Greek, he said to me: "I was in England for four and a half years, at Cambridge University. I studied economics. Then I did a Master's degree at New York University. But back here, it is hard to find a job". So I tipped him generously!

The morning session was very good, with a series of stimulating papers on various of the Sophists.

Then off in a taxi to lunch with the Fowdens. A long ride into the suburbs – Zographou – up to the foothills of Hymettos, where they have a very pleasant penthouse apartment. They welcomed us like old friends, and are indeed a delightful pair.

---

63    Costas had been a graduate student in Berkeley, working with Mark Griffith and Donald Mastronarde in the area of Greek tragedy. He now had a temporary position at the University of Crete in Rethymnon.

She, Polymnia Athanassiadi, is a lecturer in Ancient History in the University of Athens, and of very good family, we would gather, while Garth is a research scholar in Cambridge. They have a little boy, Jason, who lives here. They are both in the area of Late Antiquity, and pupils of Peter Brown – Garth has written a thesis on Pagan Philosophers in Late Antique Society,[64] under Henry Chadwick, which is very like what Peter is completing at the moment. By rights, Garth should have his book in the series.[65] He is now working on the Hermetic Corpus from a sociological perspective.[66]

Polymnia has just published a work on Julian, with Oxford, which I must buy.[67] She has strong views on most subjects, including Greek Classicists, whom she regards as the dregs of the earth (they mainly come from *villages*, she alleges – speaking as a sixth-generation Athenian – and don't know their arses from their elbows), and Andreas Papandreou, whom she regards as working for a one-party state.[68] Apart from anything else, there are, she alleges, Green Guards rampaging about (we haven't seen any!), arresting people in cafés for criticising the Prime Minister. We take all this with a grain of salt.

We only began lunch at 3.00 pm, so there was no hope of going to see the new excavations at the Agora, which Richard McK. had arranged for us to see – Dinsmoor was to show us round; they have uncovered now a corner of what must be the

----

64    This was in fact never published as a book, but was doubtless the inspiration for *Empire to Commonwealth: Consequences of Monotheism in Late Antiquity* (Princeton, 1993).

65    That is to say, the series of volumes on The Transformation of the Classical Heritage published by the University of California Press, which Peter Brown and I had founded some years before, and of which he was the general editor.

66    This emerged as *The Egyptian Hermes* (Cambridge, 1986).

67    I duly did. It is *Julian: An Intellectual Biography* (Routledge, 1981).

68    The then Greek prime minister, leader of the PASOK party., who had come into power in 1981, and was in fact a most progressive statesman.

Stoa Poikile.[69] It was an excellent, elaborate lunch – washed down with local retsina of a most villainous appearance, but perfectly pleasant. Egg and sausage pie, then a meat course, then fruit. We only broke up at about 5.30pm, and got a taxi back to the Ilissos. Garth is leaving on Sunday, but we have promised to look up Polymnia next week, when we get back to Athens.

We got in for the second half of the final session, which concerned the 'Afterlife' of the Sophists, and was enormously tedious: Schopenhauer, Hegel – even one D.D. Philippides – and the Sophists. Mr. Philippides' works, it seems, are largely unpublished, for very good reason, and this one bore has a corner on them. Philippides (end of 18th century) had views on *everything*. Finally, we had a windy closing address from Despotopoulos – after a graceful vote of thanks from George Kerferd.

After this, we rather shamefacedly slipped away to dinner with the Millers, bringing the big suitcase to leave with the McKirahans. Once again, the taximan didn't really know where Souidias was.[70] We found Steve and Stella, Richard and Megan, sitting in the garden of the School, amid the debris of a reception that Steve had just held for potential donors to the School. He gave us an impressive brochure. Then we all went off in the Directoral Mercedes to what seemed like an excellent restaurant, Anna's, which mainly specialises in game. However, no sooner had I hit the restaurant than I began to feel profoundly queasy. Delicious hors d'oeuvres were produced – eggplant, *satziki,* sausage, etc. – but I could only mumble some bread. Finally it became plain that I was about to faint, so I had to be taken back to the hotel. Very sad, but in fact we had largely had enough with the hors d'oeuvres. Just as well that I had not attended the conference banquet, as I would have had to rush from that. We persuaded the Millers to come in and meet Tony, and J. stayed down, bought everyone a drink, and talked, and apologised for me.

I lay down, taking four Lomatil, and actually recovered by

---

69      The Painted Stoa, a notable landmark in classical times.

70      It is the street on which both the British School and the American School are situated.

morning, to my great surprise and relief, as we had a long journey ahead of us.

I hope I did not offend too mortally Myrto and the rest as a result of not attending the banquet, but I think not, as she did ask us to come round on Saturday, if we were there. We do not intend to be, however, unless Tenos is *very* dull.

## DAY 4, THURSDAY, SEPTEMBER 30<sup>TH</sup>

We arose before 6.00 am, and, without breakfast, went after a taxi to the Peiraeus, to catch our boat to Tenos, the *Naias*, with Tony. We had been sold *Second* Class (= First Class) tickets, which we found to be superfluous, for a journey of 5 ½ hours. We had a cabin, and access to the front deck, where we were chased around from one perch to another by deckhands wanting to do something for us. Two gays on their way to bliss on Mykonos necked behind us on a rug. And yet it was quite pleasant. The view of Athens' smog initially was daunting. Then that gradually faded, but around Sounion a wind got up, which got brisker progressively as we reached, first, Syros, and then Tenos.

Tony was very glad to get away for a rest. As I had divined, his 'news' involved the break-up of his marriage with Kay (she has found a lecturer in Cambridge), and his taking up with Betsy Ditmars. I had certainly noticed an 'affinity' between them in Berkeley, but this went beyond music, it seems, and he really is beginning a new life. He spent most of the summer agonizing about all this, and has now resolved it. He is spending half his time in Cambridge next term as a research lecturer, in place of Myles Burnyeat, and will have Betsy with him there. Also Allan and Annie Silverman! Allan will help them (Tony Long and David Sedley) with the Stoics book.[71]

We arrived in Tenos at 1.30, in time for lunch. We found the Club Travel agent, John Armacolas, and his wife – a very pleasant pair – and they found us an excellent hotel, the Asteria (C Class), for 800 dr. a night for a double room, and recommended some

---

71    This ultimately became the basic handbook, *Long and Sedley, The Hellenistic Philosophers*, Cambridge, 1987.

good restaurants. We checked in – a nice view of the port and sea, on the north edge of town – and then went down to Lefteris' taverna for lunch – charming, cheap and excellent.

It[72] is a pleasant little town, dominated by the large 19th century Church of the Panaghia – very like Knock, the Virgin appeared to a nun here in 1822 or so, and directed her to a miraculous icon, which she dug up (!), and which is now installed in the church. It is a major pilgrimage centre (though mainly twice a year, 25th March and 15th August), and as an Orthodox shrine in a predominantly *Catholic* island (the consequence of fully 500 years of Venetian rule!), it comes across as a shrewd piece of religious politics.

Tenos as an island had no place in ancient history that I can recall (though I think that the men of Tenos behaved well in connexion with the Battle of Salamis), but there is, north of the town, a large sanctuary of Poseidon and Amphitrite, to which we walked in the evening, after a rather windy bathe.

It is still impressive in the extent of its ruins – mostly Hellenistic and Roman, I should say. Some stuff in the little museum also, of the Geometric period, from Xoburgo inland.

We had a short siesta, then drinks in the room – gins and tonics – for which we scrounged some ice from the management. Tony and I went downtown for his sunglasses, and we bought olives and nuts – there is a superb cake-shop just up from the port, and a whole street of little gift-shops and so on – a veritable *souk*!

Then down to Armacolas' second choice for dinner – *Fanaria*, in the square nearer the hotel. Excellent – and the average price for a meal is no more than £4.00 a head. Ireland will have to take drastic measures! I am already working on a plan.[73]

After dinner a short walk, and then a *metaxa* in the hotel.

---

72     That is, Tinos the town.

73     The excessive charges of tourist venues in Ireland has always been a bee in my bonnet. When my friend John Kelly was Minister of Tourism in 1981-82, I plagued him with plans for establishing an Irish system of *paradores*, on the Spanish model, by means of which the Government could establish a fair and moderate level of changes in the hotel industry – but he was not in office long enough to do anything about this, even if he had wanted to – or indeed been able to!

## DAY 5, FRIDAY, OCTOBER 1<sup>ST</sup>

In the morning, after the usual breakfast of toast and cake, we set out up the town to shop.

*We found a lovely shop which sold high-class pottery, and bought some nice ceramic doves. Then we strolled up to the cathedral at the top of the town (I dawdled behind, John panicked and went rushing off looking for me – I must have been in a shop when he passed). The courtyard was filled with hibiscus, bougainvillea, and a garden on the street on the way up had the most lovely lavender-coloured jasmine. The church inside was a mass of silver and gold lamps strung up on wires, presumably offerings. And some elaborate icons! We never found the main area of the cathedral. We decided that what we saw couldn't be all that there was of the place. Incidentally, although most of the population of the island are Catholics,this was Greek Orthodox.*

*Then down the main street to the museum, where there were mostly sculptures from the island's temple of Poseidon, and some quite elaborate pots. We then went to ask our travel agent about a bus to the middle of the island. In the meantime, we had some delicious lunch at our favourite restaurant, Taverna Lefteris, came out, and missed our 2 o'clock bus. So we took a taxi. We roamed steadily up the hills, which were very impressive. Steep slopes, with lots of stone walls, like the West of Ireland. Everywhere looked quite brown, but was obviously quite fertile, since it supports large amounts of cattle, sheep, goats and plenty of donkeys, which are still the main means of transport on the island (apart from the motor scooters!). We eventually arrived at our destination, the ruins of a Venetian fortress atop a steep mountain, 1700 ft. high. John and Tony climbed to the top, but I couldn't, because the wind was too strong, and I kept being blown over. So I went for a stroll on the lower slopes. We then made our way down the mountain to a sweet little village called Steni, to catch the return bus at 5:00 pm We called in for a cup of coffee at a local tavern, where John had a chance to practise his Greek on a gregarious lady who was dying for a chat.*

*By the time we got back to Tinos town the wind was very strong, so J and I decided not to swim, but to have a siesta instead. Tony went for a swim from the harbour in front of the hotel. We had a gin and tonic with Tony in our rooms, and then went to the restaurant Leto for dinner, where we had quite a good meal (but should have avoided the swordfish, as I think it had been frozen). Also, they had a colour TV blaring with American noise, which was a bit annoying.*

Between a loud western and 'Dallas', we were addressed at great length by an ancient politician called Averoff,[74] who I thought was dead, but is the leader of the 'Nea Demokratia' party. He seemed very dull, but was listened to keenly by the older set.

*There is a pet pelican on the island called Georgio, who is to be seen all over the place, especially where there are a lot of people, e.g. between tables at restaurants, on the steps of the bank (John remarked that he must have been there to change some fish), and his favourite place, in front of the fish market! Everyone goes about their business and he is treated as a permanent fixture. He loves to be stroked. We haven't seen him eat yet, and wonder if he does fish for himself. We've watched him skim over the surface of the water, apparently looking for fish, but not diving.*

## DAY 6, SATURDAY, OCTOBER 2ND

*The wind dropped overnight, so we walked out to the beach on the south of the town (Hagios Phocas), which was lovely. There were only six other people there. We had a glorious swim in water which was cool, but not cold, and apparently very clean. I took a little stroll while John and Tony talked incessantly about philosophy. I made a remark to them about how hilarious their conversation sounded to me, but they weren't amused. We then went back to the hotel so Tony could pack his bags and have a hair wash.*

*We went back to our favourite, Lefteris, for our lunch. Then walked down the town to get some coffee. We sat in one café for about half-an-hour and never got the coffee we ordered from a rather inane-looking boy, so we moved on down and found a self-service place. We sat there until Tony's departure. He was leaving on the 3.30 boat for Athens.*

On our way out this morning, our host was amusing. We asked him was George the only tame pelican in town. "Yes," he

---

74      Evangelos Averoff-Tositsa (1910 - 1990) was a Greek politician, leader of the right-wing party *New Democracy* (1981 - 1984), member of parliament, and author. He wrote both historical works and a number of novels. He was at this time, in fact, leader of the opposition. He had hero- ically opposed both the German occupation, and, more recently, the Junta.

said. "There *were* two, but one night a visitor from Morocco – he was very drunken – thought the other was a woman. And so – " And he made an expressive Greek gesture. A very sad little story!

*We went back to the hotel for a siesta, and later went for a walk up the hill. Back to the hotel for a G and T, and then dinner at the third recommendation of our agents, 'The Waves'. It was rather empty. I had a beef souvlaki and John had a swordfish souvlaki. Mine was very good, but his swordfish was like mine of the previous night, not absolutely fresh – probably frozen. We saw Andreas Papandreou on the TV before we went to bed.*

### DAY 7, SUNDAY, OCTOBER 3<sup>RD</sup>

*Went down to the local café for 'loukoumades' (delicious doughnuts) for breakfast. We came back to the hotel and packed a lunch of bread, cheese, sausage and wine. Took a bus, at 11.00am, for Pyrgos, on the north of the island.*

A magnificent drive along the ridge of the hills in the centre of the island. One saw the whole coastline, mainly rocky, but with a few coves, and the hills covered with carefully stepped terraces for cultivation, though brown now. Everywhere through the island are finely ornamented dovecots, with flocks of doves going in and out. At first we were confused as to the point of keeping so many doves in such luxury – possibly a religious significance, as the archaeologists would say – but the evidence is that they eat them! We met a rather stout Greek doctor on the bus, who had been out in Zimbabwe for five years, but left when the black struggle for emancipation began to take force, who gave us various bits of information. He urged us next time to visit Skiathos and Halonnesos, as being much more fertile, but praised Tenos as being 'fresh' all year round. We got out at Pyrgos, and walked about the town, which was largely asleep at Sunday noon, but very pleasant, and then got out to walk four kilometres to Panormos, on the water, where the bus route ended.

We stopped half-way for a picnic, having bought some provisions yesterday – and Jean fecked a fig and a pomegranate from trees along the way. The fig, at least, was quite delicious. I was impressed, along the way, by a shrine to Artemis, erected by the hunters of Panormos, at which we washed our hands.

110

*Went on into Panormos, looking for somewhere to swim. The beach right beside the town looked rather depressed – lots of plastic – so we walked on around the headland and had a very nice swim from a sort of beach between the rocks. There was a nice beach further on which I had investigated, but was too embarrassed to approach because there was just one family messing about with their fishing boat, and I didn't want to feel like a turkey!*

I found a nice little cove (if one didn't look *too* closely at the foreshore – the Greeks are certainly very messy) and swam there, and then found J coming back and introduced her to it. The water was noticeably warmer than on the other side of the island, for some reason. By this time it was really quite cloudy. We walked back and found the Greek doctor ensconced in the local taverna, on excellent terms with the hostess (Kyria Maria) and various other occupants. The bus was not due for half-an-hour (3.15 pm), and we had had enough of him, so we took a little walk along the other side of the harbour, where we found some ducks fornicating in a duck-pond, and one lady bathing. The bus arrived a little late, and we set out back.

Half way along there was a small drama. The bus stopped, and it transpired that a motorcyclist (who turned out to be British or Australian) had fallen or been knocked over. We rescued him – took him into the bus, and the conductor got out and drove his motorcycle back to town. He was scraped and a bit dazed, and rather surly, it seemed to us, because they really were most hospitable to him. Anyway, that ended reasonably happily, and we returned safely.

On the way back to the hotel, we found George stretching himself, and tried to photograph him, but the camera jammed. Then a young and foolish dog tried to chivvy him, and George opened his enormous jaws and routed him.

After the usual siesta and drink, we set out for dinner, and found it, unbelievably, to be raining, gently but firmly. This is fine for the farmers of Tenos, but a bit depressing for visiting Irish. We hope it is an anomaly. We were tempted by possible Greek music at the other end of the town, but not quite up to trailing all the way over there on spec. Perhaps there will be something more accessible on Thera.

Back to the hotel, then, after a stroll through pleasant back streets, for a metaxa/ouzo, and bed.

## DAY 8, MONDAY, OCTOBER 4<sup>TH</sup>

We were woken up in the middle of the night by what seemed to be a raging Aegean storm. The wind was whistling through the shutters, and the waves were lashing the pier. It was two in the morning. We went blearily out onto the balcony. The rain had cleared, and the moon was shining, but things did not look good for our projected voyage to Thera.[75] We went back to bed with foreboding.

However, by morning the wind had dropped considerably, though the sea was still rather high. J. woke up not feeling very well, so, after breakfast and paying the bill, I went to find Alka-Seltzer. They had never heard of that, so I came back with some rather indefinite pills 'for dyspepsia', and fed her one of those. She got a little better, and we checked out a little before 12.00. (The island opposite, by the way, is particularly clear this morning, and at last I asked what it was. It is Syros – although quite in the wrong direction, it seemed to me: what I thought was Syros is actually Delos!) We poked around the souk again, and J bought a few more trinkets. Then we settled down, with a coffee and loukoumades, to wait for the boat.

The Panaghia Tinou arrived almost half-an-hour late, which cuts things rather close for catching the Ios from Mykonos. However, the Ios was itself half-an-hour later than we had been told, so that turned out all right. I rushed off to try and find the Club Travel agent in Mykonos to ask about Santorini, but went off in the wrong direction and failed, so we have had to take our chances.

The Ios is a pleasant, small, oldish boat, but bowled along briskly in near-perfect conditions. The first stop was Paros, which looked more or less the same – the Hotel Kontes still in place! – but the surroundings look more developed, and the central mountains higher and barer than we remember . Most of the young backpackers got off there. On the Ios leg, we met up with a Swiss couple with two children, and swapped their wine for some olives.

---

75    I use here and elsewhere the ancient name for Santorini.

The sun went down as we sailed out of Paros, and we proceeded under a spectacular full moon, beginning as a great orange ball and slowly rising on the starboard bow as we went on. Most of the rest of the passengers, including the Swiss, left at Ios, and only a handful of the intrepid continued to Thera. We almost jumped ship, since J was alarmed at the possibility of crawling up a cliff-face on a mule. In the event, though, we sailed past the mule path, down to a place where there is a road. We arrived well after 10.00 pm, an unholy time to arrive anywhere. The moon was bright, but one could see nothing of the colours of the cliffs – just black masses towering above the ship, with lights twinkling on the top.[76]

On the pier, we were seduced, in our exhausted state, by a taxi-man, and swept away before we observed that there was a bus! However, although it ultimately cost us 500 dr., it may not have been such a disaster, since, when we arrived in Fira, we found that three hotels in succession that we picked on were full, and were finally recommended to go off to another village called Mesaria and stay there, which we have now done, finding a rather frugal place for 770 dr. a night. We would have got badly stuck with the bus.

We are now ending the evening with an excellent pizza (for J) and reasonable meatballs (for me), washed down by local Löwenbräu.

## DAY 9, TUESDAY, OCTOBER 5TH

We spent a night punctuated by every sort of noise. We are on a crossroads here in Mesaria, with two cafés opposite us, and motor scooters seems to start up violently up to 2.00 in the morning every time we looked like getting to sleep. And we were woken again at 6.00 or so with the same sort of serenades – scooters, lorries, random shouts and horn-blowing. Not much

---

76     One should explain that, when arriving at Santorini, one sails into what is in effect a massive crater, left by the great eruption of around 1600 B.C. that made the island what it is, and changed the face of Minoan civilisation.

of a night, and a rather grim little room. Still, we are probably stuck here, as we have resolved on tours for the next two days, as the best way of seeing what this island has to offer in the shortest possible time.

After breakfast, which was good, I went down to enquire about tours from Kamari Tours on the corner. An efficient young man sold me on a package of two tours, one for today on land – to the Monastery of Profitis Ilias, and to the Akrotiri excavations – then a bathe at Perissa and a wine-tasting.

*Our guide was an interesting, but fairly tough-looking, middle-aged lady. We started with a visit to the monastery, which was perched high on a hill above the village of Pyrgos. The view of the monastery was somewhat spoiled by a radar installation literally on their doorstep. The monastery itself was fascinating. It dates from 1711. The chapel was filled with very elaborate carved and painted wood (only done in the 1830's by local craftsmen), but it also had many icons, some from the 16th cent. Cretan School, which was famous for its distinctive style of light/shade painting. They had preserved (or restored) some work-rooms in the monastery, and have them displayed as kind of a folk museum – very tastefully done: the barber's room, the shoemaker's, the barley-crushing room, the wine cellar, the carpentry room (where we were slightly shocked to see a couple of cradles!); and the hour ended with a complimentary glass of the monks' own raki – potent stuff!*

*Next, we were driven to Spiro Marinatos' excavations at Akrotiri, on the southern tip of the island, which are all roofed in. It is certainly impressive, though nothing like as spectacular as Mycenae. It is like a miniature town, but they have removed (understandably, I suppose) the wall paintings to the National Museum in Athens, which rather detracts from the general effect, I would say. Excavations are still going on, in a subdued way, because funds are rather short.*

Next the tour took us to the beach at Perissa. It is, they say, eight kilometres long, with rather nice tiny little grey pebbles, but nothing to compare with our good Irish beaches. We had a leisurely swim, and a picnic of bread, cheese, salami and some revolting local white wine. The sky was sort of clouded over, but probably still capable of delivering sunburn. J worked at a sketch of a church against a background of the steep hill – Mesa Vouno – that comes down to the sea. I read Zorba the Greek – a bit windy, but quite gripping in its way. Kazantzakis is full of shit, but very capable of evoking both scenes and characters – not just Zorba, but the locals in the taverna, and Bouboulina.

The final element of the tour was a wine-tasting back in Kamari – we had to go back round Mesa Vouno, since we couldn't go over it – only mules can do that, it seems (that is where Old Thera lurks, on the top, blast it!). The wine-tasting took place in the Roussos Winery (est. 1836), and consisted of a sequence of seven of the worst wines we had ever tasted in our lives. The whites tasted weirdly of pistachio – and there were many pistachio trees growing nearby – while the reds were a sequence of bad altar wines. It was really quite sad, as the proprietor seemed very pleased with them, and was even discussing them, in fluent French, with some French tourists. We got the giggles, as I began to imagine an international panel of winetasters discussing these wines, and trying to find the *exact* adjective to characterise each of them. To make their position more awkward, we imagined them summoned in by some Greek equivalent of Idi Amin – say, a modern Dionysius of Syracuse – to judge the wine, produce of his own vineyards.

After this, we were driven back to Mesaria. After a bit of a rest, we decided to go up to Thera town and see if we could find an interesting restaurant. We got the bus up to town, and set out to explore (we met a pair on the bus who said that buses stop at 9.00 pm, so we will presumably have to get a taxi back). At first we were very shocked by Thera – nothing but turkeys everywhere! We wandered around the streets, getting more and more indignant, finding virtually no restaurants, and the only attractive ones hopelessly crowded. Otherwise, just souvenir shops and 'bars'.

We went back to our starting point, and asked the way to one restaurant named by our companions on the bus. On the way to that, we found another called Dionysos, which seemed pleasant and unpretentious. This it was, despite a rather preposterous Greek-English waitress, and we found we had a bonus, in the form of genuine Greek music from 9.00 on. Two old gentlemen appeared, one with a fiddle, the other with a mandolin, and, after some preliminary jars, really started to belt it out. After a bit, some young Greeks (no doubt retained for the purpose) rose and began to dance. One was particularly good, but all were good, and yet preserved a sense of amateurism which was pleasing. We were joined at our table by three girls whom we convinced ourselves were Irish, but rather than venture acquaintance, I proposed (perhaps wrongly) that we should quit while we were ahead, so at about 10.30 we got a taxi back to Mesaria. The evening had ended well, though – unexpected genuineness in the midst of bogusity!

### DAY 10, WEDNESDAY, OCTOBER 6<sup>TH</sup>

This morning we had arranged to go on a boat cruise round the caldera. First, though, we had to change some money – the travel agent on the corner gave a rate of 114 dr. to the £, which is daylight robbery, and we had to change £40, so that was rather ruinous. Anyhow, we paid up for the tour, taking enough money to pay all foreseeable bills, in case we leave early tomorrow morning.

We were still agonising over this when we realised that it was time for the bus. We met a pleasant Australian pair at breakfast who had been on yesterday's tour, and were going on today's. Indeed, quite a few people were going on both, and a certain amount of camaraderie developed during the day. We also met an English girl, to whom I complained that the travel agent wasn't open when he should have been, before I realised that she lived here, and was married (or otherwise allied) to the guide for the tour, a German called Gerhardt, who looks pleasantly like a Doonesbury character, and has a little puppy on a lead.

We went in an overcrowded bus to Athinios, where we boarded a pleasant little boat, and sailed first out of the caldera, round the Akrotiri Peninsula, as far as the site of the Mycenaean town, and then back into the bay, to Palaia Kaimeni.[77] There we were invited to go swimming in the hot springs (beneath

---

77    One of the pair of islands in the centre of the caldera, the result of later volcanic activity.

the surface of the water). We moored just off the shore, where there was a tiny church. J was having none of this, but I jumped in gallantly and swam to shore. The water was a turbid green from the sulphur, but not *hot*. I landed, and paid respects to the church. It turned out that the hot springs were round the corner, and were a mixed experience, as one kept swimming in and out of them, and getting *cold*.

We took what we hope will be some effective pictures of the caldera. We stopped next at Thirasia, the other half of Thera, and rode up on mules to the village of Manolas, where we had a very pleasant lunch of little fish (*gopes*). Then we walked about a bit. It is a nice little uncommercialized village – rather surprising, really, being so close to Thera! J started a sketch. I walked up to the church, and sat down behind it, contemplating the back of the island. I suddenly got an extraordinary sense of *silence* and peace. One could hear all the separate noises – birds, donkeys braying, occasional shouts of children, donkey-bells – but overall there was a silence.

*After Thirasia, our boat took us to the 'active' volcano in the bay, where we climbed up it. It is quite impressive, but the part that is supposed to be 'active' is nothing like as impressive as, say, Stromboli, where you can see bubbles and flames. All that you could see here was greenish-yellowish sulphuric earth, and steam coming out, and then only in spots. The earth was admittedly very hot to touch.*

*(Our guides on the tour were a German called Gerhardt and his English girlfriend Tricia. She was extremely gregarious and buttonholed us on many occasions during the trip. She was very amusing, and reminded us rather of my sister Clare, with her drama. She is an old hand in Thera, having been coming here for the last few years regularly, and she is endeavouring to stay here. She is fed up with England, and will move to north mainland Greece for the winter. She has a three-and-a-half year old son, Christopher, who is treated rather like a buffer, poor child. He is wheeled out and scolded in front of an audience – this we found when we met him again at supper and at breakfast in our hotel. She also told us all about how she and Gerhardt weren't hitting it off at the moment.)*

*After the volcano, we headed back to Thera, and on the way (about 6 pm) we saw a most beautiful sunset. We decided to stay in Mesaria for supper, first having a nap for about an hour. We had a delicious pizza at a restaurant a couple of doors away from the hotel. It was served to us by a very nice Irish girl, who said she had been in Thera for about three weeks, before that in Paros, and prior to that in Holland. She was working her way around everywhere, and seemed to be doing very well for herself.*

## DAY 11, THURSDAY, OCTOBER 7<sup>TH</sup>

*We decided not to try and visit Old Thera, because we were afraid we wouldn't have enough time, as it involves a longish mule ride. So we went to Thera on the bus instead – first to the bank, and then to the tourist office, to enquire about buses to the boat. We were told to get on the 1 o'c. bus. Then we sauntered through the town, first coming to the Dominican convent, where they train girls to make rugs. You can go into the workshops and watch them. Unfortunately, the designs of the rugs leave a lot to be desired, and one finds it hard to see their good points. There are beautiful embroidered linens here, but at rather prohibitive prices. I saw a rather nice tablecloth yesterday, but it turned out to cost about £80. If they'd been offering it for £8 or a tenner, I'd have been tempted. Instead I fled.*

*I can't remember if I mentioned how awful the town of Thera is. It is jammed with turkeys, and so commercial – really very unpleasant!*

We had some trauma getting to the boat. We needed to catch a local bus back to Mesaria to get the bags, before catching a bus to Athinios for the boat. That bus left at 12.45; our bus left at 12.30. They sat side by side for almost half-an-hour, until ours moved off just ahead. Then it stopped to load on school-children! But it just got us back with a minute to spare, and we scrambled onto the port bus, which was packed to the gills. Then we hung about in Athinios for about two hours – it is a most dismal hole! – until the good ship *Kimolos* arrived, at 3.30.

The *Kimolos* was not crowded. It hops from island to island in a leisurely way, arriving in the Piraeus in the morning. First Folegandros, then Sikinos – both only accessible by small boats, which come out to the ship. They look quite fun, for the hardy explorer. Lovely sunset over Folegandros – the sea and hills turned deep purple, the sky orange and purple. By the time we got to Ios, it was night. Ios had attracted us, but we were warned (by both Tricia and Eileen) that it had been taken over by bums and potheads – a selection of whom boarded the boat, indeed. We met a very pleasant girl from Kilkenny on the boat – now a nurse in Glasgow, married to a nice, very quiet Indian psychiatrist, and she talked at us much of the way to Paros, where we arrived (after Naxos) at about 10.45 at night.[78]

We were full of anxiety about the Hotel Kondes being full or much declined, but it was neither. The pleasant owner was there to greet us, and seemed pleased to see us, and we were soon lodged in a room with a balcony at the back of the hotel – 751 dr; obviously up from last time, but still not bad. Then out to have a meal (at 11.00!) at our favourite taverna round the corner (*Aligaria*), which was still open. We had delicious meat balls and stuffed eggplant, for 315 dr.

And so to bed, after a short walk on the front. It is hard to tell yet how much the island has changed.


DAY 12, FRIDAY, OCTOBER 8TH

We slept well, though the beds are a bit hard, and the plumbing slightly eccentric. Had a good breakfast of eggs and sausages in a self-service across the square, since none seemed to be on offer at the hotel. The Kontes is a pretty low-key institution. We then decided to take the 10.00 am bus to Naoussa, and have a bathe there, and possibly lunch. Thoughts of renting bikes or moped we regretfully set aside.

The ride to Naoussa was pleasant, and we saw a little beach on the outskirts of town, which we headed back to. Plainly, Naoussa is growing as a place for holiday homes. The water is perfectly clear, but the slight whiff of sewage as one dived beneath it was somewhat worrying. Certainly nothing visible, though, and the beach was clean (by Greek standards!).

We read for a while, and then headed back into town, to

---

78    This was a return visit, as we had been here previously in May 1977; see p.19 above.

stroll around back streets. All very pleasant – the usual little lanes and crannies, adorned with bougainvillea, etc. We reached the main square again at 12.15, and decided after all to go back on 12.30 bus and have a (frugal) lunch in Paros. In fact, we went out in search of a *souvlaki,* found a rather bogus restaurant on the seafront, and had a *large* lunch. J had 'lamp shops'[79] (230 dr.) and I had a plate of whitebait, which were delicious, if a little unnerving, as one has to munch them down head first; and a bottle of retsina. Not bad, though.

Then back to the hotel, exhausted, and slept for two hours, planning to go to the Valley of the *Petaloudes* at 5.00.[80] When we enquired, though, we found that the tour was off, so we decided just to walk out south of town, to see if we could find an Asclepieion which was marked on the map. On the way we observed what has been happening to Paros since we were last here. Discos, bars along the front ('Your favourite *koktail* for only 120 dr.'!), large new hotels and apartment blocks and private houses sprawling out of town in either direction. It is all very sad. And of course the garbage dumped along the roads is indescribable – puts the Moyne Road[81] in the shade entirely!

We were joined, as usual on our perambulations, by a faithful dog – we have gathered as many as three – who accompanied us out and back from the outskirts of town.

On our way back, we fell in with an aged couple walking into town, who engaged us in conversation. He was Greek in origin (from Melos), she Belgian. They had spent their working life in London and Los Angeles, doing I know not what, but obviously doing it successfully, and fifteen years ago, after much deliberation and study of Mediterranean watering-holes, decided to retire to Paros. They loved it, but now they were much depressed. It is apparently scheduled by the Greek

---

79    A private joke: we had seen lamb chops advertised thus in a Greek menu some years before this.

80    See earlier diary, p. 20.

81    A country road leading down from our house in Old Portmarnock to the coast, which was vulnerable to dumping.

government to become the major holiday island (for *basic turkeys*) after Mykonos, and the signs are already on it. Traders become nastier, tourist shops and other traps more vulgar and obtrusive, the niceties of life disappear. One can't get servants now, they complain, and shopkeepers no longer have time to pass the time of day. *Now*, they said, it was comparatively quiet again (though it seems pretty crowded to us!), but in July and August it was unspeakable. They live out of town, but the town is creeping out towards them. I tried to console the husband by suggesting that a slump in tourism may be at hand, but he wasn't convinced. And just today they inaugurated the new Paros *airport*, with daily flights to Athens! We left them in town with mutual expressions of goodwill.

*We went back to the hotel and had a couple of ouzos – then to dinner at our favourite restaurant around the corner – Aligari. I was disappointed that they had run out of those delicious beans – gigantes – but we had a good feed of souvlaki and stuffed eggplant.*

While dinner was coming, I rushed up to see if the bookstore we had noted earlier was open. It was, and I went boldly in to buy some books. They did not have Samarakis, but I bought the original of Zorba, to work on with the translation, and two slim volumes of poetry, one of Ritsos, *Petrinos Khronos,* and one of Elytis, *Maria Nephelê,* the latter of which is a sort of play, and sounds interesting. I toyed with a novel of Vasilikos, but decided to postpone it. The lady was amused that I was making these purchases without being able to speak much Greek, but was very good in helping me to say what I wanted in Greek, and getting me to say it correctly. She much regretted that I was only staying a day, since she could otherwise have exchanged English and Greek lessons with me. I will have to complete my collection in Athens. I should try to get something from all the finalists on the competition.[82]

After dinner, we strolled for a little along the front, rather depressed by the discos.

---

82    That is the competition for the Europalia Prize for Literature, 1982, for which I was on the committee, as the prize was to be awarded to a Greek, and a Professor of Greek was required from each EU country – but I was, of course, a Professor of *Ancient* Greek! See next diary.

## DAY 13, SATURDAY, OCTOBER 9<sup>TH</sup>

Up by about 8.00, and went across to the self-service, where I had a yoghurt (excellent) and J the usual bread and butter. Then up the north shore of the bay for a brief swim. Again, the water seemed clean, but one can't be sure. I floated, meditating, until stung by a small jellyfish, when I fled back to shore. Then we went to call on the Katapoliani church, which is most impressive. I had remembered only the baptismal font. Then we called at the museum, which is as atrociously presented as ever – the Archilochus inscription still in a corner, with no explanation at all. A few labels scattered around, all in Greek. I didn't see the piece of the Parian Marble.

The boat, the *Lemnos*, arrived on time, and was packed to the gunwales. We were lucky to get a seat (on the side deck), but those who got on at Syros really had to scrape around. Of course, like ourselves, everyone is ending holidays. We arrived duly in the Piraeus, after a pleasantly calm voyage, got the subway to Omonia Square, taxi to McKirahan's flat by about 8.30, and, after a cocktail and *mezes,* took Megan out for a pizza round the corner (Richard is off to Delos and Mykonos with his students for the weekend). We called in to the American School on the way to see if there was any mail, but only an obsolete note from Steve welcoming me to Athens, and doubting that he could put us up on Oct. 9. But no news is good news, presumably!

## DAY 14, SUNDAY, OCTOBER 19<sup>TH</sup>

A friend of Megan's – a fellow-teacher at school – called Pat came to breakfast at 9.30. Megan served an excellent omelette, and Pat brought croissants. She is an interesting girl – Hungarian-Italian parentage, brought up by her mother in Athens. Her mother is now dead, so she carries on by herself as a teacher's aide in the school where she was educated herself. From Megan's account, the school sounds a thorough rip-off. It is for ex-pats, mainly Americans – high fees ($5000 a year), large classes, enormous size (around 1500 kids). Personnel from American bases use it, and Andreas[83] has pretty well phased them out, it seems, so the school will lose some customers.

After breakfast, we resolved to go down to the Hilton and see if we could change some money, as Costas Yialoucas is taking us to lunch – I phoned him up yesterday, and he's booked for dinner, so lunch was decided on – and we wanted to have some money to hand. But the Hilton wouldn't change money, the swine, except for guests, so we are left with a few hundred drachmae.

We agreed to meet Costas at the entrance to the Agora at 1.30, since the ladies wanted to visit the flea market which blossoms in the Plaka on Sunday mornings. We took a streetcar to Omonia, and walked down Athinas St. Lots of junk about, but we finally found a very reasonable little rug shop, and bought a pleasant coverlet for 250 dr.

Costas was there to meet us, and to our alarm took us to a most luxurious restaurant called Dionysos, round the south of the Acropolis, and with a fine view of it, for which one paid through the nose. An indifferent lunch for four (beef estofado and Greek salad, and two bottles of white wine) cost him 3900 dr. (we peeked!). The poor man will be on bread and water for the rest of the month, but nothing would do him only this gross place! It is good to see him in such good form, though. He had recently returned from a tour in East Germany, as delegate of the Cypriote government, so he must be well-connected there. It sounds very much the same programme that I went on back in 1967.[84] His thesis on Euripides and the Sophists is to be published in Cyprus, which I hope will help to set him up with the powers that be, but he says that much still depends on patronage, and his foothold in Rethymnon is precarious. He is keeping in with Livadaras, though.

We walked back over the Acropolis, which was closed, and

---

83    Sc. Papandreou.

84    In the summer of 1967, as a result, as I recall, of an invitation issued to my father at a conference in Romania by a colleague from the DDR, I had headed off to a summer course in German at the Humboldt University in east Berlin, an adventure which in fact proved quite entertaining.

round the Agora, meeting a mad book peddler on the way, who became ferocious when we took an interest in his wares. I was inclined to buy the collected poems of Seferis. He wanted 500 dr. I offered 300, and he became abusive (not much bargaining goes on any more, it would seem); so I became abusive. Then I bought a modern translation of *Iphigenia in Aulis* for 100 dr. (far more than it was worth!), and he offered me the Seferis for 300. But then I didn't *have* 300, so he became abusive again. Finally, after I had roared at him, he shouted 'Go to your village!' We concluded that we had been grossly insulted, but Costas claimed that it was not a Greek insult familiar to him: *pêghaine sto khorio sou!*

We decided then to take a taxi to Lycabettus and go up the funicular to watch the sun set. It was a superb day to do this, as it was perfectly clear – one could see the Peloponnese and Corinth clearly, and of course all of Attica within range. As it happened, we had decided to leave the camera behind!

### DAY 15, MONDAY, OCTOBER 11TH

Up in time to see Megan off to work. Then Polymnia Athanassiadi phoned (I had got on to her mother yesterday). We agreed that lunch would be out of the question, so we parted with promises to get together somewhere in the future. Then we went for a walk on Kolonaki, to see if we could find bookshops or record shops. We found both, and bought cassettes of Maria Farandouri and Theodorakis (doing Ritsos' *Epitaphios*), and then novels of Samarakis, Vasilikos, and more Ritsos. The bookstores really are far better than in Dublin – especially Kaufmann's on Stadiou.

At about 1.00 we decided to move out and find a taxi. Just outside, at a little coffee shop on the corner, we found Jim Clauss and Nancy Tersini[85] having a coffee! Jim's wife Louise had a baby boy just before he came over last week and he is

---

85    Both former graduate students in Berkeley. Jim became a professor of Classics at the University of Washington, where he remained for the whole of his career.

rather lonely, since she is back home. Just as we moved to find a taxi, Jim remembered that they were *on strike!* The issue is a reasonable one – they are being asked to convert to diesel *at their own expense* – but that didn't help us. There are a few blacklegs around, but not many. Jim and Nancy helped us with bags down to the main drag, and Jim enquired in the Hilton, but no bus till 2.00 at least.

Then, fortunately, a moonlighter came along – wouldn't say what it would cost to get to the airport, but I grabbed him anyhow, reckoning we could fight him when we got there. In the event, I presented him with 600 dr. – twice the going rate – which pleased him greatly. No argument at all! I felt rather foolish.

In the queue, we met a rather know-it-all Irish old-timer in Greece, called Francis Barry, who (of course) had come out on the bus for 25 dr., which completed my sense of foolishness. He has a house on Paros, knows Desmond O'Grady[86] (who is still there, now a good deal soberer, and with a part-time appointment in Harvard), and likes to attend Easter on Thera. I must check up on him!

On the plane, we were greeted with the news that the catering staff of Aer Lingus are on strike, so no food. No great harm, but a token of the state of the country! We are on tenterhooks to hear whether Charlie has been overthrown, but I'm sure he has outmanoeuvred them again.[87] Much better for us[88] to have him at the helm, in any case!

---

86    A (rather bibulous) Irish poet, whom we had known in Limerick in the mid-1960s, and who had 'retired' to Paros.

87    He was in fact overthrown in a vote of no confidence on Nov. 4th, an election was held, and a Fine Gael-led government under Garret Fitzgerald installed on Dec. 14th.

88    The reference is to Fine Gael, of which I was at the time a fairly active member.

# 6: THE BRUSSELS JAUNT:

## OCTOBER, 1982

*It may seem extraordinary to set off again so soon after returning from Greece, but this is business. As might be gathered from the previous diary, I was the Irish representative on the jury to choose a (Greek) recipient for the Europalia Literary Prize for 1982, and this was the final stage in the process, where we all had to gather in Brussels.*

### DAY 1, TUESDAY, OCTOBER 19TH

I was rescued by Jean from college at 1.30 pm, and taken home for lunch. Got to the airport in time to buy some chocolates for Brigitte.[89] I was hoping to finish off Samarakis' novel, but got in beside a most voluble Professor of Electrical Engineering from Cork, Michael Sexton,[90] who gave me no respite. He also knew the man across the aisle, working for a Belgian company based in Waterford (though *he* is from Ballydehob – it really *does* exist!), and the Belgian firm is a licensee of Westinghouse. They are involved in electronics. Sexton knows everybody – he knew that Tom Mitchell's[91] uncle was Registrar (I think) in Galway – had Gerry Wrixon[92] under him in his department – and so on. So I got nothing done.

---

89    Brigitte Wyckhuyse, a family friend (in particular, of my sister Elizabeth).

90    Sexton was indeed a distinguished member of the UCC community. He died in 2016, in the fullness of years.

91    My colleague Thomas N. Mitchell, Professor of Latin in Trinity, and later Provost (1991-2001).

92    Gerard T. Wrixon, Professor of Microelectronics in UCC, later President of the University (1999-2007). We got to know him when he was studying in Berkeley in the early 1970s, and remained good friends since.

On landing, we found Mark Clinton and Frank Cluskey[93] waiting to board a plane for Dublin, and greeted them warmly – again, Sexton knows everybody! Then collected bags, and we went into Brussels on the train – very simple. I shared a taxi to the Hotels Metropole and Atlanta (150 fr. from the Gare Centrale). I found myself expected at the Metropole, with a folder of bumf. Some daunting news: we start tomorrow morning at 10.00, with a decision expected at 11.00. Then a press conference, and so on. I have a mortal fear now of being exposed as a total fraud, and also of coming down with a severe relapse of pneumonia. The whole expedition may be a great disaster, even fatal! I think of Dad's last expedition to London, and it bothers me.[94]

Anyhow, I went out for a sandwich and a drink with Michael Sexton, and conversed in a splendidly bibulous way about the problems of the world. His most immediate problem is that he has a meeting tomorrow to fix where a nuclear fusion centre for Europe is to be situated – Padua or somewhere in France – and the French and British (who favour Padua) are both after his vote. The French think they can claim him, since he studied there, but he favours the British. He has to face the French at breakfast tomorrow. Almost worse than my problem! Then we got onto Dev, Michael Collins, and the problem of the North.

I parted from him finally at about 10.00 pm, and came up and phoned Brigitte. Finally got her, and arranged to get together on Saturday afternoon, and she can get me to the airport on Sunday – if I last that long! Then phoned J and reported progress. Then a little reading of bumf and novel, before collapsing. I hope I get a chance to see some of the exhibits and performances.

---

93    Both prominent Irish politicians, Clinton Fine Gael, Cluskey Labour, at this time both members of the European Parliament.

94    I had actually come down with a severe cold, which turned into pneumonia, on our return from Greece just ten days previously. My father, some ten years earlier, in June 1972, had returned from a lecture trip to London with what was diagnosed as Legionnaire's Disease – a very severe pneumonia – and died over the following weekend. But his constitution had been weakened by a previous long visit to India.

Woke up at 5.00, feeling awful – headache, apparent fever – cursed my stupidity. I took a disprin and drank some water, and gradually got a bit better. It may be only a bit of a hangover, as I *did* drink three beers last night with that old boozer Sexton.

Breakfast was served in my room, at 8.00. A very pleasant croissant, roll and coffee. I shaved, and settled down to study the literature again. I am still not well – distinctly shaky, and a bit headachy. I must get more aspirin, and perhaps a thermometer. I went down to the lobby, found there was a *pharmacie* just round the corner, and bought some aspirin. But by this time I had taken a Contac and was feeling somewhat better. Then I waited in the lobby for some signs of life.

The first sign I saw turned out to be Philip Sherrard and his wife[95], both quite charming – he a bit like Oisin Kelly, she a bit like Kirsty Leonard[96] – and they made me feel better about the whole thing. I am in very daunting company, though. Everyone else is an accredited Neo-Hellenist, talking fluent Greek (as well as French and German, in most cases). We were greeted by various officials, Van Hoeck and Dawas, and by a nice girl who gave me some money, and then the Sherrards and I set out to walk to the Palais des Beaux Arts – a pleasant walk, during which I learned that they live in Euboea, she runs a small publishing house in Athens, he is connected with the British School, and is currently working on an anthology of Byzantine writings on spirituality – a later Philocalia.[97] He is unhappy about the choice before us, but favours Samarakis over Ritsos, since he

---

95    The distinguished authority on modern Greek poetry and Orthodox Christianity, who was representing Great Britain, but lived in Greece, and his wife Denise. Much more will be heard of them in future diaries.

96    Oisin Kelly, distinguished Irish sculptor, father of my brother-in-law, Fergus Kelly, distinguished scholar of Old Irish, who had been a student of my father's, and had married my sister Elizabeth; Kirsty was the wife of my old friend, Nicholas Leonard, then a journalist with the Irish Independent.

97    The Philocalia is a collection of extracts from the Church Fathers.

does not regard Ritsos as a very high-powered poet – too facile.[98] He doesn't think Samarakis is a genius, but as a prose-writer there seems more point to honouring him than another, well-honoured poet.

At the Palais we were welcomed again, and all the distinguished persons assembled: Mario Vitti, of Italy; Jean Bingen,[99] of Belgium; Isidora Rosenthal-Kamarinea of Germany (Greek in fact, and a funny old trout); a nice youngish girl, Sysse Engberg[100] of Denmark, formerly a Classicist, now in Byzantine and Modern Greek studies; a jolly poet called Leo Ross from Amsterdam; Henri Müller from Luxemburg – all published authorities and translators on the subject. The President is a French slob called Jacques Lecarrière,[101] also an expert (he has translated Seferis, Ritsos and Vassilikos), and seems to have written also about the Gnostics.

Lacarrière tried to steer the meeting straightaway to a certain kind of decision, by suggesting that we should really be choosing a writer "not entirely unknown, but not too well known, who would have work still in him (or her)." This was certainly not our charge as it had been conveyed to me, and Sherrard plainly didn't think so either. We were to choose the

---

98    Philip's real problem with Ritsos was that Ritsos was a Communist. Philip, as I learned later, didn't like Communists.

99    Jean Bingen (1920 – 2012), Belgian papyrologist and epigrapher, specializing in Greek and Roman history and civilizations, especially ancient Egypt, was another Classicist, but probably at least knew Modern Greek pretty well.

100    Actually slightly older than me – born March 8, 1939. She was Professor of Modern Greek and Balkan Studies in the University of Copenhagen.

101    Jacques Lacarrière (1925 – 2005) was a French writer, born in Limoges. He studied moral philosophy, classical literature, and Hindu philosophy and literature. Professionally, he was known as a prominent critic, journalist, and essayist. He wrote also on the Gnostics. I don't quite recall why I am so rude about him!

greatest Greek writer (excluding Elytis in my mind, and in almost everyone else's, as having a Nobel Prize already). The comments round the table centred on Samarakis and Vassilikos, tending to exclude Ritsos as too honoured already. I spoke up – in English, with apologies, blaming my cold – for Vassilikos, as being more interesting, and younger (and so with more promise). The first vote produced a close thing – Samarakis 4, Vassilikos 3, Ritsos 1, one abstention. So we voted again, and I switched to Samarakis. Result: Samarakis 6, Vassilikos 3 – a clear enough decision. Nobody very happy – least of all, it seemed, Lecarrière, who announced the result to the press with a very ill grace. And indeed we will have to explain to the public why we *didn't* select Ritsos, I would say. He *is* the towering figure, after all!

A few glasses of ouzo with the Press (whom I avoided), and then lunch. Old Mme. Rosenthal got at me in a friendly way, to see what Greek I knew, and I had to reveal that I knew very little. I really am a bit of a scandal, but I can only say that I didn't *cause* any decision arrived at to be worse than it was. *They* chose Samarakis!

After an excellent buffet lunch, with Greek wines, I went round the exhibition of classical statuary and pots, which had many excellent pieces. I have the catalogue. Various famous pots, such as Odysseus and the Sirens, the heads of Socrates and Euripides, and some comely Venuses. Then I felt a bit weak, and went back to lie down for a while, taking an aspirin. I was a little better by 6.00 pm, so I rose and went off to the reception. Just as well, as Couloubaritsis[102] was waiting for me, and most anxious that I wasn't there (in fact I got lost for a while in the bowels of the Palais with dear old Müller and his wife, and Mme. Rosenthal). He is determined to entertain me. Since there is a reception at the Greek Embassy tomorrow evening, we fixed on Friday lunchtime, which may be inconvenient, but there's no way round it. I don't know how long I can stay at the Metropole, for a start.

---

102     Lambros Couloubaritsis (1941- ) is a Belgian scholar of ancient philosophy of Greek origin, who taught at the Free University of Brussels for many years.

I just about survived the reception, which was very half-cocked. We were meant to meet Belgian writers, critics and academics – but I only saw Couloubaritsis! I talked to Jean Bingen also, though, who is on the council of FIEC![103] He had been in Helsinki, and took part in this decision not to publish proceedings. Afterwards, Sysse Engberg seemed at a loose end, so I proposed that we go and find a beer and a sandwich in the Grand Place. This we did, very pleasantly. Her English is perfect, fortunately (she spent two years in Dumbarton Oaks, for one thing). I had bought a ticket for Menander's *Arbitration,* and she was going to some movies, so we got back to the Palais about 8.30 pm.

My play was excellently done, by a director called Evangelatos,[104] but perhaps a bit *too* clever. Each act (of the five) was performed in a different tradition (ancient, Italian Commedia dell'Arte, French 17th century, Victorian, modern) to emphasise the continuity of the Menandrian tradition. Each was excellently done, but really, dramatically, it would have been better to stick to the original form, masks and all, which they did very well.

On returning to the hotel, I found Philip Sherrard and his wife having a beer on the pavement, and joined them. We talked of Plotinus and Platonism for almost an hour, and then there was an eruption from taxis, and many Greek literary figures emerged – most notably Katerina Anghelaki-Rooke,[105] who seems a most ebullient lady. At this point I retired, since it was 11.30, and the party might go on for many hours more. Samarakis himself was about to arrive, in another taxi.

---

103   The Fédération Internationale des Études Classiques, which had met that year in Helsinki.

104   This would have been Spyros Evangelatos (1940-2017) one of the most important Greek theatre directors of this period.

105   She was in fact a most distinguished poet, and translator of poets. She was married to an Englishman, Rodney Rooke, and her godfather was Nikos Kazantzakis, who was a good friend of her parents. I got her later, in 2003, when I was Director of the Irish Institute in Athens, to take part in a reading with Seamus Heaney, reading her Greek versions of various of Seamus' poems. Born in 1939, she died in 2020.

I had a peaceful night, and seem a bit better this morning – though by no means over it yet. I am increasingly bothered, though, by our choice of Samarakis.[106] The bookstores are full of both Ritsos and Vassilikos, and their instincts were surely right. I hope I'm wrong, but I sense no enthusiasm for our decision. And yet *To Lathos* is an excellent novel – I still haven't quite finished it!

Brussels is an impressive town, though various old hands complain of its being spoiled by being modernised. We are really right downtown, on the Place Broukere; the walk to the Palais brings one past the Cathedral and the Gare Centrale. I haven't really explored much further yet. I hope to do so this afternoon, if I stay well.

The ceremony was a grand affair, and much encouraged me that we had in fact made the right decision. We were presented first to the Queen – a charming lady, who looked me in the eye in the friendliest manner, as if to say 'We both know we're just playing a game, but we won't tell on each other!' – and Andreas Papandreou, who conveyed no such message. There was a succession of addresses, from the president of the jury, Lecarrière (who managed to explain why we hadn't picked Ritsos), the head of Europalia (Comte d'Ursel), then van Hoeck. Then Samarakis himself spoke, after being presented with the prize by the Queen, and was excellent – on a banal theme, perhaps: the duty of writers to oppose nuclear war and other forms of madness – but still excellent. Then the Prime Minister, Maertens, then Gaston Thorn of the EEC, then Papandreou. The TV and Press were there in force, and we were sweltering under klieg lights on the podium.

---

106    I don't know why I was fussing, really. Antonis Samarakis (1919 -2003) was a Greek writer of the post-war generation, whose work explores themes related to humanism, the dangers of totalitarianism and alienation, and was a writer of considerable distinction. I should say that he would be about on the level of Graham Greene. *To Lathos* (*The Flaw*, 1965) is indeed an excellent novel.

Afterwards, there was another reception, and then an excellent lunch. I left the reception early, with the Sherrards and Katerina Anghelaki-Rooke, and we ensconced ourselves in the restaurant, drinking their approved aperitif – champagne and raspberry cordial! Everyone else eventually drifted in, and I found myself in the alarming situation that Samarakis took a violent *liking* to me, as an Irishman, and pledged eternal friendship, kissing me on both cheeks. He is actually a delightful old boy, and the life and soul of the party. He is plainly very pleased with his prize. I have promised that he shall have a state visit to Ireland. Many toasts were drunk, and much wine flowed. Katerina also plans to visit Ireland, and is acquainted with Seamus and Marie Heaney, so we should have a good time when she comes.

After lunch, it was too late to go out to the exhibition of Byzantine Art, so I just walked around Brussels, starting with the Parc de Bruxelles, to get the feel of the place. It flows downhill from the Palais to where the Metropole is, via the Grand Place, and is on the whole a very fine town. I also bought Ritsos' trilogy, and a record of Theodorakis' version of Neruda's *Canzon General*.

I came back to the hotel and lay down for a while, before facing the reception at the Greek Embassy. Then down to the lobby, where various others had gathered, and decided to share a taxi. Unfortunately, I ended up as the odd man out, having ushered Katerina A-R into a front seat, so I had to take one on my own, costing 210 fr. The party was very crowded, with lots of military men, and doubtless the usual embassy crowd. The Sherrards were not there, so I mainly consorted with the A-Rs, and a bit with old Müller and his wife. Papandreou swept in, flanked by bodyguards, shook hands all round, then collogued for a bit with Samarakis, I'm glad to say (I was afraid he might be at odds with him), and disappeared (into a back room somewhere, it would seem, because the police were still around when we left). Otherwise, nothing of interest at the party – good nosh, though.

I took a taxi back with the A-Rs, and then sat around in a café (after phoning J and reporting progress) for an hour or so, trying to decide what to do next. Katerina finally decided that she wanted to go down to the Grand Place and have some seafood, so we set out. The Grand Place is splendid at night, and flanked by a maze of little streets, which seem to be solidly eating places, mostly seafood. We settled finally on one, and had an enormous dish of assorted cockles, mussels, crabs, and bits of lobster, which was exciting, but rather frustrating at the same time, since none of them much liked being parted from their shells. The A-Rs are a jolly pair. He is English, and did Classics at Cambridge (with John Rist and Henry Blumenthal[107]), and then went and settled in Athens, marrying Katerina. He works in a library. She is a god-daughter of Kazantzakis, and is something of an authority on him, lecturing at Harvard from time to time – and is, of course, a poet. I hope she comes to visit Dublin in the spring, as she is good fun.

Finally got back the hotel about 1.00 am, full of the direst presentiments about the mussels – which were not, fortunately, fulfilled.

### DAY 4, FRIDAY, OCTOBER 22$^{ND}$

Rose moderately early, but breakfast wasn't brought to my room till nearly 9.00. I had a plan to rush out to the Byzantine exhibition, but this was delayed by a phone call from Marie-Claude of Europalia, asking me to look at my honorarium cheque. It was in fact made out to Bingen, and he had mine! Just as well *he* noticed. So she came round, and made the exchange. I paid the hotel bill at the same time, paying for the last night myself (1500 fr.), and two phone calls to Dublin cost another 1700 fr. – more than a room for the night! I am greatly shocked!

I set out for the exhibition on the Metro to Merode. It was in a magnificent museum, set in a large park (Parc du Cinquantenaire), and was most impressive – silks, icons, manuscripts, reliquaries in ivory and gold; Byzantine art was actually more lively and varied that I had thought. I was amused,

---

107     Two distinguished Classical philosophers, and old friends of mine.

134

for instance, by a rather crude plate from Corinth with an 'amorous scene'. Some statues of the Virgin '*Hodêgêtria*' were also very fine, and the ivory carvings were excellent. I went through rather hurriedly, though, in order to get back to the Metropole in time to be picked up by Couloubaritsis at 12.15.

I got back with some time to spare, and bought some little marzipan figurines round the corner which I had noticed previously. I eschewed lace, though there was lots of attractive stuff. Couloubaritsis arrived promptly, and took me to lunch in a little café near the Palais des Beaux Arts, where we met a student of his who is interested in Philo, to whom I gave some suggestions. We had an excellent plate of cold meats and beer. Couloubaritsis gave me his book on Aristotle's *Physics* and a sheaf of offprints, of which I have broached one on Anaxagoras, which is relevant to my talk next week.

Then he got me on the train for Louvain, just before 2.00. It rolled along pleasantly, stopping at every station (one little town whose name particularly pleased was Erps-Kwerps – two little towns or one?), until we got to Louvain/Leuven. It is all completely Flemish down here. I feel, unreasonably, as if I were moving into Orange territory – but they are all Catholics, in fact! Yet there is some similarity, as opposed to the Walloon part of Belgium. They seem sort of solid and hard-headed, like Northerners – not unfriendly, though it is better not to speak French to them.

I got a taxi to the Institute of Philosophy, where I found Carlos Steel[108] beset by business until 6.00 – exam results have to be discussed and published. We decided that I should explore the town, an idea that pleased me, so he walked me up to the Cathedral (which is now also a museum, and very impressive) and left me at it. I cut short my visit to the Cathedral, because it was as cold as the tomb, though the weather was quite fine outside, and walked down the main street (Naamsestraat) in the direction of the

---

108    A distinguished authority on late Greek philosophy, and an old friend, who had been helping me greatly with my translation of Proclus' Commentary on the *Parmenides*. He was currently director of the Institute of Philosophy.

Beguinage. The whole town is charming, being essentially a 17<sup>th</sup> cent. (or earlier) walled town, and now a university city. The only other product is beer, it seems – Stella Artois! The Beguinage is a remarkable haven of peace in the middle of the town – originally a quasi-monastic retreat, it is now inhabited by students and faculty – like a large Oxford or Cambridge college, with cobbled streets and quads, and rows of residences. A little stream – in two forks – flows through it, and there are various bridges over it.

I moved on from there to visit the Irish College[109], since Carlos suggested that I look in on them. I hadn't known there still *was* one, and indeed it is only hanging by a thread. I rang the bell and was greeted by a very jolly Franciscan friar, called Isidore – something of a Friar Tuck figure, who is actually the cook, as he revealed – who showed me round the church and grounds, gave me a cup of coffee, and gossiped about Ireland and Louvain. He has been here for seventeen years, but is still much interested in the fate of Charlie Haughey. He had heard that Jim Gibbons has had a heart-attack also, which would really put the tin hat on the situation.[110] (I saw also in the *Times* that the economic plan is published, and that the IRA are on the way to winning *five* seats in the Northern elections!) The fate of the College actually hangs in the balance, since they have only two monks there, and can't afford to keep it up. They are hoping to make it into some sort of centre for European Studies – but of course it is in a Flemish-speaking area. Still, I will take an interest in this cause![111]

---

109    The Irish Franciscan College in Leuven, was co-founded in May 1607 by Aodh Mac Cathmhaoil, Irish Franciscan, theologian and aide to Aodh Ruadh Ó Domnaill. The College was founded under the patronage of Phillip III of Spain.

110    Jim Gibbons (1924-1997) was a Fianna Fáil politician who had been a government minister under Jack Lynch, but came out in opposition to Charles Haughey, and suffered for that. He had recently been attacked outside the Dáil by a group of Haughey supporters, and suffered a heart attack shortly after that.

111    In fact, in 1983 the Irish Institute for European Affairs was opened in the College, and this has kept it going until the present.

Back then to the Cathedral – I had a beer in a café across the street from it – and so back to the Institute, where they were just breaking up, a little after 6.00. Carlos then drove me back to his pleasant little house, apparently on the edge of open country, but in fact within the old town walls, and within walking distance of everything. It is small, but very well arranged, on *four* levels. He has to house *four* riotous sons, aged from ten to three, who were very pleasant children, really, but *loud.* They also talked to me incessantly in Flemish, which was confusing. I produced chocolates, which were popular, and then a 'magic' spider, which ran up and down paper, which very much interested them. His wife, Ann, teaches in a boys' school, and was exhausted after a hard day, but bore up gallantly, and served a tasty supper – leeks baked in cheese sauce, with slices of ham and cheese.

After dinner, Carlos and I went down to his study and looked at Proclus for an hour or so. Then a friend of his who is a rare book dealer came round to call, and the upshot was that we went down to his shop at 10.00 at night, to see what he had. He had lots, and is an excellent man. In the event, I decided to plunge, and buy an *incunabulum,* Julius Caesar, 1494! – needing binding, but a good bargain at 20,000 fr. I took his address, as he is much better value than Barney Rosenthal.[112]

## DAY 5, SATURDAY, OCTOBER 23RD

I spent an adequately comfortable night, only wakened by children around 8.00 or so. Rose before 9.00, and, after a good breakfast, Carlos and I went off to the Institute for a morning's work. There we ran into John Dudley, who has actually landed a four-year position in Nijmegen, which gives him some security. It is good to see Carlos in his environment. It is ideal for this sort of work. We solved most problems, but some remain. I must see what Westerink has to say on them.[113]

---

112    My rare book dealer in San Francisco, from whom I had in fact bought a number of volumes over the years.

113    Leendert Westerink, of the University of Buffalo, was my other great

We went back for a good lunch of roast beef, *with stewed pears!* – actually very tasty. Then to the station, and so back to Brussels Central, where Brigitte[114] collected me. The day was dull, and began to drizzle, but we went off to an Antiques Market, where she was looking for little scent bottles. She found some, and I bought what looked like a *netsuke,* but turned out later to have a piece broken off it. It cost 2200 fr., so I don't know if I was swindled or not.

Then back to her house for a rest. I am lodged in a room normally occupied by a student lodger, who goes away at the weekends – so really there is no room *chez* Brigitte during the week. We planned to go out to dinner and a movie, but then Brigitte revealed that she had been pressed to come to a party being given by the wife of her psychiatrist, so we went to the movie (an excellent Turkish one called *Yól* – 'The Journey' – made by an inmate of one of their prisons, but, though clandestine, not really anti-regime), and then back, in the rain, and on to the party. The party seemed to be mainly for clients of the psychiatrist (mostly less than fully cured, I should say), and was quite wild. It was mainly a hard rock disco, and she got me to dance wildly a number of times. We met some Irish people also, who were *not* dancing. Brigitte seemed to enjoy herself, though not wildly, and we left at about 1.00 am, having done our bit.


DAY 6, SUNDAY, OCTOBER 24TH

I slept well. Rose about 10.00, and before breakfast we went out to the market in the adjacent square, and bought cheeses and *würst* for breakfast, and to bring home. It is a very pleasant neighbourhood, really, to all appearances. I bought cheese of Maredsous,[115] among other things.

---

resource in dealing with the complexities of translating, and commenting on, Proclus.

114    Brigitte Wyckhuyse, see above (p. 126).

115    A Benedictine monastery, the mother-house of Glenstal.

After breakfast, Brigitte suggested a concert in the Cathedral – the Artists' Mass, composed for the occasion, and performed by various distinguished members of the Brussels artistic community. The curate of the Cathedral is by way of being a bit precious, it seems, and well in with the artists – and a very good fellow, says Brigitte – and he gets this together. It was actually very good, but we got cold after about an hour and a half in the Cathedral, and went off to the Grand Place for a spot of lunch. We had each a *cannibale*[116] at one of the main cafés, and gossiped – Brigitte being very 'Berkeley' in many ways. She much enjoys slumming and being a student, 'hitchhiking' across the Caribbean on yachts, and yet having a pad in Florida, and dealing in antiques and diamonds.

Then back to the house, collected my bags, and so to the airport, without a hitch. On the plane I met a rather bewildered Irish lad, seconded by Bord na Móna to Rwanda, who was returning after a spell out there, having had a very good time, but was quite uncertain whether anyone would be there to meet him.

J was there to meet me, and so I went happily home, though still not quite recovered from my cold.

---

116    I can no longer remember now what a *cannibale* was, but I think it is a steak tartare sandwich.

# 7: STUDY TRIP TO GREECE

## AUGUST — SEPTEMBER 1983

*This was an expedition to take a summer course in Modern Greek offered by the University of Thessaloniki, which was provoked by my meeting in Brussels, the previous autumn, with the distinguished scholar of Modern Greek, Philip Sherrard. I was there to award the Europalia Prize in Literature to a Greek writer, Antonis Samarakis, and was serving (rather bogusly) as the Irish representative, and Philip the British. Philip covered for me, but gave out to me at the same time, for, as a Classical scholar, only paying attention, as he expressed it, to the ruins in Greece, and ignoring the fact that there is a living people and culture there. So he had provoked me to take a summer course in Modern Greek, and promised to entertain me in his home on the island of Euboea afterwards if I did that. The result of that challenge is contained in this travel diary.*

### DAY 1, MONDAY, AUGUST 1ST

So here I am, at 7.15 am, in a little café in Athens airport opposite the domestic (west) terminal of Olympic Airways, having had to come here in a taxi – quite a journey, quite a different airport (unless the taximan was having me on!). The actual flight only took three and a half hours, but we gained (or lost?) two hours, so it was just dawn, 5.50 am, as we arrived in the terminal. No problems, except a full 747, mainly composed of youth.

A typical airport scene as we checked our passports: a small knot of Arabs, small, dark men, gathered at a special desk, gesticulating (and being gesticulated at by) Greek officials – negotiations carried on in (fractured) *English*. No doubt their papers are in absolute chaos. But at last one representative was allowed through for some purpose. End of scene.

First mishap: the plane to Thessaloniki was delayed an hour, to 8.30 – hence my presence in this café, enjoying a pleasant breakfast. A curious coincidence: as I walked in, I recognised a bearded man, talking to a lady who had been near me on the plane. I accosted him, and he turned out to be Francis Barry, a man we had met at the end of our last Greek expedition, in the queue for the plane home. He lives on Paros, and was waiting to take the new airbus out there. The lady was his wife Jane.

The flight to Thessaloniki I hardly noticed. There was a heat haze, so no view, and I must have dozed. It only took 35 minutes. I could have taken the airport bus, but took a taxi, and got a most garrulous and amiable taxi-driver, who showed me the sights, and on whom I practised my Greek, but who went rather a long way round, and cost me 350 dr.!

The Hotel Capsis is large and modern, near the centre of town. We are getting a *very* special rate, as the normal rate for a room for the night is 2260 dr. It is not a place in which one would normally stay on holiday for very long. The staff at the desk were pretty surly to start with, but one gets used to them. I met the hotel representative of the summer course, who was very pleasant. He couldn't fix me up with a *non*-English speaker (we have to share a room), but with a young German, who is most amiable, and will speak German – and I hope Greek eventually, though he knows very little.

I walked up-town to the Institute, where they gave me the placement test, and I sat down rather groggily and did it. It was a comprehension test, which I comprehended, and answered as best I could. Then I went off to a lecture, and caught the end of the first lecture on Modern Literature, which was on Cavafy. It sounded rather *Greek* and waffly, but the lecturer, Mitsakis,[117] is a man of great distinction, it seems. We will see!

---

117    He was indeed. Giorgos Mitsakis (1921-1993) was a Greek composer and lyricist of numerous *rebetika* and folk songs, as well as a skilful *bouzouki* player. He was also known by the nickname *the teacher* (*ho daskalos*).

Back to lunch on the No. 1 bus. I met a few of the students, English, American, German, French, *Bulgarian* – but average age about 20, so I feel rather middle-aged and out of it. I don't see anyone that I would much want to consort with. Again, we will see. That would rather put a damper on the fun.

When the results of the test came out, I found I had been placed, not in the intermediate, but in the *advanced* class. I'm afraid I'm just too proficient at passing exams for my own good. I may have to retreat from that, but I'll give it a try. I had a good, but rather sticky, siesta (no air conditioning) till 5.00 pm, and then went up for a bathe to the roof pool. It is an excellent facility. I met some Oxford students up there who are pleasant.

Then down, from 6 to 8, for Modern Greek Dance with Mr. Papachristos, an excellent teacher, from whom I learned as much Greek as I did Greek dance. I learned the basic principles of the *kalamatianos,* anyhow, sweating copiously, and then got lost in the intricacies of something from Epirus. Perhaps next week will bring more enlightenment.

Out for a beer, and wrote to Jean. Then back to a *modest* dinner, looked at an interview with Bunuel on TV, and so to bed. It is still very hot.

DAY 2, TUESDAY, AUGUST 2ND

I actually woke up at 7.00, since my room-mate is used to rising at 6.00 – though he was out quite late last night, jarring (I must remind myself of his name). Had a good breakfast – met a girl from Amsterdam who is studying Byzantine Art. Then off on the bus with everyone else to the School, at 7.45. Public buses, we may note, are *free* up to 8.00 – because workers use them to go to work! What an excellent idea, if a gloriously uneconomic one! I wonder how they justify it economically. If someone can tell me, I will recommend it at home.

I find the Advanced Class with Mr. Lialias just about possible – worth pushing myself for. I am certainly not as fluent as some, but I can manage to understand, and I have the grammar. I must force on the fluency. The tendency to speak English is

142

reprehensible, but I hate stumbling along like an infant. I met a pleasant elderly American lady professor in the break, and went and had a coffee frappe. Then up to the Institute and bought a text book, and some stamps. Then home to the hotel on the bus, to hear Mitsakis' lecture, in the Vergina Room. It was good, on Cavafy (some readings), and then poets of the 20's and 30's – mainly Seferis, Elytis and Ritsos.

Then lunch (3 *psaria,*[118] with tomato and cucumber salad, grapes), and a siesta, where I didn't sleep, but did some homework. Then, at 4.30, I decided not to swim, but to go up and visit a nearby Byzantine church, that of the Twelve Apostles. A fine exterior, in decorative brick (14th cent.), but inside sadly vandalized by Turks, and the mosaics and frescoes in a very fragmentary state.

I got back in time to book in for the special trip to Mt. Athos from the 13th to the 15th, which I greatly look forward to (I had to hand in my passport, though, which I may find annoying if I run short of money!). Then a bus tour of the city, which took us first to the Acropolis, where we had a lecture on the history of the city, and a brief walk around, and then down to the White Tower, and up to Panorama, a rather posh suburb (formerly a separate village), with a fine view of the bay and the mountains. We passed a rather sumptuous American College – 'Anatolian College' – on the way up. I wonder what that is! But it was really a rather sketchy tour. I think I will walk up to the Acropolis one afternoon – or perhaps take the bus?

A modest supper of *dolmades* and a slice of cheese, and then I took a walk along the seafront, witnessing a demonstration and march (probably communist) in support of the unity of Cyprus and ending of U.S. bases, and taking a beer. I wrote to Jean, and read Henry Miller – silly man that he is.[119]


DAY 3, WEDNESDAY, AUGUST 3RD

Up again good and early, Alexander being an early bird. The

---

118    Sc. small fish.

119    I think I was reading *The Colossus of Maroussi.*

class was again manageable – though this time Lialias read out a children's story, and expected us to understand and précis it, for tomorrow morning. I only got the plot vaguely – about a cuckoo in the nest! Mitsakis has switched his lectures to the hotel, so one toils back at 11.00 to hear him. This has advantages, though. He is still very poor in delivery, but a fund of good information when one can hear him. He has taken us through Cavafy and the other '20s poets, and is now bringing alive Seferis and Elytis. I must say that he arouses in one a desire to read more, which is a good thing in a lecturer, but it would help if he distributed a few specimen texts.

I must buy some Seferis and Elytis.[120] Seferis also appears in the loathsome Miller's effusion to advantage – one keeps on reading, since he has a certain rough facility, but the bombast really annoys me.

In the afternoon I decided to take another walk and see another church, the Panaghia Chalcheôn, which looks interesting, so I went on up to St. Demetrios,[121] past the Roman Forum (also sealed off). In the process, I found an apparent bus terminal for such places as Haghia Triada, which I might avail of one of these days! St. Demetrios was also a disappointment – destroyed in the fire of 1917, and rebuilt as a modern church. Only bits of the old church, frescoes and mosaics, still survive, but very dim. I visited the crypt, which contains the saint's tomb, and is a little museum (with very little in it!). I bought a set of slides for 150dr., which at least show some frescoes to best advantage. Then took a beer across the street, and back for a swim in the pool.

The evening was unusually interesting, because there was an excellent show of Northern Greek dancing after dinner (which was itself good) – Macedonian and Pontic, done by two amateur groups, who were very lively and competent. The Pontic war-

120     I subsequently obtained both – Seferis' *Collected Poems* in the edition of Edmund Keeley and Philip Sherrard, signed by both authors in September 1983, in Sherrard's lair in Katounia, where I proceeded after this summer course. Keeley happened to be visiting as well.

121     St. Demetrios, a 4th cent. martyr, is the patron saint of Thessaloniki.

dances were particularly exciting, involving a quivering of the whole body, working up to a sort of frenzy. At the end, we were all invited to have a go, so we rose and danced a sort of *syrtaki*.[122] I felt quite pleased with myself.

And so to bed, I thought – and had climbed in, when Alexander appeared, all set to go out, and no one to go with. So I roused myself, and went out with him. But we couldn't find any action, though we walked as far as the White Tower and back along the Tsimiski and then Egnatia. There was one centre of action near the White Tower, but it was very crowded with students and would-be Hell's Angels, and didn't seem very friendly. Finally we found a little *kafeneion* back near the Capsis, and had a beer. Alexander is an interesting fellow – a sort of intellectual drop-out, who decided to be a carpenter, but likes studying as well. A little like Heinrich Boll's 'Clown', perhaps.

## DAY 4, THURSDAY, AUGUST 4TH

Up betimes – at breakfast met two interesting people, one a retired English civil servant who lives in Cyprus, Robin Knights, the other a young man from Coleraine, Gerry – who is at the University of Warwick, but counts himself as an Irishman. But I still see no congenial companions on the horizon. I found myself beside an elderly German schoolteacher (Herr Eisen) at dinner last night, who is decent, but very solemn – talks Greek laboriously and dutifully, as of course one should! The callow youths and maidens, though, I can't really relate to – I just feel *old* – though I met a very bright young Australian from Melbourne at lunch (David Meldon), who had lots to say on both Irish and Australian politics!

The class was OK again, but I wish that he would use the text-book more, since he got us to buy it! I found an excellent bookstore on Tsimiski, on the way back to the hotel, which I must return to. No money now, though, because no passport. Fritz – lent me 500 dr. to buy Prinj's dictionary (480dr.) – the Divry is no bloody good!

---

122    That is, more or less, Zorba's dance, in *Zorba the Greek*.

Another composition to do in the afternoon, so I composed some of it – which I had understood much better, I'm glad to say! – and then fell asleep, as did Alex. Up just in time to get into the pool, and sunbathed and read grammar. I sent a birthday card to the Mouse, who will probably eat it![123] I decided to give the evening lecture – on regional development in Thessaloniki – a miss, and went down to change some money, as I got my passport back (changed £30, at 126.62 dr.), and bought Elytis' *Axion Esti,* in Greek and English (800 dr. in all!) – so much for my limit for today! I began *Axion Esti – Genesis* – over a beer in a taverna on the square. Excellent stuff! I am moved to try a few poems myself. We will see what comes out.[124]

The drachma was devalued against the $ a day or so ago – down to 84 to the $ – and a great political row has broken out, even within PASOK,[125] but presumably Papandreou had no choice. As for me, I think I will change a few dollars on Visa, perhaps.

Supper was a rather good potato stew – just potatoes cut up and stewed in spicy tomato sauce. Must have cost *nothing,* and, with soup, a piece of white cheese, and some tinned peaches, it satisfied me amply. We are certainly on simple rations, but we are getting it all for nothing.

I am writing this now at 10.45 pm in a rather nice taverna in a park, up from the hotel, to which I might return for dinner – Pieria Family Taverna!

DAY 5, FRIDAY, AUGUST 5TH

Alex only got in about 1.00 am, drinking just across the road. I told him he was 'burning the candle at both ends', and this amused him greatly, since it is not a German expression.

Once again, I survived class, and feel I am absorbing a good deal. Mitsakis again was barely audible, but good – this

---

123     Our daughter Ruth, who was to be 1 on August 10th.

124     Nothing did, so far as I can recall.

125     The ruling party in Greece, led by Andreas Papandreou (formerly a faculty member in U.C. Berkeley).

time on Ritsos, notably *The Moonlight Sonata,* which he dwelt on at length. I asked him afterwards whether Elytis was influenced by Neoplatonism, when composing the *Genesis* part of *To Axion Esti,* and he was delighted. Indeed, he assured me, Elytis is much influenced by Plotinus, and acknowledges the debt. I have enjoyed the first part of *To Axion Esti,* and must now approach the *Passion.*

A tolerable lunch. I talked to the lad from Coleraine again (he has no desire to return there, but lives in Chania, teaching English), and a nice Polish lady, a Balkan historian, who is solid for the Pope's Solidarity, admires Lech Walesa, but thinks 'it is all finished'. So I tried to encourage her, saying that it did not sound finished to me.[126] But what do I know? Anyway, she has a job in the University of Warsaw, and is here studying Greek, so all is not lost for her. She wanted to know if I had seen a Catholic church, and it happens that I had, walking back from the lecture, so I gave her directions.

In the afternoon, I did some of tomorrow's exercise (on prepositions), and then went for a walk (or No. 10 bus-ride) to the Arch of Galerius, the Rotunda, and whatever else.[127] The Rotunda and another church were *closed for repairs* – most of the bloody churches in this town are closed for repairs, and the rest aren't worth seeing. I bought some shampoo and deodorant (for a total of 300 dr.), and went back and used both. The shampoo actually smells as if it was designed to discourage lice and scurvy – but t'will serve.

There was an excellent lecture at 6.00 – *in Greek,* but very clearly and helpfully presented – on writers of the 1930's – especially Stratis Tsirkas and Karagatsis, but also Stratis

---

126    I think I was right in the long run, but it took till 1989 before Walesa and Solidarity triumphed.

127    The 4th-cent. Roman Emperor Galerius commissioned these two structures as elements of an imperial precinct linked to his Thessaloniki palace. Archaeologists have found substantial remains of the palace to the southwest. These three monumental structures were connected by a road that ran through the arch, which rose above the major east–west road of the city.

Mirivilis. Not sure if I got the finer points, but certainly derived something from it.

I learned from David, the Australian, that a petition is being got up against the food. That I will not sign, since I think we are getting more or less what we are paying for, but tonight I decided to break loose, and go up to the Acropolis, to see if I could find anything better. I walked round the ramparts at sunset, which is indeed an exhilarating sensation; you look down on the whole city spread out round the Bay, but the whole area is just grotty without being quaint, and the walls are grossly neglected. The central citadel I made towards – it looks rather like King John's Castle in Limerick, with houses built into it – and found it was a *jail*!

Now I am sitting, at 10.00 pm, in a pleasant taverna near one of the gates, having a humble but good meal of veal cutlet, french fries, and *melitsana-salata,* washed down with a bottle of retsina (350 dr.).

I took the 22 bus back. It gets you to Eleutheria Square.

### DAY 6, SATURDAY, AUGUST 6$^{\text{TH}}$

Not much to report today. Lialias read out quite a moving short story of Stratis Mirivilis, called *Katapanios,* about a faithful dog that had to be put down. I changed £20 stg. more, just to be safe for the weekend, though I *hope* this lasts me well into next week.

Mitsakis' last lecture was good. He dwelt on the remarkable juncture of music and poetry since the late '50s – Theodorakis and Hadjidakis popularising Seferis, Elytis and Ritsos. The Irish cultural scene could learn much from this. Properly it should arise in *Irish,* though. Seán Ó Riada might have been the man, had he not drunk himself into the grave.

In the afternoon, I read *Axion Esti,* and snoozed. I was woken by Alex at the door, then went up to the pool, where I sunbathed, swam, and did some work (am reading more of Runciman's *Byzantine Civilisation*), but was increasingly annoyed by some American military specimens who were getting louder and louder on beer (loudest came from North Carolina, and proud of it!). There was a black serviceman in a corner, significantly, who just sipped a soft drink and glowered at the whites, over a book.

I came back down to the room, and had just gone over to the phone to call management about jax paper, when the room began to shake, and we were in an *earthquake* – about 5 on the Richter Scale, I should say. Things swayed about for what *seemed* an age, with *two* separate shocks, and then calmed down.

I had an interesting talk at dinner with a student of Westerink and Kustas in Buffalo,[128] currently in search of a thesis. I urged Syrianus[129] on him. He has visited Vlatadon Monastery,[130] where they have microfilms of all the Mt. Athos manuscripts.

After dinner, I just crossed the road to a *zacharoplasteion*[131] (where Alex, Fritz and some girls were ensconced), where I had a beer, coffee, and *baklava,* and read for a bit. I also wrote most of an article on Greek tourism, which I hope to send to Aengus Fanning[132] (via Jean for typing!).


## DAY 7, SUNDAY, AUGUST 7^TH

Today was taken up with an excursion westward, to Pella, Vergina and Edessa, taking in also a fine monumental tomb at Lefkadia Naousis. We moved out at 8.00, in three bus-loads, and reached the excavations at Pella.[133] A most impressive spread of villas have

---

128    That is to say, Leendert Westerink (1913-1990), a mentor of my own, and George Kustas (1922-2016), both professors of ancient philosophy at the University of New York in Buffalo. The student's name was actually George Mellon (see below).

129    Distinguished Neoplatonic philosopher, teacher of Proclus

130    The Vlatades or Vlatadon Monastery is a monastery in Ano Poli, Thessaloniki. Built in the 14th cent. during the late era of the Byzantine Empire, it is a UNESCO World Heritage Site, one of the 15 in the city.

131    That is, a pastry-shop.

132    My editor in the *Sunday Independent.*

133    Pella was the ancient capital of the Kingdom of Macedon, and birthplace of Alexander the Great.

now been uncovered, with some splendid mosaics – dating back to the 4th cent. B.C. – in the museum. They used sea-pebbles, and thin wire to pick out the details. It was good to see where Euripides, and Agathon, and Zeuxis, came to visit Archelaus.[134] In the mountains rising behind, Euripides might have witnessed bacchic revels! More is being discovered all the time. They are now working on the palace of Archelaus. Last year they uncovered one portico of the Agora. Pella was abandoned by the Romans, so it is an excellent example of a Macedonian city uncontaminated by Roman remains. I bought an illustrated account of the contents of the museum for 200 dr. Excellent photos of the mosaics.

And so on to Vergina, where we viewed the elaborate royal palace on the acropolis, the theatre, which they are just excavating, where Philip was murdered (it is now clear that Vergina is Aegae)[135] – and then saw (from outside a fence) the tomb of Philip, on which Andronikos[136] is still working.

I got talking, on the way, to a pleasant German student from Munich (beside me on the bus), a Croatian-German school-teacher (at lunch), and a Bulgarian professor of historical linguistics from Sofia – this last a rather dim fellow, but a pupil of Georgiev's, he told me.[137] We stopped for a picnic lunch at a fine, but unfortunately collapsing, tomb at Lefkadia, with paintings still preserved on its front. But they will have a devil of a time now preventing it from collapse.

And so on to Edessa, which is *not* Aegae, but which sits on a Macedonian city, which is now being excavated (though only Roman stuff has been recovered so far), and where there is a fine waterfall, or a number of them. Beautifully situated on the edge of hills – it is said that the Aegean once came up

---

134    Euripides and Agathon were distinguished Athenian playwrights, and Zeuxis an equally distinguished sculptor. Archelaus was King of Macedon from 413 to 399 B.C.

135    King Philip was assassinated in the theatre in Aegae in 336 B.C.

136    Manolis Andronikos (1919-1992) was a Greek archaeologist, and Professor of Archaeology at the University of Thessaloniki.

137    Vladimir Georgiev (1908-1986) was a prominent Bulgarian linguist, philologist and educational administrator.

almost to its outskirts, and one can see that possibility from the view. All the plain between Edessa and Thessaloniki was, first, sea, and then a malarial marsh, until it was drained, when it became very fertile and prosperous farmland, growing fruit of all sorts, cotton, tomatoes, and tobacco. I had an interesting talk, at a pleasant café in Edessa, with some American ladies – two younger ones very brisk and purposeful, going all over Greece and Turkey and Yugoslavia.

And so back to the hotel to do homework, about 7.30 pm

## DAY 8, MONDAY, AUGUST 8TH

A new set of lectures began. I first decided on Modern Greek History, but an enormous crowd headed for that, so I went off to Prof. Petsas, on Macedonian Art and Archaeology, which I could well learn more about. He is the excavator of Pella (from 1957 to 1975, I think), so he should be most interesting. The first lecture was just on Macedonian history, but even that was interesting – especially the founding folktale reported by Herodotus, which I had missed, and must check up on.

In the afternoon, it actually looked like rain, but I went up to the pool, after doing some homework. I forgot my towel, though, so I just sat. I finished *The Colossus of Maroussi*. The overall effect is not bad, I must admit, but I still think that Miller must have been a bit of a pest. Durrell put up with him, though.

Later, another shot at Greek dancing. I will never be a dancer, I fear, despite Mr. Papachristou's best efforts, but I think I have mastered the simplest form of *kalamatianos,* at least. Then quite a nice supper of eggplant, at which I talked to Gerry from Coleraine, and the Indonesian girl, and then we thought that a meeting was to have been held about Mt. Athos, but it is actually fixed for *tomorrow* night, at 9.00. Rumour has it that no transport has been planned – and that on the Greek equivalent of the August Bank Holiday![138] No way can we get to Athos if that is so.

---

138    August 15th is the feast of the Assumption of Our Lady into Heaven, and a major festival in most Mediterranean countries.

After that, I went out drinking with Alex, Fritz and Hendryk (from Denmark) – the Bulgarian was going to join us, but ducked out at the last moment. I am sure he is a KGB man. The wretched 'professor'[139] is very cowed.

I am making progress with *To Axion Esti,* but it is tough going. I bought Ritsos' *Tetarti Diastasi,* with the *Moonlight Sonata* in it, and his House of Atreus sequence (500 dr.). It is much easier than Elytis.

## DAY 9, TUESDAY, AUGUST 9TH

I sent a consignment of clothes to the laundry this morning. We will see what the damage is, in every sense! Lialias appeared somewhat muted today, to begin with. He cheered up, though, but he concentrates rather too much on the Italian girls in the back row, who are certainly quite attractive, but *karakatzes,*[140] and pests. Petsas is most interesting, since he has started in on Pella.

After a siesta, I spent a while at the pool, and then, instead of listening to a propaganda lecture on Civil Rights and the Cyprus Issue, I went off for a bus ride, which involved taking the No. 5 bus to the end of the line, at Nea Krênê, one of the easternmost suburbs. It was a delightful jaunt, though the suburb is in a way depressing, with vacant lots dotted about, and the seashore full of junk. We drove out along the shore, through Kalamaria, and out beyond the point of the bay.

In one vacant lot, there was a tiny church, apparently constructed out of cardboard and tin cans, from which loud chanting was coming. I sneaked cautiously in, and found a service in progress, with a cantor chanting lustily, and a *papas* going about in the sanctuary, incensing the altar. Then he processed out, and solemnly incensed me, which abashed me not a little, before proceeding back into his lair. Then old ladies began to filter in, in ones and twos, so I thought I should beat it, and did.

---

139    That is, the Professor of Historical Linguistics from Sofia, mentioned earlier.

140    That is, chatterers (lit. 'magpies').

I walked down to the seashore, and sat and read a little Steven Runciman, and contemplated the garbage. Then I walked along and found two pleasant fish restaurants, 'Miami' and 'Brachos', to which I must return, preferably with companions. I found a plastic soldier, and presented it to a small boy, who was very pleased with it. Then back to the bus, and so to town – I was deposited on Mitropoleos, just behind Molcho's bookshop.

The meeting at 9.00 am about Athos solved nothing, except to show that the secretary had made no plans for how we were to get there. He might as well have said, "Hands up all who would like to go to Albania!". This is a bank holiday weekend! He discoursed in Greek on places to see there, but had no *practical* advice, really. So – the Germans (of course!) had come up with cars, but we outsiders have to find public transport. We will work that out tomorrow.

I watched a rather grim American film on TV (subtitles) about safety in nuclear power plants. And so to bed.


DAY 10, WEDNESDAY, AUGUST 10$^{TH}$

In the morning, instead of dear Prof. Petsas' lecture, I decided to go to visit the Vlatadon Monastery and Institute, with a pleasant graduate student from Buffalo, George Mellon, the student of Westerink and Kustas mentioned earlier, who is looking for a thesis subject. We went up in a taxi. The Institute is quite modern as to its library – one could actually work there if one were in Patristics and didn't want *all* the journals! – and they have all the manuscripts of Mt. Athos on microfilms, together with some of their own (I actually looked at a microfilm of a manuscript of Galen, which contained the essay *On his Own Doctrines,* which I *thought* was only known in Latin translation – but this *can't* have been overlooked, surely? I was trying to persuade George to take on a Neoplatonic subject, but he seems scared of that – though Syrianus' *Commentary on Hermogenes* might suit him. Anyhow, I am glad to have visited the Vlatadon, which is beautifully situated.

In the afternoon, not much time to do more than

snooze, since we were going to the Museum at 4.30. In fact, we got a private tour of the Museum, led by Petsas, and it was very worthwhile. It is a new museum, well laid-out, and now enriched with the finds of Derveni, Vergina, and, most recently, the tombs of Sindos, a site not far from Thessaloniki, to the west, going back to the 540's or so, very rich and civilised – and at a time when the area was not Macedonian, as far as we know, but Thracian, with Greek colonies, and some mixture. There is certainly a strong Athenian influence in these tombs, but they were only discovered in 1979, and not published yet. I viewed again the bandy-legged greaves,[141] and challenged Petsas on them, but he is not convinced by these – he maintained that Philip's wound would not have left his left leg shorter. Ah well!

After this, I went off with Gerry and the nice retired English official from Cyprus, Robin Knights, for a drink and dinner up on the Acropolis. We found a very pleasant place a bit down from the Acropolis, with a fine view of the bay, and had a very good meal. Excellent conversation, chiefly with Robin Knights about Cyprus. He has been in an interesting and important position for some years now, as 'interpreter', but also 'adviser' to U.N. troops, chiefly Irish, whom he gets on with very well, he says. He provided much insight on the Cyprus problem – and its insolubility. Gerry was also interesting. He gave up the law, after a spell in Toronto, to settle in Chania and teach English. But where does that end? It is almost reliving my problem in Ethiopia.

And so back down the hill, and to bed. But an amusing detail from the dinner: we were approached at the table by a beggar-woman – probably gypsy – and her pretty little daughter, very well dressed. She seemed to be selling holy pictures. We all gave her 10 or 20 dr., and she floated off. A little later we walked down the hill looking for a taxi, and there they were at the bus-stop – but they didn't want a *bus*. Round the corner came a taxi, and they bagged it before us. So that was where our contributions went!

---

141    A pair of slightly irregular greaves (that is, shin-guards) that I was inclined to claim for King Philip of Macedon, by reason of his having been wounded in the left leg.

## DAY 11, THURSDAY, AUGUST 11<sup>TH</sup>

Niko is really a bit inconsequential in class – jumping irresolutely from the book to some grammar to the magazine to popular songs. All useful, though – but little chance to *converse.* The *karakatzes* in the back do all the talking, in a kind of Eurobabble that sounds vaguely like Greek, and which he seems to understand. Petsas was good today, with splendid slides of tombs and grave ornaments – remarkably shaped bronze and silver vessels.

I snoozed after lunch, did some homework, spent some time at the pool, and then went out to Molcho's and bought a beautiful book on Athos – only 250 dr. Then back for a beer, but then missed supper, because we had to leave at 7.30 for a performance of Aristophanes' *Lysistrata,* at an open-air theatre up above the city, in the pines, at Seikh-Sou.[142] The play only began at 9.00, so I had a long chat with Robin Knights before that. The paper today reported a rather sensational foiled kidnap attempt on Galen Weston in Ireland, with *four* kidnappers shot dead and three wounded! No police casualties. There may be a row about that![143]

The play was excellent, though I couldn't follow most of the dialogue; but it was done with great gusto, good music and choreography. It came across as good folk theatre, and the audience loved it.

## DAY 12, FRIDAY, AUGUST 12<sup>TH</sup>

I am finding it always more difficult to get up in the mornings. Alex is always up at about 7.00 am, despite getting to bed between 1 and 3 most nights. I roll out at about 7.20, and just get the bus after breakfast at about 7.55.

Niko ended his class early, for some reason known only to

---

142    Otherwise known as Kedrinos Lofos, Cedar Mount. Seikh-Sou is a Turkish name, meaning 'Sheikh's Water'.

143    It was an IRA operation, but the police were on to them. In fact only two were shot, and five arrested.

155

him, promising to meet in the afternoon at 4.00. I hung about a bit, and then decided not to go to Petsas, but to return to the hotel to do some work on Greek and Athos, so I did that. I also went out and bought a Greek cap, and a water bottle – neither of which I will need, probably!

After lunch I worked a little more, and wrote, reproachfully, to J, since I have still received no letters. But there hardly would be, I suppose. I only hope that mine have got through, though.

I attended the beginning of Niko's afternoon *conversazione* in a café across from the hotel, but then we grabbed a no. 10 bus at 4.30, and headed off for the Chalkidiki station to catch our bus to Ouranopolis. We arrived in very good time, in fact, and found, to our surprise, that there was no great fuss or crowd. The Greeks all got on the bus at the last moment, to avoid the heat, and more or less filled it. There was no unusual traffic on the road. Fine scenery – this part of Chalkidiki is prosperous. We passed through Stagira, birthplace of Aristotle (there is a statue to him, on a fine look-out point). It is much changed, I fear, since his day – there is even a disco, with some vulgar American name; it occurred to me that, if there *must* be a disco, they should have called it 'The Unmoved Mover'.

We reached Ouranopolis around 8.00 – on schedule – and found it fairly crowded, mostly with foreigners (Germans). It is a nice little beach resort, but not quaint or old. We walked up to the first Room for Rent that we saw (i.e. Andrew, Kolya and myself – the Spaniards, surly as usual, preferred to try the beach). The proprietor rushed out to welcome us, and produced a very pleasant room overlooking the sea, with a balcony, for 850 dr. He then promised a further one downstairs for me. So I called to the two lads out the window, and asked them did they want the room. They came up to look, and liked it. So I was taken downstairs to the *next* house, actually, where the man, in order to persuade the lady who owned it, said that *my two sons* were in his only free room, and I had nowhere to stay. So she took pity on me, and fitted me into a room for 500 dr. But the fiction of my two sons rather got out of hand, as our host was greatly tickled by the idea of myself and my two strong sons setting out for the *Agion Oros,* and Andrew and Kolya were admired by both himself and my hostess, and I was congratulated upon them (They asked had I no *koritsia,* and I said, 'Yes, one, but I had to leave her at home with her Mummy.') Anyhow, the idea of the 'sons' went down very well, but we then had to remember to maintain the fiction (they had the next morning to enquire where their 'papa' was). It was touching to me to think that, in Andrew's case at least (he is 20), we might well have had a son of almost that age, whom I might have been taking to Mt. Athos. But then he might have been any sort of strange fish, brought up, as he would have been, largely in Berkeley!

Anyhow, we went out and had a pleasant dinner – *kalamarakia* and *mydia* (mussels), round the corner, and so to bed.

Kolya is a lively lad – obviously of very good family in Belgium – but also half-Russian, and prefers his Russian name, Nikolai, to his Flemish one, Werner. He is studying Art History, in a rather desultory way, I should say. Andrew is doing French and Modern Greek at Lincoln College, Oxford.

## DAY 13, SATURDAY, AUGUST 13<sup>TH</sup>

Our slumbers were disturbed in the middle of the night by a most curious *funeral* procession (I think) – much mourning and wailing, past the windows. I thought of Cavafy's great poem, *God Abandons Antony.* It sounded most uncanny, and we hope it is not a portent. Otherwise, I slept well. The old lady had coffee and a sweet biscuit waiting for me when I appeared, and fussed over me most charmingly. I went round the corner, and found Carsten and the Germans ensconced in a café – they had got down in good time for the 8.00 am boat. So we all assembled, and embarked. It was a little steamer and pretty full. It cruised down the coast, past three or four monasteries, calling in at every pier, and loading or unloading something or somebody. We caught glimpses of monks peering out from nooks and crannies. The monasteries are vast conglomerations of buildings, most imposing, and mostly now uninhabited. St. Panteleimon is particularly impressive, with Russian onion domes.

We landed at Daphni, the port for Karyes, the 'capital' of Mt. Athos, at 10.00, and boarded a frightfully overloaded bus, which struggled (successfully) up the steep incline to the 'capital'. Karyes is a very grotty little town, both headquarters of the Greek administration and of the monastic central administration. We got our papers (a finely inscribed *diabatêrion* in Classical Greek), and went off for lunch, to deliberate what to do next. We were joined by a pleasant young German, Thilo Schmidt – a refugee from Carsten and his *peculiar* sense of humour, I think. Anyhow, after a rather dire lunch, of *very* well stewed *kotopoulo* (chicken), we decided to set off for Vatopedi, to the north, and then work our way back from there.

Thilo acquired a good map and guide from an Austrian monk that he met in the square, and, armed with that, we set off, though slightly in the wrong direction (we intended to head for Stavronikita – just as well we missed out on that, as it turned out!). We set out on the inland route to Vatopedi (along the ridge of the peninsula), but took a wrong turning, which cost us three-quarters of an hour, and ended in an isolated farmhouse, inhabited by a rather eccentric monk – who set us right, however. On the way, though, we stumbled upon a most curious deserted (Russian) *skêtê,* in one room of which Kolya discovered row upon row of *skulls,* arranged carefully in sevens, on shelves, with bags and bags of bones in sacks on the floor – not a place to come upon in the middle of the night!

Finally on the right path, we walked for four hours across the ridge of Athos, north to Vatopedi, mostly on a carefully laid out, but dilapidated, antique road, which must have required thousands of man-hours to construct. We learn that there are wild boar, deer, foxes and even wolves on Athos, but we saw nothing much larger than a mosquito – not even much bird life. There are apparently quite dangerous snakes as well. I was too exhausted to notice most of the time, even if a rhino had stumbled across our path.

We came in sight of Vatopedi[144] and the sea at about 6.00 pm.

---

144    The meaning of Vatopedi is disputed, but it seems plain enough to me that it means 'Blackberry Plain'. There are blackberry bushes everywhere,

A marvellously welcome sight – a massive complex of buildings, like a small mediaeval town. We were warmly welcomed, with coffee and lots of water, and then I declared that I was going to swim, and that if any monk tried to stop me I would punch him on the nose. Thilo and Kolya followed me – only Andrew hung back. In fact, no one bothered us, and we had one of the most welcome swims I have ever had. The water was just perfect, hardly a ripple, and the evening sun still warm. I floated on my back and contemplated Vatopedi, the mountain and the sky, and felt marvellously peaceful.

Then back to our dormitory, which has a balcony with a splendid view over the bay, and we sat on it, demolishing most of a bottle of *ouzo,* until dinner at 9.00 (8.00 their time) – this being signalled by the lights coming on. By dinner time, other guests had arrived – four Italian businessmen, amiable (especially one elderly interior decorator whom I'm sure is queer as a coot, but none the less companionable for that!), but speaking no Greek, and some Greeks. The dinner was undistinguished – pasta and bean soup, with bread and olives; the wine was simply vinegar, unfortunately! After dinner, there was nothing to do but go to bed – not enough light to read.

## DAY 14, SUNDAY, AUGUST 14^TH

I arose brightly at 6.00 am, having slept well, and decided to go down to the church, whence chanting was to be heard. How long they had been at it by the time I arrived I don't know (perhaps even since 2.00 am, on other evidence!). I listened for half-an-hour or so, and then went on a stroll round the courtyard, not finding much. They don't weed the cobbles, which gives the place an abandoned look, but then on the other hand a profusion of flowers arises (especially blue ones like a sort of daisy), and these are frequented by bees, who produce the monastic honey, so excessive tidiness would deprive them of that!

The others got up about 7.30, and I returned to find everyone gathered round the font of the *phialê,* or baptistry,

---

in fact, and fine juicy blackberries on them, just now coming ripe.

blessing the waters. This was a most elaborate ceremony, at the end of which we were all invited into the *phialê* to kiss the Abbot's hand and a large icon. Then back to the church, where things continued for another *two hours* or so, down finally to an Our Father and communion, which we didn't venture to partake of. We were wrecked, but we were stuck, because breakfast was to be served immediately after.

And so it was, finally – just a spoonful of jam and a cup of Greek coffee, though. A most interesting figure appeared in church, and later, in the shape of a *Japanese* monk, with a friend of his. He turns out to be from Tokyo, but studied in Athens for four years, and has a Greek wife. There are 30,000 or so Orthodox Christians in Japan, it seems!

We were promised a guided tour of the church at 12.00, so we didn't feel we could swim before that. We have decided to take the boat down to Iviron, or even the Grand Lavra, at 3.00, and will swim before that. The tour turned out to be excellent, by one of the monks, a succession of wonderful treasures, leading up to a laying out of the relics, for our veneration: a fragment of the True Cross (naturally!), the Girdle of the Virgin Mary, the skulls of two eminent saints whose names I forget, and the Index Finger of John the Baptist (one of the more significant parts of him, presumably!). We were then invited to venerate them. Kolya (as Russian Orthodox) and I venerated away lustily, but the Protestant sensibilities of Andrew and Thilo found this altogether too much. No offence taken, though!

After this, lunch, which was actually better than dinner – a tasty vegetable stew. The same awful wine, though – it would do well for cleaning the silver. After a discreet interval, we packed up and repaired to the beach, having thanked everyone and left 100 dr. each for the church. I would have liked to see the manuscripts, but it didn't seem possible to ask for that, after the tour of the church.

We had another fine bathe, but 3.00 o'clock came and went and *no boat*. We asked some fishermen on the dock, and they said no boat, because *too much wind*. This seemed ridiculous at the time, but in fact a storm *did* get up later, and raged most of the night. We set out to walk to Pantokratoros, the nearest monastery down the coast. It was a hard slog uphill at first, but we got magnificent views of Vatopedi in its green valley, presiding magnificently over the curve of its bay. I'm sure there was an ancient site here – it is such a fine location. We also got quite a good view of Thasos. The storm came on as we walked, rumbling blackly over Mt. Athos. We were accompanied by the four Italians, who made a jolly procession, raising our voices disconnectedly in song. We first whistled national anthems, then some opera, some Gregorian chant, Edith Piaf – whatever. The walk took about three hours, and we arrived just as the rain really began to come down.

We were met by a very jolly (but actually rather cracked) guest-master, Abba Petros, who served coffee and ouzo, but then distributed to each of us a prayer of his own composition (*not* very original), and showed us a book he had written about the Grand Lavra, where he was previously stationed.

Here are some views of Abba Petros on tourists, in his own words (I conned Andrew into buying a copy, from which I quote, since I didn't have any spare cash – in fact I will be lucky to get back without having to borrow!). He sees three categories of visitor: (1) "the pious clergical servants, Christians and Foreigners, who, when entering the Churches, bow piously, fall on their knees, and humbly venerate the sanctity, and, tears in eyes, drop their drachma to light a candle for their souls" – 5 -10 %; (2) 30-40%: *Explorers*. He doesn't mind these too much, as they are in search of truth (I hope we fit into that category); (3) 40-50%: "I call them *tourists*. They run the one behind the other, as muttons go to butchers. They don't know where to go to, nor do they know the purpose they visited the Mt. Athos for. They have no interest whatsoever neither to see nor to hear anything... Some of them tell me, 'Open, Father, the Church. We wish to go in and pray.' They come out virgins alike to what they were when they went in. They didn't light a candle, nor did they even make their sign of the cross. Why, etc.?" He then tells a little tale of how he excoriated some tourists. Good for Abba Petros! God save Mt. Athos from tourists!

We were afflicted by a lunatic Greek who flattered himself

that he spoke Italian, and so fastened himself upon the Italians, to whom he spoke incoherent drivel, and they were most patient. During dinner (which was not bad – a vegetable stew, but *revolting* olives, and no wine), he purported to interpret Abba Petros' views on wearing short sleeves in church, and other matters, and was really rather offensive. Plainly a few screws loose.

We all bedded down in a dormitory, with blankets, but no sheets, and an oil lamp, so we could only go to sleep. I was fearful of bugs, but actually there weren't any.

### DAY 15, MONDAY, AUGUST 15<sup>TH</sup>

This is, of course, only August 2<sup>nd</sup> on Mt. Athos, and so it is not the Feast of the Panaghia, as in the rest of Greece. We were woken at 2.00 am, though, by the calling of the monks to prayer with the *semantra,* a wooden gong. We dozed off again, then, till 6.00, when we rose for a bit of church, and then some coffee and a biscuit. We viewed the beauties of the church, and then returned to say goodbye to Abba Petros, who kissed us all on both cheeks, and tried to make us stay for another cup of coffee, but we had what turned out to be vastly exaggerated ideas of how long it took to get to Karyes, and insisted on setting off at about 8.00am.

In fact, it only took two hours, and fairly pleasant walk – or else I am getting fitter than I was on Saturday. We strolled along, eating blackberries and the odd less-than-ripe fig, and singing snatches of song, ranging from the Internationale to Gregorian chant, until we hit the main road to Iviron, and found ourselves almost in Karyes. We passed some jolly monks on a tractor, which is a sign of the times.

No sign of Carsten and other Germans when we got to Karyes, so it is still a mystery as to where they got to. We had a 'brunch' of fried eggplant *swimming* in oil, washed down with coca cola (100 dr.). I bought J a mould for making Easter bread, and some slides. Then we decided to walk up and visit the monastery of Koutloumousion, just above the town. It has obviously suffered from a recent fire, and much is being rebuilt, but the *katholikon* is unharmed, with excellent frescoes and icons.

We were entertained to *loukoumi, raki* and coffee, and then strolled back to Karyes, and to the bus, which was full, but not crowded this time. The Italians are going to stay another day, and got off at Xeropotamou. We all feel that we should quit while we are ahead, fascinating as it all is. The boat was more or less on time. We finally came upon the Germans, not at Daphni, but up the coast at Panteleimonos. They, in characteristic krautish fashion, had seen three times as much as we, starting from Iviron, then to the Grand Lavra by boat, then walking round the base of Athos up to past Daphni. Bloody Huns! But we saw enough, I think. I only regret not asking to see the monastic library in Vatopedi.

The bus was waiting, and left promptly, at 5.00. We got seats, but it was very full. Just as well we didn't try to get back to Ierissos. A good drive back, though. We got a taxi back to the hotel, and the driver told us that he *hunted* on Athos – wild boar and deer – and had two friends who were hermits there! There was still some supper when we got back – and guess what? Fried eggplant!

### DAY 16, TUESDAY, AUGUST 16TH

Very bleary today! Not much achieved. I think my Greek has slipped back a bit, whatever about appreciation of the culture in general. I picked out Prof. Denis Geanakoplos[145] of Yale on 'Byzantine Influence on the Slavs and the West'. He is rather batty – pours out a stream of consciousness, mainly about his own works, but is full of information. So perhaps I'll stick with him.

A letter finally arrived from J, and is most welcome. It took ten days in coming. In the evening, there was a visit to the Folk

---

145    Denis Geanakoplos (1916-2007), Professor of Byzantine History at Yale, was actually a renowned scholar of Byzantine cultural and religious history and Italian Renaissance intellectual history. Author of 13 books and over 100 articles, he was considered one of the foremost Byzantine scholars in the world. I am being a bit irreverent about him here, I'm afraid.

Museum of Macedonia, which was actually most interesting, I was particularly interested in the evidence of fertility rites, passion plays (the goat-men), and ecstatic fire-walking in Thrace.

I wasted some time in a café across the road drinking beer and *metaxa* with Keith and George, and didn't sleep very well in consequence.

## DAY 17, WEDNESDAY, AUGUST 17<sup>TH</sup>

Things picked up a bit in Greek class, but I still don't know if I'm learning anything or not. I went off, rashly, in break to look at a record shop in Aristoteles Square, and came back with Theodorakis' version of *To Axion Esti* – 800 dr. Not bad for two records, but still, I am leaving myself short.

Geanakoplos is still rambling, but promises a bibliography and lecture notes. I went for a swim in the afternoon. Then there was a lecture from a Dr. Kôphos (?) on Balkan Cooperation – *very* small turn-out, but a good talk, and a cheerful man. I asked him afterwards about the rumour that Zhivkova (Todor Zhivkov's[146] archaeologically minded daughter) was done in by the Russians, as Steven Runciman suggested, but he scotched that; she died of natural causes.

After supper, George Mellon appeared, bringing to visit me the Irish-American he had found who is studying Orthodox theology here (and has been for the last seven years), Philip McGee, who turns out to be not too crazy, and really very pleasant. He is anxious to search for his ancestors in Island Magee in the North – all solidly Presbyterian, though, and he *was* a Catholic. He found another Philip McGee, teaching in the Law Department in Cork. I might check on him. We went across the road and had a beer and a *krema,* and discussed Orthodox theology.

And so to bed.

---

146    Todor Zhivkov (1911-1998) was leader of the Bulgarian People's Republic from 1954 to 1989, when he was deposed. His daughter Lyudmila died in July 1981, it seems, of a brain tumour.

## DAY 18, THURSDAY, AUGUST 18TH

I forgot to mention that the same George (who is really in manner rather like a milder version of Allan Silverman[147]) asked Geanakoplos would he like to come for a coffee yesterday afternoon, and he accepted willingly, so George asked me along. Geanakoplos still comes across rather nutty, but more sympathetic. Born in Minnesota, of Greek parents, he first became interested in the Italian Renaissance, then in Greeks in the Italian Renaissance, and so to Byzantium. He studied under Dvornik[148] at Harvard, whom he reveres. His son is on the faculty at Yale, in mathematics, and he is very proud of that. I got his lecture notes off him, and they are indeed useful (I had checked out of his class yesterday, to a good one on Greek Foreign Policy – which, however, inevitably reverted to Cyprus).

Not much happened today that I can recall, except that in the evening we went to an interesting, but rather randomly constructed, film on Greek Folklore, in the theatre near the White Tower. The most interesting items were dances of the Goat Men, fire-walking in Thrace, and ceremonies in Crete involving sacrifice of a bull – disgusting, but most interesting.

## DAY 19, FRIDAY, AUGUST 19TH

The Greek class was unremarkable. I can't say if I'm improving or not at the moment. Certainly I can't *speak* Greek with any facility.

At lunch, I was talking with George and an American lady,

---

147    A former student of mine in Berkeley, now a distinguished professor of Ancient Philosophy in Ohio State University. When he first arrived as a graduate, he marched into my office and asked me out for a coffee. I was Chairman of the Department at the time. He explained that it was his policy to get to know the faculty.

148    Francis Dvornik (1893 -1975) was a Catholic priest and academic. He is considered one of the leading twentieth-cent. experts on Slavic and Byzantine history, and on relations between the churches of Rome and Constantinople. He taught at Harvard from 1949 to 1964.

Karen, and agreed to go up and visit the University at 4.00, which we did. A nicely laid out campus, virtually deserted at the moment – the faculties open only in the morning, we learned. Much disfigured, though, with endless green and red PASOK and KKE slogans. It is really a disgusting practice, and no law against it is enforced, plainly. Then we went off for a beer, and Karen told us most of her life-story.

We had quite an interesting lecture in the evening from Bishop Panteleimon, of the School of Theology of the University of Thessaloniki, on Orthodox Liturgy. He took Geanakoplos off for a slap-up meal afterwards. Philip McGee came round after dinner, and we had another beer across the road, with George.

## DAY 20, SATURDAY, AUGUST 20<sup>TH</sup>

Classes as usual. Geanakoplos ended his lectures with a spate of total rambling, which began with the Serbian Empire and ended with his family history, and what he was going to do for the next week.

I had a swim in the afternoon, and did some homework. Then, in the evening, we went off – about fifty or so of the School – to a *rebetika* concert in the football stadium by Soteria Bellou,[149] a well-known *rebetika* singer, now quite an old lady – assisted by a younger woman called Mimi. They both had magnificent voices, but the whole thing failed to grip me enormously. *Rebetika* is just basic Greek music, really, such as one might hear on a bus, quite Middle Eastern and repetitive. Yet Sotiria Bellou is the grand old lady of *Rebetika* – rather like Bessie Smith – and it was a privilege to hear her. Curious features of the concert were: much applause at the beginning of a song, many of which

---

149    Sotiria Bellou (1921 –1997) was a Greek singer and performer of the rebetiko style of music. She was one of the most famous rebetisa of all, mentioned in many music guides, and a contributor to the 1984 British Documentary entitled 'Music of the Outsiders'. On March 14, 2010, Alpha TV ranked Bellou the 22nd top-certified female artist in the nation's phono-graphic era (since 1960).

the audience knew, and little at the end. Sotiria just sat on a chair – no fuss, no taking bows, no palaver. Then various young men got up to dance – one even escaped onto the field – and their action was respected and applauded, not interfered with. They appeared to be in a kind of trance – perhaps high on pot or something. So one felt one was witnessing something. I must learn more about it. Alex has a German book on the subject.

## DAY 21, SUNDAY, AUGUST 21<sup>ST</sup>

Up early (6.00 am), to go on an excursion to Meteora. We headed off at 7.00. Alex wouldn't come. He is rather depressed at the moment. His relation with the French girl didn't seem to work out too well. He headed off to Chalcidice for the weekend yesterday, but was back by the evening, gloomy. Admittedly, there was a violent thunderstorm, but that shouldn't have deterred him. I think he rubs people up the wrong way by expressing radical opinions. He is much interested in the Resistance Movement in the War, and has bought a number of books on the subject. Well, I'm glad I'm not 20 again. Too much agony. Come to think of it, I think I am physically and mentally in far better shape now than I was then – which is not, one might say, saying much, but still…

Anyhow, off we headed. Once again, the plains of Macedonia appeared fertile and well-cultivated. Our first stop was the Vale of Tempe (we saw Mt. Olympus rising up on our right before that, but it was rather misty). Tempe was spectacular, though really there are better spots *physically* in the Sierras of California. Towering cliffs flanking a ravine, through which the Peneios flows to the sea. A shaky bridge (specifying only 10 *atoms*[150] at a time, but there must have nearly 100 when we crossed it!) led to a little church built by the railway workers who constructed the narrow-gauge railway through the gorge, and to a little café where we had coffee. As the only real entry to the rest of Greece,

---

150     That is to say, 'individuals'. Notices of this kind in lifts, prescribing only 5 *atomoi* at a time, always used to amuse me.

it was a problem for Xerxes[151] to get through. Round about here, he must have begun to wonder why he came.

We drove past Larissa – a dismal-looking modern town – and Trikkala, and then suddenly the valley narrowed, and we came in sight of these extraordinary rocks – vast stalagmites rising from the plain, of various heights and sizes, and on a number of them – impossibly, as it would seem – are perched substantial monasteries! As we drove closer, the picture became more bizarre.

These monasteries are on towering, apparently sheer, cliffs. The only way up used to be by rope-ladder or basket – rather like the *ambas* of Ethiopia. Now of course, for the tourists, an easy path is carved out of the rock, and bridges connect the main monasteries with the 'mainland'. We only actually visited one monastery, Barlaam, and that in a vast crowd, so it was about the worst way to do it – one had to think away all the pullulating turkeys – but still it was spectacular.

We had a pleasant picnic on the way home, in the grounds of a church. I lunched with Edward, a pleasant German school-teacher. On the way home from there, we stopped to visit a Frankish castle at Platamon, and then had a swim. The castle is perched most scenically above the sea, but I doubt that the Franks cared much about the view!

DAY 22, MONDAY, AUGUST 22ND

I can't summon up anything remarkable about today, except that we performed some more Greek dancing in the evening – and I went up to the Vlatadon monastery in the afternoon.

AY 23, TUESDAY, AUGUST 23RD

I bought Gail Holst's book on *rebetika,* and am now delighted that I heard Sotiria Bellou. The lectures this week have been pretty dismal, and I have ceased attending them, except for the Greek

---

151    The King of Persia, who invaded Greece in 480 B.C., but was ulti-mately defeated, at the battles of Salamis and Plataea.

language. I am trying to finish Cousin Gervase's[152] book, and get stuck into *Ho Monarkhês.*[153] I walked up with Keith and Christine to the Church of St. Nikolaos Orphanos, but found it closed.

## DAY 24, WEDNESDAY, AUGUST 4TH

Damianos Tsekourakis from the university surfaced, back from holidays in Samothrace, and asked me to lunch tomorrow. He is a former student of Tony Long[154] in London, with whom he worked on Stoic ethical terminology.

In the evening, I got together an expedition (Keith, David, George, Christine, Thilo) to go back to Nea Krini, on the No. 5 bus, and explore a fish restaurant there. It was actually very pleasant, right on the water, and only expensive – 900 dr. for me and Keith – because we decided to have *glôssa.*[155]

## DAY 25, THURSDAY, AUGUST 25TH

I walked up to the University at 11.40, met Tsekourakis at the Classics Faculty, and had a talk there. I met a girl who is currently studying with Giangrande[156] in London – doing a thesis on

---

152    This was Byzantine Aesthetics (John Murray: London, 1963), by my cousin Fr. Gervase Mathew, who was a great authority on things Byzantine, and who was University Lecturer in Byzantine Studies at Oxford.

153    A novel by Vasilis Vasilikos (1934- ), distinguished Greek author, diplomat and politician. His most famous novel, perhaps, was Z. I note that there is still a marker in my copy of this book, about half way through!

154    My old friend Prof. A. A. Long, distinguished authority on Greek Philosophy, and in effect my successor in Berkeley (from 1982), had taught Classics at University College, London, from the late 1960s to 1973, when he moved to Liverpool as Professor. Tsekourakis actually published the results of his studies with Long as Studies in the Terminology of Early Stoic Ethics in 1974.

155    That is to say, sole. Big fish is expensive in Greece, as I have remarked before.

156    Giuseppe Giangrande was at this time professor of Classics at Birkbeck College, University of London, and an authority in the area of Greek poetry. Antipater was a Greek epigrammatist of the late 1st cent. B.C.

Antipater of Thessalonica – very suitable! Then he drove me home, to an excellent lunch cooked by his wife, with liberal doses of ouzo, retsina and a liqueur made by her mother. They have two pleasant teenage children, a girl and a boy, and a nice flat. The lunch went on till 4.00, and they urged me to phone them again after the weekend.

I snoozed when I got back, but revived in time for the evening entertainment, where enterprising members of the course proposed to show their talents, especially in song. It was all surprisingly good, really, though I was ashamed not to be able represent Ireland in any way. The Bulgarians led the way with some rousing choral songs, but Italy was also well represented, mainly by our ladies, Silvia, Gabriella, etc., and the expatriate Greeks performed well. Our class actually stood up and sang our songs at the end. My loony friend Valeriu from Roumania stood up and sang some songs of his own composition, which actually weren't too bad.

## DAY 26, FRIDAY, AUGUST 26<sup>TH</sup>

I proposed today to slip off, with Keith, David and George Mellon, in a hired car (from a hole-in-corner company discovered by Keith) for a tour of Chalcidice, cutting out at 2.00, and skipping the evening lecture (which would actually have been quite interesting, on Modern Greek Music and Poetry), and tomorrow's classes.

We went up the rental place at 2.00, and were presented with a Volkswagen Polo, which was comfortable enough, but proved to possess a number of eccentricities. First, the passenger door wouldn't open, and then it wouldn't close, but we settled that. Then we found that it wouldn't go into reverse, and we never did solve that – we used the 'manual reverse', though, with great success. Then the front seats shot back and forth, according as one accelerated. But our worst shock came about half-an-hour out of town, when the temperature gauge went right up, and radiator began to boil, at a place called Galanitsa. Fortunately, we were able to pull into a gas station, which gave us water, and, after giving it time to cool down, we found that there had been *no* water in the radiator. We also decided that there was no oil in the engine, and rather over-compensated, as it turned out, by putting in two pints.

But in fact the old crate got us all the way down Sithonia to Torone, a fine beach adjacent to the site of the ancient town, which covers a promontory jutting out between two fine bays, the southern one, Porto Refto, being the finest natural harbour in Greece. After a good dinner, we decided to camp on the beach. Only George had a little tent. The rest of us wrapped up in sheets, etc., and just flopped down, protected by mosquito repellent. But we had seen flashes of lightning in the distance earlier, and about 3.30 in the morning large drops began to fall, with thunder and lightning to accompany them. George stayed in his tent, and Keith retreated to the car, while David and I took refuge in an adjacent taverna, where I rigged up five chairs side by side, and slept reasonably well till morning. All very unfortunate for our spirit of adventure, since in fact we had been perfectly comfortable and asleep until the rain came.

### DAY 27, SATURDAY, AUGUST 27TH

I rolled off my chairs at about 7.00, before anyone appeared to hunt me, and joined the others in a very pleasant early morning swim. The rain had cleared away, to reveal a lovely calm morning. Then Keith decided to have a 'Captain Cook' under the hood of the banger, and spent a while titivating and messing (he cleaned the distributor and the air filter – or rather, the place where the air filter should have been!), until we got impatient, and demanded to go and visit the mound that was Torone. He's an amusing man, Keith, excellent rough Australian humour when he's in good form, and then periods of lassitude. He also likes tinkering. He knows more Ancient History than I do, and wanted to be a teacher, but works as 'a sort of personnel manager', he said, cryptically. He is divorced, and speaks of a girl-friend possibly coming to join him later. He has taken a year's leave from his job to mess around and do what he wants.

We climbed up to the Acropolis, through piles of shit and assorted debris – both tourists and Greeks to blame here, I think – and surveyed the whole site. There is precious little left above ground, except on the foot of the promontory, and that is largely mediaeval. The Australians were excavating here, but there is little sign of their work. And yet Torone was a considerable city. Only the fine situation of it is now visible. We went down again to the small stony beach to the south of the fort and had another swim. The stones were slimy and unpleasant, though, and I stepped on a sea-urchin, which leaves me with a spine in the ball of my right foot – very annoying.

Then back for lunch to the same little taverna (our great plans for picnics tend to dissolve in face of the pleasures of lounging in tavernas), and then decided to go for a spin round the foot of the peninsula, to visit Sykia and Sarti. Sykia was touted as an exciting village, but it is about as exciting as Swords.[157] We had a coffee there, waiting out a thunderstorm, and then went on to Sarti – also praised by Nico and others, but just a modern seaside resort. However, we had a third swim there, Keith being ribald about various exposed boobs. A nice item noted from a restaurant menu opposite where we parked: *Kalamari – Inkstand.*

We decided then to go on round the coast, much as we liked Torone, to see if we could find anything picturesque. Actually, we found the only picturesque town in the whole peninsula, I think, in Hagios Nikolaos, where we stopped for petrol, and the garage proprietor ended up selling us a bed for the night, in the upstairs of his house (as so often, they are building an upper storey for their son's anticipated marriage). Mrs. at first drove a hard bargain, insisting that we should take *two* rooms, at 800 dr. each (= 400 dr. a head) – not unreasonably, in fact – but she then obviously felt a little bad, and kept bringing us things that evening, and the next morning – grapes, figs, coffee, cakes. She also sold George two litres of excellent local red wine for 120 dr, which we sampled, but which he wants to save for a final party on Tuesday.

---

157     A village near us in North Dublin, which is in fact not without scenic features!

172

We walked up the town to a little square, with nice old houses – a Communist *kafeneion* and a PASOK one on the square, it seems! – and finally dined in a little taverna on *souvlakia* and all the trimmings, for the enormous price of 150 dr a head!

## DAY 28, SUNDAY, AUGUST 28<sup>TH</sup>

Up not very early – around 9.00 – and managed to divert George from a notion he had to climb a nearby hill, to explore an alleged prehistoric site. Madame brought us various things for breakfast, mainly coffee, bread and fruit, and we feasted on some of Keith's cornflakes, about which we had been giving him a bad time. Then, about 10.30, we set off in the direction of Olynthos. Keith took over the driving again, to my relief, as I wasn't looking forward to driving back to Thessaloniki.

Olynthos is most impressive, though one would have liked more signposting. It is a unique example of a classical town plan – most of the northern part of the city, in grid pattern, is still visible. Then we moved on to Potidaea, at the top of the first prong of the peninsula (Kassandra), for a bathe and lunch. We looked at the eastern side of the peninsula, and found it crowded to the gills with holiday-makers, so we retreated over to the western side, under the shadow of the ancient walls, and beside the canal, and had a perfectly pleasant bathe, and then lunch in an uncrowded taverna built out from the walls.

Then we ventured down the coast a bit, to view the sanctuary of Zeus Ammon and Dionysus at Aphytos, and took another bathe on the beach of the Zeus Ammon Hotel. The sanctuary is pleasantly situated, and quite well preserved as to its foundations, but the Grotto of the Nymphs was guarded by two Alsatians chained there!

Lastly, on the way home, we paid a visit to the most interesting Cave of Perachora, where prehistoric settlements of 500,000 B.C. or so have been discovered, including (in 1960) a skull which was originally thought to be pre-Neanderthal, but now is agreed to be Neanderthal. There were also fine stalactites, some thin as needles, covering the ceiling of certain grottoes.

Many bones of cave-bears, hyenas, lions, mammoths, and so on have been found, and are in an adjacent museum, together with engagingly awful paintings, to show what life was like in those days. Keith was also delighted to find a coprolite – i.e. a fossilised turd. He decided to announce himself as a professor of coprology, especially *contemporary* coprology!

And so back to the Capsis, through intense Sunday evening traffic. In fact, the old banger got us there and back with hardly a hitch, and was thus excellent value. The expedition to Kavalla got back later than us, about 10.30. We ended the evening, after a beer across the road, by watching *The Eagle Has Landed* on TV.

## DAY 29, MONDAY, AUGUST 29TH

I found out that my laundry bill (for three lots) came to about 2500 dr.! It was naïve of me to involve myself with the Capsis for any service whatever. Robin Knights incautiously went and had a haircut, for 600 dr.! So I will have to change $100 on Visa, or I can't even leave the city!

We had exams this morning in language, which were not demanding, and which I completed successfully in less time than anyone else, which astonished me – but in fact it is in written work that I can defeat all facile prattlers, like Manolis and the Italian *karakatzes*. I had a coffee with Robin Knights, then back to the hotel.

I spent some of the afternoon at the pool, and then noticed, among the personnel of the next conference in the hotel, on International Law, a Dr. Connolly from Ireland (U.C.D.), and phoned up his room to see if we could have a drink. He turned out to be a she, quite a nice girl from the North (or North-ish!), like so many. We had a drink at the Snag Bar, and explained what each other were doing. She is stuck here for three weeks, which I do not much envy her for.

I also did a final bit of Greek dancing, but dropped out half-way. I think I have got as much out of it as I need.

In the evening, we all went out to a taverna to honour Nikos, and an excellent evening it turned out to be. The *Gephyra* is an old-style taverna, with genuine *rebetika* – a group of three old gentlemen, on *bouzouki,* flute and organ, and dancing. We rather took the place over. I even got up and danced like a madman with a group of young Greeks – the result of much excellent retsina from the barrel. Andrew has photographs of this event, which may have to be suppressed. The party broke up at about 2.00 am, and we got home by taxi.

## DAY 30, TUESDAY, AUGUST 30TH

The final class took place over coffee round the corner. I still can't carry on a conversation comfortably, but I can't really expect to. My study of the language has only extended for four months. I think I have learned a great deal. We went off then to bookstores and record stores. I resisted all further books, but bought a cassette of Markos Vamvakouris off a stall for 150 dr. – a cheapo type which will probably be useless. Then I changed $100 (at 91 dr. to the $) without fuss, and bought a bus ticket for Athens, for tomorrow at 8.10, for 1200 dr.

Then up the university, to commune again with Damianos. We found *both* of my books in the library, which is most impressive.[158] It actually seems quite a good library, though he says it lacks back numbers of periodicals. I learned that the Derveni Papyrus, after being sat on in Thessaloniki by two gobshites for an unconscionable time, was published last year without their assent – by Merkelbach in *ZPE*.[159] Damianos agrees with Merkelbach's decision. I must get hold of it, but I'm not sure if we have *ZPE*.

---

158     This presumably refers to *Iamblichi Fragmenta* (1972), and *The Middle Platonists* (1977).

159     This was a document of great importance for the history of early Greek philosophy, discovered in a burial site of the Classical period at Derveni, not far from Thessaloniki. It posed many problems for a prospective editor, and those into whose hands it fell were plainly not competent, but did not want to surrender it. So they were outmanoeuvred by the distinguished archaeologist and papyrologist, Reinhold Merkelbach, who published the document in the *Zeitschrift für Papyrologie und Epigraphik.*

In the afternoon I decided not to go to the pool, but had a siesta, packed, and read. Then, in the evening, a final ceremony for the distribution of certificates was held in the Yacht Club of Thessaloniki. Very pleasant, except that a thunderstorm began during the presentation of the certificates, and we had to retire precipitately indoors, where dinner was then served. Not bad. I sat with the American ladies, Ruth and Lou, and Keith. The ladies are a hilarious pair, thoroughly divorced (though Lou is on her third husband), and hard as nails – I should say in their late 30's. Ruth works with the N.E.A. in Washington, and Lou is a professional lobbyist. They have been travelling indefatigably around Greece, and propose to continue to do so – as, of course, does Keith. As for me, I want to go home.

The party broke up about midnight, and Niko gave me and some others a lift back to the Capsis, after we said goodbye to innumerable people.

## DAY 31, WEDNESDAY, AUGUST 31<sup>ST</sup>

Rose at 6.30, to give myself good time to get to the bus. Dear old George actually arrived to rouse me at 6.00, and I would have strangled him, had I had the strength. He came back at about 7.00, though, and insisted on carrying my bag down to the station, so we said goodbye there, and resolved to meet again somewhere or other. I must write to Westerink on his behalf.

The bus ride was tedious but uneventful – except that I found Ruth on it, and Manolis, unexpectedly going off to visit an aunt on Skiathos, with that weird little American with the dyed hair (were *all* the dashing young blades on this course gay?). Keith certainly thought they were, but he had a jaundiced view. Certainly young Helena was breaking her heart over a splendid specimen that I would have had no doubts about. The indomitable Ruth was setting off into the wilds of Mt. Pelion. They all got off at Volos. I warned Ruth against centaurs, but my sympathies would actually be with the centaurs.

I got into Athens about 4.30, and took a taxi to the Hotel Ilissos, which I was actually glad to see again. About £17.50 a

176

night, for bed and breakfast – much better than the Capsis, I must say! The manager *pretended,* at least, to recognise me from last September! Tried to phone Moschatos Travel, but no reply. Then I had an ouzo and a coffee round the corner, and at 7.30 set off to have dinner with Polymnia,[160] as arranged yesterday – via Syntagma, where I picked up a box of chocolates. The usual dialectic with the taximan as to where Chrysanthemou Street might be, but we got there. Polymnia in good form, excoriating all things Greek, as usual. Garth is away in Holland finding a house, preparatory to their moving to Gröningen, where he has secured a position. He turned down the Berkeley job – Peter's position[161] – perhaps wisely, since he has this other one, but otherwise he should have gone. We went on chatting till 2.00 in the morning, and then I luckily found a taxi out on the main road. An entertaining but exhausting evening.

## DAY 32, THURSDAY, SEPTEMBER 1ST

Up this morning at 8.00, all set to do battle with Moschatos. Set off after breakfast on the No. 5 bus, and found them still shut, at 9.00. The janitor said they might open at 10.00, so I went off pottering down Hermou and Mitropoleôs to see what I could find to bring home. I set my heart on a Mycenean female idol in an antique store, but it cost 30,000 dr. Not bad, actually, but I wasn't too sure if my Visa card would stand it. I went and explored the Roman Agora instead – almost deserted, and quite restful. All the turkeys are in the Greek one, and on the Acropolis. The city is full of foreigners – hordes of Americans!

I got back to Moschatos at 10.30 and found them open, and indeed was assured that there was no problem about the plane, though they could only issue me with a ticket at the airport, and I had to turn in my existing one. So with that residual small anxiety, I went off shopping again. I bought two rather nice little

---

160    Polymnia Athanassiadi, distinguished authority on later Platonism, and formidable character, then married to Garth Fowden (see earlier diary, p. 103).

161    That is to say, the distinguished ancient historian Peter Brown, who had passed on to Princeton. Garth had been a student of his, as had Polymnia.

Macedonian rugs – or rather a rug and a cushion cover – which I *could* have bought in Macedonia, if I had had the gumption! Here, in a nice shop on Mitropoleôs, I paid 1500 dr. each for them. Still, not bad. Then over to Kaufmann's, and bought Seferis' *Collected Poems* (for Philip to sign), and Woodhouse's *History*.[162]

Then back to the hotel to collect my gear. I left the big case and my briefcase in their storeroom, to be collected on Sunday, had a beer and *tost* round the corner, and caught the No. 5 bus for Omonia Square, to get a taxi to the bus terminal at *Treis Gephyres,* for the bus at 2.30 to Limni.

The bus ride was splendid (after Chalcis, at least!), but rather exhausting. One rides first along the ridge of Euboea, through pine forests, and then into inhabited valleys on the northern end, with grapes, figs, olives and corn, and finally down to the sea at Limni, quite a respectable town.[163] Philip and Denise were there to collect me, and we drove back to Katounia in their jeep.

Katounia is a fantastic corner of the world. It is about five kilometres south of Limni along the coast. It consists of a valley which was occupied by a mining company (mining magnesite, I think it was said!) which abandoned it after the War, and then couldn't sell it. Finally Philip (who was working in the British School at the time), with two partners (one of whom, Jack Rivaz, is still here, the other having dropped out) bought it in the early 1960s – *six* houses, and a whole valley, with a stream flowing through it – for £1800! It is somewhat reminiscent of Fallen Leaf[164] – the pines and the wildness – except that here one has the warm Mediterranean in front of you, instead of the ice-cold mountain lake!

---

162     *George Seferis, Collected Poems,* translated, edited and introduced by Edmund Keeley and Philip Sherrard, Princeton, 1967; and *Modern Greece: A Short History,* by C.M. Woodhouse, London: Faber, 1968.

163     Indeed, Limni, or rather Elymnion, goes back to antiquity, having been a member of the Athenian League in the early 5th cent. B.C. – though it preserves little, if anything, of its early life.

164     A favourite resort of ours in the Sierra Nevada, south of Lake Tahoe, when we lived in Berkeley, California.

Had a very pleasant cocktail at Jack's house, just down the valley, before dinner. There I met Philip Sherrard's daughter Liadain, and his first wife, Anna, from whom he is amicably divorced (and lives just up the hill from Jack, in a house which both Sherrards used to occupy).

I also met Jack's daughter Jane (his wife died giving birth to Jane, and he has never remarried – the Sherrards helped to bring her up), a pair called Robin and Anne Baring, who are relations of Lord Revelstoke,[165] and of the banking family – though Robin appears to be a gentleman of leisure. She is a psychiatrist, and is writing a large work on 'the Female Principle', on which she is consulting Philip, to his despair).

Last but not least, I met Edmund ("Mike") Keeley,[166] and his Greek wife Mary – a most pleasant company. It is remarkable that Keeley should be present – I will get them *both* to sign the Seferis book![167]

Later, we went back and had a little snack, with some more wine – we had stuffed ourselves on *mezes* at Jack's. And so to bed.


DAY 33, FRIDAY, SEPTEMBER 2ND

Philip and Denise occupy a simple but pleasant residence which used to be the estate *hospital,* and they live there most of the year, surrounded by books, almost self-supporting in vegetables and fruit, and attended by a faithful dog, Rocco. They also keep a flat in Athens. Philip showed me the guest houses (they rent these to make ends meet), and they are truly splendid – a majestic view

---

165    Proprietor of Lambay Island, just to the north of Howth, which we would visit from time to time, when out sailing. Robin Baring is actually the younger son of the 6th Baron Ashburton, and a pretty competent artist. His wife wrote a number of books under her maiden name, Anne Gage.

166    Edmund Leroy "Mike" Keeley (1928 – 2022) was an American novelist, translator, and essayist, a poet, and Charles Barnwell Straut Professor of English at Princeton University. He was a noted expert on the Greek poets C.P. Cavafy, George Seferis, Odysseus Elytis and Yannis Ritsos, and on post-Second World War Greek history.

167    And so indeed I did. The result is still on my shelves.

down to the bay, through pine trees. I would love to take one, and bring Jean and Mouse to enjoy it, for at least two weeks – perhaps next May might be possible?[168]

Philip and Denise like to work in the mornings, so, after a leisurely breakfast, I went down to explore the beach. Philip gave me an article on Gnosticism by Henri Corbin,[169] a great authority on Persian religion (in particular), now dead, but whose works I must investigate. I am also reading Seferis as fast as I can. All in all, I spent about four hours on the beach, since they only came down towards 2.00, and only then did we go up to lunch, so I barely escaped sunstroke. Gradually all the characters of the previous night assembled, to bathe and chat. Jack is much interested in Irish politics, going back to Parnell and my grandfather, about which we talked. He says his mother's family was Irish, but left Dublin in 1916, when it seemed that things were descending into anarchy.

After a long lunch, lasting till 4.30, a siesta was declared, and then drinks on the verandah, with Keeleys and Liadain, with whom we then went out to a favourite taverna in Limni – again protracted by entertaining conversation. Mary Keeley appals us by having a sheep's head for dinner. Philip and Mike are enraged by their English publisher's decision, in a reprint of the Cavafy translation, to put a rather crude David Hockney drawing on the cover, and are planning a blistering manifesto on the subject.

## DAY 34, SATURDAY, SEPTEMBER 3RD

Rose at 9.00, and had a leisurely breakfast. Philip and Denise have the remarkable habit of beginning each day with a clove of garlic, a device for preserving good health which they

---

168    In fact, this began a long history of visits to Katounia, extending over the next thirty years or so. See later diaries. In 1992, when we moved to Howth, we re-named the house we bought there Katounia.

169    Henri Corbin (1903 – 1978) was a French philosopher, theologian, Iranologist and professor of Islamic Studies at the Ecole pratique des hautes études in Paris. I did indeed give much attention to him in later years.

recommend! That may very well be so, but it is easier to do in Katounia than in a more populous environment. I find myself rather burned this morning, having spent an excessive time on the beach yesterday, so I decided to spend the morning in the shade of the verandah, reading Seferis, and Tsekourakis' offprint on the Cynic diatribe, attended faithfully by the wasps, who, however, are really not very troublesome. Philip and Denise put out a bowl of water for them, anointed with jam, and they drown in that in great numbers, but there are always more.

## DAY 35, SUNDAY, SEPTEMBER 4<sup>TH</sup>

Philip and Denise drove me down to Athens in the jeep, called round to their flat, collected my luggage from the hotel, and we went out to dinner in a delightful taverna somewhere on a hill, following which they left me to the airport somewhat after midnight, where I got on what turned out to be a full flight – so I was lucky!

# 8: EXPEDITION TO BARCELONA

## MAY, 1984

*This was organised by Prof. Montserrat Jufresa, of the University of Barcelona, to bring me out to lecture both on 'Joyce and the Classics' and on a theme in ancient philosophy. It was in fact my first visit to Spain.*

### DAY 1, SUNDAY, MAY 6<sup>TH</sup>

I am now in the departure lounge at Dublin, indignant at being put on a plane which gives me a *four-hour* wait in London – but it seems that that is the penalty for getting a 'cheap' flight. It is a great pity that Jean wouldn't come, but she is working herself up to coming to Athens (if I go!). Still no rain (it is over two weeks, now, and very serious), but it is quite cold and foggy today. I have brought Spanish grammars and phrase books, but it's a hopeless cause, I'm afraid. Anyhow, they speak Catalan in Barcelona, presumably.

Now (5.30 pm) sitting in Terminal 2, Heathrow, *Croissant Corner*, having coffee and an almond-filled bun – some days old, but obviously quite good in its prime! I wish I was leaving on the 6.15 to Casablanca and Marrakesh. I have been reading *Ulysses* with enjoyment, but am in general bored and stiff. I haven't seen traces of bomb devastation, but there is a notice appealing for information. I sat beside a gentleman reading an Arab newspaper who had a briefcase, and couldn't help feeling a frisson of concern. I realise now that I have left behind my Spanish phrasebook – and the *Classical Lexicon to Finnegans Wake.*[170] I hope I can function. I saw a crash course in Spanish in three months on sale – how about *three days?*

---

170    A large volume, edited by Brendan O'Hehir and myself, back in 1977.

*Hotel de Ville, Brussels*

*University of Barcelona*

*The Agora, Athens*

*Naoussa*

*University of Tel Aviv, Israel*

*The Sea of Gallilee*

*John and Mouse, Aix en Provence*

*Waimea, Hawaii*

It is now midnight (the Cathedral clock has just chimed), and I am safely in bed in a pleasant little hotel in the old part of Barcelona, the *Regencia Colon,* just inland from the Cathedral. Carlos and Montserrat[171] met me very efficiently after a less than two hour flight from London, and drove me here. Barcelona is pretty vast, it seems (about 3m inhabitants in all), but the old city is clearly demarcated and compact. I walked about a little, and had a beer round the corner. I look forward to exploring further tomorrow. I have no engagements till 7.00pm. There is a formidable array of Joyce scholars lined up. Am reading *Ulysses* as fast as I can. Apparently I am expected to give three discourses!

DAY 2, MONDAY, MAY 7TH

Woke about 8.30. Slept well, after I had divested myself of the right amount of bedclothes – the weather is quite warm. Breakfast of rolls and coffee. Then strolled out, first to the Cathedral, where I sat in on 9.00 Mass in a side-chapel, then looked around it. A sound of geese during Mass proved to come from the cloisters, where a flock of geese flourish, strutting and posing absurdly for the visitors. Lovely old buildings and streets all round the Cathedral. I found a possibly good restaurant, lots of antique shops, and some museums. There is an exhibition on in honour of the Catalonian patriot Francesc Macia,[172] which sounds interesting – the 1930's. Catalan, by the way, is quite different from Spanish – more like French, if anything[173] – and not unreadable, in fact, though quite incomprehensible orally.

---

171    That is to say, Prof. Montserrat Jufresa, of the University of Barcelona, and her husband.

172    Francesc Macià i Llussà (1859 – 1933) was a Spanish politician from Catalonia who served as the 122nd President of the Generalitat of Catalonia, and formerly an officer in the Spanish Army. Politically, he evolved from an initial regenerationism of Spain to the defence of the Catalan Republic, becoming the first president of the restored Generalitat and achieving the first successful establishment of the self-government of Catalonia of modern history.

173    It is in fact much akin to Provençal, and a Romance language in its own right.

Now 11.30, after a visit back to the jax, and to read more of Stuart Gilbert's *Ulysses* book. It is a *very* small room that I have – though all I need, after all. Wandering round a town such as this while reading *Ulysses* is a curious experience. One feels very like Leopold Bloom.

Out again, then, and walked down a main thoroughfare (Via Laietana) as far as the sea – but the port is very commercial, and didn't look inviting. I turned back along the Rambla, the lower part of which seems to be a red-light district, with whores standing placidly along the street, and a few sex shops. I had a beer, and then a reasonable lunch of paella and roast chicken (more than I wanted), for 350 pesetas, which I hope will not lay me low. Back then through various charming squares, and retired for a siesta, and more reading of Joyce.

When I awoke, it had clouded over, and was actually attempting to drizzle. I went out for a short walk at 6.30, but got back to be collected by Montserrat at 7.00, for a lecture at 8.00. We walked to the university, conversing on the way. She is ashamed of her English, but it serves very adequately. My Spanish is in practice non-existent. I met a number of members of the department – the Vice-chairman, Carles Miralles, and Jaume Portulas, both interested in early Greek lyric, and who have cooperated in a book on Archilochus (translated into English), which they presented to me.

The lecture, in Catalan, was obviously good, but incomprehensible to me (the audience was large and appreciative), given by a fellow who has translated *Ulysses* into Catalan, Joaquin Mallafré.[174] We went out after the lecture and had a good German meal, with Montserrat, Portulas and himself. Much lively discussion about Catalonia, Ireland, and the role of the writer. He promises to send me a copy of his translation.[175]

---

174     Joaquim Mallafrè i Gavaldà (b. 1941) is indeed a major Catalan translator of literature. His version of Ulysses appeared in 1981, but he has also translated Beckett, Pinter, and Kipling.

175     This he never did, but I fear it would have been to no purpose!

Rose a little late, and went out after breakfast and bought some anti-diarrhoea pills, just in case, since I felt a bit queasy this morning. Monserrat collected me at 10.15, and we took a taxi to the university. I got confused, and thought I was doing Platonism this morning, but I was meant to be doing *Joyce*. I was introduced to a Professor MacDermot (cousin of John Dudley), a nice enough lady – a good friend of Eilis and Vivian,[176] and a remote cousin of theirs and mine, but strangely unforthcoming in view of all that. She didn't come to the lecture.

The lecture was delivered to a large and appreciative audience – they laughed at jokes, so understood English well enough – but I didn't get through all the topics promised. I thought it best to finish after an hour, though. I promised to send the full text to the Chairman, after Rosemary[177] types it up. Went off for a coffee afterwards, with the Chairman, Montserrat, Jaume and Carlos Miralles. Then back to the hotel.

This time I lunched frugally off a ham and cheese sandwich (*bocadillo*) and beer, and took a siesta till 4.00, when the Picasso Museum would open. The Picasso Museum was a marvellous experience, if rather exhausting. He spent his formative years in Barcelona, from 1895, when he was 14, to 1900, when he went to Paris. Most interesting was the great amount of work preserved from this early period, which shows his brilliance in all traditional modes of painting – giving him the perfect right to goof off later, I suppose (which it still seems to me that he is doing), after the Blue and Cubist periods, which are at least structured. But what do I know? I was bombed disastrously by a pigeon on the way back, while strolling through a tiny mediaeval alley. That is the penalty for that. My suit is out of action, and must be cleaned. A decent fellow came to my rescue with Kleenex, and showed me to a fountain, where we cleaned the coat, but I hadn't noticed that it had gone down the leg of the trousers as well.

---

176    My second cousin Eilis Dillon, distinguished novelist, and her husband Vivian Mercier, distinguished literary critic.

177    Our departmental secretary in Trinity.

That exhausted me, so I read until it was time to go to dinner with Carlos and Montserrat. At 8.15, I got a taxi to their apartment – very well appointed, in surroundings rather like that of the Fowdens in Athens.[178]

An interesting company assembled there (Carlos is Carlos Marti – I forgot that everyone keeps their own name in Spain), Carles Miralles again, a lady and man from the English Department of the *other* university (whose names I must get) – she is a good friend of Eilis and Vivian also – and a girl from the Classics Department, Eulalia Vintró,[179] who is also a Communist deputy in the Catalonian Assembly, and the most cheerful Communist I ever met! All the party were at least Socialist, and were much depressed by the recent landslide victory of Conservative Nationalists under Pujol.[180] I started things off by asking about the recent election – floodgates of misery! So I tried to console them by maintaining that now was an awful time to be in government. Catalonia has gone conservative partly in reaction to the central government, which is Socialist, but partly, they maintain, because Pujol has managed to corner the market in Catalonian patriotism – rather like Fianna Fáil!

We had an excellent dinner – asparagus in cheese sauce, followed by a shellfish plate – cockles, prawns, crayfish, monkfish, in good Catalonian sauce, washed down by Catalonian white wine. The party went on till 1.00, when I moved to break it up (thinking they might be waiting for me to do so!). Miralles kindly gave me a lift back.

---

178    See above, p. 103.

179    Eulalia Vintró Castells (b. 1945) has indeed had a distinguished career, both as a parliamentary representative (she retired from this in 1999), and as a professor of Greek.

180    Jordi Pujol i Soley (b. 1930) is a Spanish politician from Catalonia who was the leader of the party Convergencia Democratica de Catalunya (CDC) from 1974 to 2003, and President of the Generalitat de Catalunya from 1980 to 2003. He had just won re-election.

I did some washing of shirt and underwear – we'll see how that works! I hope my suit trousers are not permanently ruined by the pigeon. After breakfast, I wandered up to the cathedral and poked around, mainly admiring the side-chapels, reading the guide. Then I went and communed with the geese in the cloister. It is remarkable how quickly one develops a sense of proprietorship. I find myself resenting the busloads of turkeys who clutter up my cathedral – and there *are* fair droves of them, even at this time of the year! Mainly geriatric funsters, though.

Montserrat collected me at 11.30 for a lecture at 12.00. She revealed to me the names of the two guests I didn't catch – Arancha Usandizaga and Josep Maria Jaumé, both of the Universitat Autonoma de Barcelona. Arancha is Basque, as she told me (though she no longer speaks Basque), and she feels Basque. Josep is a very pleasant character from Carlos' home town of Reus (as was Gaudí!). Carlos' father, it seems, was mayor of Reus, and is a senator. This from Montserrat by way of apology for talking so much politics last night – no apologies needed, though, I assured her!

The lecture was remarkably well attended – the library was full to capacity – and, though they really cannot have understood much, they all had their summaries, so they will have derived something. I had to summarize the last bit, since we started late. No questions, not surprisingly. Miralles revealed that he would like to publish the talk in a new journal they are planning to produce, so I agreed.[181] It is not meant to appear till next spring, so that will give me time to use the talk in America in the autumn a bit. It is a bit erudite for a very junior audience, but the main theme, 'the female principle', is comprehensible enough. After the lecture, I went off and had some beer and tapas with Montserrat and Jaume, and then back for a siesta and a read of Joyce.

At 4.30 or so, I rose and got a taxi to the Placa d'Espanya, to visit Montjuic. An impressive pile of a palace belonging to

---

[181]     It did in fact appear, as ' Female Principles in Platonism', in *Itaca* Vol. 1, 1986 (reprinted in *The Golden Chain,* Ashgate: Aldershot, 1990).

Alfonso XIII now houses various exhibitions and the museum, but it all closes at 2.00. I climbed up, and walked around it, finding nothing but a congress of driving schools conducting lessons, and a group of old age pensioners playing cards. I walked on to the Miro Foundation, hoping that would be open, and it was. Another excellent encounter with a great painter – and I prefer the late Miro to the late Picasso; less pure rubbish, I think. Then I walked down the hill, into a rather dismal area, and, becoming exhausted, hailed a taxi, which was a bit of a mistake, since he had to drive me all round the city to get to the Cathedral. But my feet *did* hurt.

I set out a little before 8.00 to the university, to hear Valverde's lecture on Joyce (he is the latest Spanish translator, and quite a poet and philosopher himself [182] – was in exile from Franco in Canada for six years). In fact he was so popular that we couldn't get in, even after a larger room was found – Montserrat advertised *too* well! – so we went and sat and talked in the Classics library. Jaume and I carried on a lively conversation in a mad mixture of French and English, with some Catalan thrown in. I met Valverde only after the lecture, and very pleasant he is – as is his wife. He was in Dublin for Bloomsday '82. He says his most vivid memory is of strolling along with Borges, [183] singing Irish ballads. I am sad to have missed that! I remember only just having got back from Berkeley, and deliberately avoiding that event, suspecting it would be bogus.

Then back to the hotel, driven by Carlos Miralles, and decided to go out to dinner in the Restaurant Ternell (?), just

---

182     José María Valverde Pacheco (1926 – 1996), was a Spanish poet, essayist, literary critic, philosophy historian, and Spanish translator.

183     Jorge Francisco Isidoro Luis Borges Acevedo (1899 – 1986) was an Argentine short-story writer, essayist, poet and translator, and a key figure in Spanish-language and international literature. His best-known books, *Ficciones* (*Fictions*) and *El Aleph*, published in the 1940s, are compilations of short stories interconnected by common themes, including dreams, labyrinths, philosophers, libraries, mirrors, fictional writers, and mythology. Borges's works have contributed to philosophical literature and the fantasy genre, and influenced the magic realist movement in 20th cent. Latin American literature. His late poems converse with such cultural figures as Spinoza, Camoes, and Virgil.

beside the Cathedral. It was excellent, in fact. I had a fish soup, and veal parmegiano – it is French-style rather than Spanish, and slightly posh, but still not expensive. It all came to about 1400 pesetas, with wine.

## DAY 5, THURSDAY, MAY 10TH

Today I resolved, despite the advice of all at dinner, to go to Montserrat (the Benedictine monastery), and accordingly walked up to the Pullmantur terminal on Gran Via at 10.00. Miralles kindly gave me a letter to a monk in the monastery, but as it turned out I had no real opportunity to use it.

The drive there is most impressive, enlivened by the demented comments of our geriatric guide, whose English was baffling. The suburbs of Barcelona proliferate into neighbouring 'villages'. There are said to be six million people in the greater Barcelona area. The mountain of Montserrat ('serrated mountain') rises above the plain rather like Meteora,[184] except that the 'meteora' are separate peaks, which makes them weirder, though not necessarily more impressive. It has the same sort of rounded lumpiness, though – knobs formed into curious shapes. It is a long drive up to the monastery, which is nestled (if that is the word!) between two mighty crags, the right-hand one of which might easily fall on it (and has in the past, I believe!).

A frightful mass of turkeys (and pilgrims, I suppose) met our eyes. I counted over *thirty* coaches. We proceeded in a pullulating mass towards the church. The church is actually quite modern (18th cent., I believe), though the foundation goes back to the 11th cent. (there is one Romanesque door preserved). We went in crocodile formation to see the Black Madonna, who is impressively stern. She is the patron of Catalonia, and must be reasonably pleased at the moment. The decoration is rich, but rather vulgar.

After this, I sat in the church for a while, to wait for the singing of the choirboys at 1.00, but it went on for more than half-an-

---

184    The spectacular mountain-top monastic complex in Thessaly (see p.167 above).

hour, and I got bored, and went to view the museum instead, which I was able to do alone, since *everyone* wanted to listen to the choir. Perhaps I missed a great experience, but I doubt if they would match the King's College choir in Cambridge. Downstairs there are paintings, mostly pretty dull (though old – 15th, 16th cents.), but among them a Caravaggio and a Velasquez.

Then quite a good lunch was served – after which, however, it was too late to go up the funicular, even if one wanted to, so I sat in the sun for a while, and did a Spanish exercise. There is a pleasant young Australian couple on the tour, and he had very much wanted to get up to the top and photograph. It is actually a bit misty, though the view is spectacular.

And so back, via a rather pointless visit to a perfume factory. I was not tempted by the perfume. It was rather of the quality of that wine on Santorini, in the winery we visited.[185]

I contented myself with a *bocadillo* of sausage and a beer, but was tempted then to go out to a flamenco show, in the Plaça Real, *Los Tarantos*. They were actually excellent, but the audience was *very* thin (I went to the *first* show, 10.00 to 12.00!). Very good guitar playing, and singing and dancing. It cost 1800 pesetas, with a jug of sangria, which saw me through the show. Not bad value.

DAY 6, FRIDAY, MAY 11TH

I sprang up just before 6.00, to catch the tour bus at the terminal at 6.30, for a trip to Andorra. I actually made it quite comfortably, but no breakfast. It has been raining, plainly – still black clouds around – but it cleared up as we left town and drove through Catalonia. It is pretty cool, though. I am not dressed for the mountains, come to think of it.

The visit to Andorra was interesting. It is much afflicted by tourists, however, and subsists on the sale of duty-free goods. I actually bought a pair of 'Stan Smith' tennis shoes.

Back, then, for a quiet evening in the old town, and an uneventful return to Dublin the next day.

---

185    See above, p. 115 – the Roussos winery.

# 9: *ISRAEL*

## MAY — JUNE, 1985

*The occasion for this visit was another conference organised by my
friend John Glucker, of Tel Aviv University, on behalf of the Israeli
Classical Association, this time on more general Classical themes. On
this occasion I was able to visit the household of my god-daughter,
Miriam Shtaierman (née Farrell), and once again fit in a brief visit to
Jerusalem, at the invitation of Samuel Scolnicov.*

### DAY 1, TUESDAY, MAY 28TH

This trip may prove to be *very* short. The goddam plane has now
been delayed *twice,* through 'technical difficulties', and I am in
grave danger of missing my connection. This is a penalty for being
patriotic, and going Aer Lingus to London instead of BA. If I
had gone BA, *they* would have been responsible for getting me to
Israel. These bastards are not. The airport is almost deserted. The
public must have known they were going to go walkabout tonight.

I had a rather hectic day, rushing into town to get the last
few pages of my talk off to Rosemary[186] – brinkmanship! She did
a great job, though. Then Jean picked me up, and had bought
me a new wardrobe for the tropics! A nice pair of pants didn't
fit. It is depressing trying to get into clothes one hasn't been
into for a while – some which I now *can* get into which had been
put away years ago as too voluminous. I really will have to face
up to the Great Diet – but all that generally happens is that I
end up with a bad cold, and relapse to my natural weight, which
seems to be about 13st. 7lb. Sorry 'bout that, but that's how I was
programmed, long ago.

---

186     Our excellent departmental secretary.

*8.15 pm:* I am now considerably mollified, on board a BA flight to London, just about to leave (I hope). A very pleasant young official rescued me when I protested that I had an APEX connection to catch, and got me on this flight. The weather is still blustery and confused, as I leave, but will presumably clear up greatly while I'm away. I leave behind me a very wretched Fine Gael Portmarnock Branch preparing for a campaign,[187] in which we are going to get a pasting. Mr Barron[188] was in *great* form last night as he was demolishing our diseased trees. I am meant to be composing a few speeches for Tom Houlihan.[189] Am I to compose them *in character*? (A pheasant has just run across the runway in front of the plane! A nice touch. Less ominous than a rabbit, certainly!)

*10.10 pm:* So far so good. The flight to Tel Aviv was actually leaving from Terminal 1, since it is BA. The now familiar super-security. The metal detector here is the only one that picks up my penknife. It is mildly absurd to see security staff frisking elderly rabbis – but, after all, if a terrorist really wanted to disguise himself, how better than as an elderly rabbi? A large group of the orthodox, as we wait, are filling in the time praying and bowing at one of the walls – presumably that facing Jerusalem.

### DAY 2, WEDNESDAY, MAY 29TH

*7.45 am:* Now sitting in Ramat Aviv, having breakfast – usual mess of things, very good. I am showered, and changed, but still feeling a little groggy. The flight was OK – a 747 – a few squalling kids, and absolutely full – almost all Jewish, so far as I could judge. It took 4 hours, 20 mins., and got into Tel Aviv just at dawn, gaining two hours. I changed $50 at the airport, and got 1000 shekels to the $ – a spectacular development from 1981, when it was about 10. That's inflation! But costs have not

---

187    I was at this stage, and for many years afterwards, involved in Fine Gael at the local level. We were indeed about to face local elections in June, in which Fianna Fáil greatly increased their representation.

188    Mr. Barron was our tree cutter. We had a number of dead elms, as I recall. He would cut down a tree in exchange for taking half the wood!

189    Our local Fine Gael candidate.

gone up greatly, The hotel now costs $30 a night – actually down from $33 in 1981! The bus into town was 590 shekels – about 50 cents. I got a taxi to the hotel, who took me for 2400, but even that's not bad. The temperature on arrival was 80° – already going up, I should say. I will carry on today as long as I can. No point in going to bed now.

*5.20 pm:* Just back in my bedroom after a pleasant bathe in the pool. I actually skipped the afternoon session, which was historical, since I felt a bit dim, and decided I needed a siesta. Also, there was a degree of messing about lunch. John Glucker has fallen and hurt himself *in the bath,* and is hobbling about miserably. He brought a sandwich himself, to eat on the premises, and waved vaguely when I enquired about lunch. All the people I knew (Wasserstein, Appelbaum, John Dudley) had mysteriously vanished, and only a gaggle of unknowns, talking animatedly in Hebrew, were left outside. No one offered to take me to lunch, which I found strange, since we were welcomed elaborately at the outset, as distinguished foreign visitors, so I said 'Fuck 'em all', and went home. But I needed a rest, anyhow.

It was quite a good morning session – nothing ground-breaking, but four good sensible papers, following an amiably scatter-brained discourse by Dean Gabriel Cohen. John G. produced an amusing squib about Zeno consulting the Delphic Oracle, and being told to *synkhrôtizesthai tois nekrois.*[190] I think it's a piece of comedy-based 'biography', but one can't be sure. I was glad to see old Yehoshua Amir[191] again. I must check up as to what happened to *Studia Philonica.*

*11.00 pm:* I have had an eventful evening. I decided to set off down town to check out a Yemeni restaurant in the Old Quarter of

---

190     That is to say, 'have intercourse with the dead'. This story is actually told in Diogenes Laertius' *Lives of the Philosophers* VII 2.

191     Yehoshua Amir (1911-2002) was a distinguished Jewish scholar, and authority on Philo Judaeus, among other things. He had been born (in Germany) as Hermann Neumark, but escaped to Palestine at the beginning of World War II, and changed his name in 1951. I must have met him on my first visit, though I do not record this. I also cannot recall what the connection with *Studia Philonica* was; it is an American publication.

Tel Aviv, after waiting around to see if John Dudley would return. I got the 24 bus all the way to Allenby, and then struck off in search of Shaul's Inn. I almost went into another instead, which looked good, but persevered – and then found John Dudley, with Gerda Schwarz and the whole Glucker family! So we had quite a party. Dinner was OK, though not *that* exotic – hummus and tahini, and then *shishlik* – came to £7. A *bit* touristy, but on the other hand clean and pleasant. The Gluckers returned by taxi, while JD and myself went for a promenade on the seafront, had an ice-cream, and discussed the state of the world. The academic situation in Holland is quite savage, it seems – they can just close departments and put people out in the street. We actually lead a charmed life in Ireland. We came back eventually by taxi – cost $2 or so. I am developing a pair of blisters, I'm afraid.

## DAY 3, THURSDAY, MAY 30TH

*11.45 am:* In my room, after returning to the hotel and taking a coffee on the terrace, since the proceedings turned into Hebrew at the conference, after the first paper by Gerda Schwarz of Graz, on Vases and Tragedy, which was actually very good. An interesting pot illustrating Phineus, which I must get Stephen Jackson[192] to follow up, and a good illustration of the Amphiaraus-Eriphyle-Alcmaeon story, for which there was no clear literary equivalent – earlier than Euripides' Alcmaeon play of 406. I am contemplating a bathe, but am quite involved in Krämer's *Ursprung*, which is good on many points, though not, I think, on Xenocrates. I learn that busses go every few minutes to Natanya from outside the door, which actually makes life slightly more than less complicated. How can I be met?

I went back for the end of the morning session, and we all went over to the Faculty Club for lunch, at the university's expense. Dr Amit-Freundlich walked me over – a most amiable man, as befits his name. Once there, I sat with Prof. Wasserstein, John Dudley, and Samuel Scolnicov, whom I didn't recognise at first, but who is

---

192    A graduate student of mine, who was working on the *Argonautica* of Apollonius of Rhodes.

actually speaking this afternoon – in Hebrew, which is why I hadn't deciphered him yet (I should have asked!). We had a good chat, about Plato and Italian scholars (I must check up on Romano and Catania[193]). He is writing a book on Plato's theory of education, and still planning a study of the *Parmenides*.[194]

Samuel in fact gave the first talk, and had an English version of it – it is essentially a review of Bolotin's edition of the *Lysis* – so I stayed for that, but the other two – including one from Yehoshua Amir on *Youdaismos* – were in Hebrew, so I slipped off back to the hotel for a swim. After the swim, I read Krámer and drank arak on the terrace, waiting to see if Dudley would return, and would be interested in an excursion. He returned at 7.00, and was, so we headed off on the 25 bus to Jaffa – only 250 shekels, right across town! We explored Old Jaffa, beautifully done up by the Israelis, but really very bogus – the old streets don't even *smell*! An Armenian family live in the house of Simon the Tanner, and hospitably invite one to ring the bell – but when one does, there is no answer. We dined at a non-touristy restaurant at the bottom of the hill. I tried fish – sea-bass – which wasn't bad; 5000 shekels, though, more expensive than meat, as in Greece. Then I ate a sweetmeat from a wayside stall, which I know I shouldn't – and, right enough, I have got the runs! However, I have applied various pills, and perhaps I will pull through.

## DAY 4, FRIDAY, MAY 31ST

*9.00am:* I have just phoned Miriam,[195] and promised to be with her about 10.30 – depending on the bus! Dudley has set off by train to Haifa and Akko; we may make contact later. Buses to Netanya (605) are *meant* to go every ten minutes.

---

193    Francesco Romano, Professor of Greek Philosophy at the University of Catania in Sicily, whom I in fact had much to do with in later years.

194    Both of these projects duly came to fruition.

195    My first cousin once-removed, and god-daughter, Miriam Farrell, who had married an Israeli, Koby Shtaierman (whom she had met while on holiday in Greece), and who was now living happily in Netanya, near Tel Aviv, having converted to Judaism.

The bus was as good as its word. I just caught one as I got to the bus stop, and it drove non-stop to Netanya. My hotel is really very well situated from the transport point of view. The usual grim succession of high-rise apartments, first in Hertzliyya (though a lot of fine villas visible there also), then Netanya. The coastal highway is quite pleasant, otherwise. We passed through the Vale of Sharon, which under the Turks was allowed to degenerate into malarial swamps, but is now all highly cultivated, though with patches of original sand-dunes and scrub.

I had some difficulty in finding a taxi, and getting him to find MacDonald Street, but there was no mystery about it in the end, so he was just ignorant. It is quite a well-established street near the sea, though new high-rises are all around, and a few hotels – Netanya is quite a resort town. Koby and Miriam were there to greet me. They have a nice apartment, as these things go. I found them in some excitement, since Koby's brother Nahman is getting married on Tuesday – I will just miss that, unfortunately! – but there is a preliminary party tomorrow, beginning at the synagogue, and going on to the Shtaierman's house. Koby had to go out to get some wine, to deliver it, so Miriam and I settled down to a chat. She is embarked on a computer course, which should lead to a job in the autumn. Meanwhile, Koby is trying to change his job, since he is not being paid enough. They lose out on inflation every month. The apartment costs $200 a month to rent – not bad by *our* standards, but... – but it would cost $60,000 to buy. The average wage of a worker is about $150 a month.

Koby came back, and he and I went off to the beach, armed with cans of beer. He proved most amiable and talkative. We swam, then sat on our beach chairs and drank beer, and discoursed. He tried to explain the computer projects he is engaged on. He sounds very bright. I wonder whether I might be able to get him some sort of fellowship in Trinity for a while? We sat for about an hour – only later did I realise how burned I had got!

We had a cup of coffee back at the flat, and then set out, in Koby's magnificent BMW, for Caesarea. Caesarea is actually a bit disappointing, for a Classicist, though a very fine site otherwise. First, the amphitheatre – rather restored, but a fine sight – decked out for a performance tomorrow night of the Dutch Ballet, with Galina Panov and her husband,[196] doing *Romeo and Juliet.* So it's in use. Apparently, the first inscriptional evidence of Pontius Pilate was found here – a dedication by him of something (a statue, perhaps?) to the Emperor Tiberius. The rest of the town is slightly to the north, and circumscribed by a Crusader wall – only a fraction of the ancient town, presumably. Again, buildings have been adapted for use as restaurants and boutiques, which is not quite proper. Koby didn't come in, as having seen it all, so Miriam conducted me round the ramparts of the Crusader town. Everywhere one can see the usual phenomenon of fragments of previous civilisations being cannibalised to form parts of later ones – Roman pillars built into Arab walls, and so on.

Then back to the flat, and had a siesta till 6.00 or so. Then John Dudley rang, rather to my alarm. He had got to Caesarea, when things closed down for the Sabbath, and then somebody gave him a lift to Hadera, and now a taximan was prepared to drive him to Netanya. Miriam gallantly asked him to dinner, but the next we heard from him he was back in Ramat Aviv! The taximan had found the centre of Netanya dug up, and refused to proceed – so he took John back to the hotel.

Miriam served an excellent dinner of tandoori chicken, and we then drove over to John Glucker's party. This was, once again, a rather grim affair.[197] Miriam met Dudley, and worked out that her brother Bernard had been at school with his younger brother Peter. Small world! Old Appelbaum was in good form, telling us the story of his life. I seem to remember he told it to me last time as well, but no matter. He was one of those who came out and founded a *kibbutz* (in 1938 in his case) in mosquito-infested marshes, such as much of Palestine then

---

196    Galina and Valery Panov, both distinguished ballet dancers, had defected from the USSR to Israel in 1974

197    Cf. the account of the Glucker party in my diary of the First Visit, p. 62 above.

consisted of, thanks to the loving care of the Turks. Anyhow, we left at about 11.00, since it wasn't very thrilling for Koby and Miriam.

And so to bed.

## DAY 5, SATURDAY, JUNE 1<sup>ST</sup> (SHABBAT)

Koby went off early to get the ceremonies started. Miriam and I followed about 10.00, getting a taxi across town to the Shtaierman house, and nearby synagogue. Koby's parents are very respected citizens, being among the founders of the town, and live in the original part of town – unpretentious little villas, but any sort of house is a luxury in Israel these days. The synagogue (*bêt ha-knesset*) is a friendly little neighbourhood one, and presents a scene of amiable chaos. All the men gathered in the main part, with a group in the centre, including the cantor and his assistants, apparently arguing vigorously, but in fact shouting out readings from the Bible and blessings, for all they're worth. The women are behind, in their section, chatting and preparing food and drink. Koby doesn't go to synagogue very often, but he interpreted valiantly for me. I was greeted warmly by all, put on a skull-cap, and was invited to participate – though I obviously couldn't read the Bible in Hebrew. Finally, Nahman, as the bridegroom, stepped forward and did his bit of reading, and was then pelted with sweets and nuts, which were frantically harvested by the children.

Then they broke out the beer, the brandy, and the hors d'oeuvres, and everyone feasted enthusiastically. It was a sort of communion, as it must originally have been, and doubtless still should be. A good deal of the ceremonial reminds one of what Christian ceremonies must originally have been. The cantor has a tremendous voice – could be an opera singer! Koby says that on Yom Kippur he sings like that all day, without food!

The family, including the bride, Yael's, parents, whom I found very pleasant (originally from Holland – he was sheltered during the War by a Dutch gentile family) repaired then to the Shtaierman house, and a large lunch began, with whisky, beer and wine. Old man Shtaierman has a heart condition, and they are watching him carefully, but he longs to have a drink with someone, and picked me as an excuse. He was disappointed that I wouldn't drink whisky before lunch, but I had some with him afterwards. At lunch, the courses kept coming – all delicious – but one rapidly ran out of space. Mrs. S. is an archetypal Jewish mother – made far too much food, and then tried to get us all to eat it! Much was inevitably left, and given to Miriam and Koby to take home.

We left in mid-afternoon, fairly stocious, with some notion of going to the beach, but I am quite burned after my exposure yesterday, so we actually all retired for a siesta, which lasted till 7.00. We finally got up, had some tea and cake, and then headed off to Tel Aviv, to Koby and Miriam's favourite 'pub' – a hostelry on Dizengoff, run by a pleasant fellow called Nissim – originally from Libya. He served excellent snacks – 'cigars' and samosas – with our beer. We found we couldn't face a real meal, but sat there till almost midnight, communing with Nissim (an amiable but taciturn man) and watching the fish and other fauna in his coral fish tank. Great business being done, despite the economic crisis – mysterious, like Ireland.

## DAY 6, SUNDAY, JUNE 2ND

This is a week-day, of course, but Koby doesn't have to leave early, since it is his day for attending the Technion in Haifa, where he both studies and teaches. He took me down to the bus station, to catch the 11.00 bus to Jerusalem, *via* Petah Tikva and Lod. I had fixed with John Glucker to meet him, if at all, at the bus station in Jerusalem at 4.00.

I shared a taxi with a pleasant, elderly lady journalist to Mt. Scopus and checked in to Bêt Maiersdorf. Things look even more splendid up there now,[198] and the reason is that a whole new Humanities Faculty block has been built adjacent to the Faculty Club, on very modern lines – without a right angle in the whole complex. I wandered up there, to see if I could find the Classics Department, and actually came upon Abraham

---

198    Sc. than back in 1981, when I visited it previously; see p. 93 above.

Wasserstein,[199] who was most hospitable, invited me to dinner tomorrow, and drove me down to the bus station, where I had agreed to meet John Glucker, if he actually turned up. I waited duly, and he did not turn up (in fact so badly was he limping after his fall that he hardly could have), so I then walked across to the Hilton, just opposite, and, after waiting a little while, and buying a present for the Scolnicovs, who are having me to dinner, I took a taxi over to the Academy of Sciences.

There I was entertained to tea by the Secretary, Nathan Rotenstreich, a Kantian philosopher, and Urbach the President, and a number of others, and at 6.15 I delivered another edition of the much-travelled "Female Principles in Platonism'. It is hard to say whether it went down well or not – Samuel liked it, as did Yehoshua Amir, who gallantly turned up, but the others were non-Classicists. Pines[200] was apparently there, Samuel said, but I missed him.

Dinner with the Scolnicovs was very enjoyable. They are still in the same flat, though they are about to move to a house. His wife Hanna is very pleasant. I had forgotten that Samuel is Brazilian by birth. He has also taught himself good Italian, and is well in with a coven of Platonists in Catania led by Francisco Romano.[201] We planned a possible visit by me next winter or early spring to do a seminar on the *Parmenides,* but that is all very optimistic, I think.

## DAY 7, MONDAY, JUNE 3RD

I was duly collected by my tour coach from the Faculty Club at

---

199     Abraham Wasserstein (1921-1995) had actually taught in the University of Leicester for a number of years, before coming to Jerusalem. He was Professor of Classics in Jerusalem from 1969 to 1989. He was a most widely learned and entertaining man. His son David was teaching in U.C.D. at the time.

200     Shlomo Pines (1908 – 1990) was an Israeli scholar of Jewish and Islamic philosophy, best known for his English translation of Maimonides' *Guide to the Perplexed.* He was a professor in the department of Jewish Thought and of Philosophy in the Hebrew University.

201     I had a number of pleasant visits to Catania, in northern Sicily, in later years, at Romano's invitation.

7.45 am for a day trip to Masada – armed with a water bottle lent by the Scolnicovs, which actually proved essential. We called into the bus depot opposite the Jaffa Gate, and then headed off on our drive down to the Dead Sea, along past Qumran and Ein Gedi, until the splendid bulk of Masada rose up to the right. The Dead Sea is drying up, so far as I can see, as a result of irrigation works. They plan ultimately to drive a pipeline in from the Mediterranean, and generate electric power in the process, but at the present they are too broke.

Fortunately, at Masada there is now a funicular to the top – although one *could* walk, in 120° heat! The tour was well conducted, but about all one could take in that heat. Fortunately, we were not invited to explore the lower levels of Herod's palace, interesting though that would doubtless have been! We saw the bath-house and the synagogue. Quite a lot has been reconstructed – enough to give the idea. Water is piped now to the top, and we simply poured it over ourselves at intervals. It dried in minutes. We inspected the still-impressive Roman siege-works – what pig-headedness impelled them to besiege the place for two years? Why not just *leave* them there? But that's the Romans for you!

Anyhow, we drove back *via* a spa on the Dead Sea. I got in and floated a bit, but it is really rather foul. I largely ruined my best black shoes by using them to walk down to the water's edge – too hot for bare feet! Then we went to the oasis of Ein Gedi, made famous by David. We walked up to the waterfall, and plunged under that. It is now a nature reserve, and we were warned to beware of leopards, but they were far too smart to appear!

We got back to Jerusalem before 6.00 pm – I was dropped off at Maiersdorf on the way – coming in on a back road. Wasserstein kindly collected me, and drove me to his house. Dinner was very pleasant, and included the Wigoders, originally from Dublin, and the Wassersteins' son Bernard, an historian at Brandeis. All the sons are professors, in fact! A typical Jewish intellectual scenario. Wasserstein himself is a most courtly old man. I really must entertain his son when I get home.

# 10: EXPEDITION TO AIX-EN-PROVENCE

## AUGUST, 1986

*This was a family holiday, to meet up with old friends from Berkeley, now in Cambridge, Peter and Elizabeth Garnsey, and their three children, Monica, Julian and Silvia. Peter was (and still is) a distinguished authority on Roman History, and Elizabeth a sociologist. They had taken a house in Aix for the summer, and had secured a flat for us nearby. Jean's contributions, being less on this occasion, are in italics.*

### DAY 1, THURSDAY, AUGUST 7TH

We are starting ominously – the boat is delayed by gales, and won't sail from Rosslare to Le Havre until 7.30pm, rather than 5.00 pm (this announced at 11.00 am). If so, that would not be too bad, but it may be worse.

*10.00 pm:* Now safely on board. The boat actually left at 8.45, having promised 8.30, which I suppose is not too bad. It only got in at 6.45 am. We drove down very comfortably, stopping in Enniscorthy for 'tea' – actually very vile coffee, and an OK pastry. The Mouse[202] had a gross ice-cream, which had to be collapsed into a bowl. Once in Rosslare, we walked along the cliffs, then had drinks in the hotel (quite pleasant), and then joined the queue.

Eileen had fixed us up with a two-berth cabin, which is just not quite enough. I wasn't thinking – or rather, I *thought* it was a four-berth. We are having to sleep Mouse head to tail, which

---

202     Our daughter Ruth was just on the eve of her fourth birthday (August 10th).

may not work. There is a bit of a swell, but the wind has certainly dropped. It will probably now clear up beautifully in Ireland – indeed, I hope for Grimes'[203] and the sailors' sake it does.


## DAY 2, FRIDAY, AUGUST 8TH

We had a pretty good night, despite top-and-tailing with the Mouse. Mouse moved up to Mummy at 4.30 or so, and we carried on till 8.15. Then up, and had a leisurely breakfast, gazing out to sea. At about 9.30, we emerged into blue skies, a situation we have almost forgotten the existence of!

*8.00 pm:* Now at a very pleasant Relais Routier, laid out as an old Normandy farmhouse, about 50 km down the road. We have settled down to the 45fr menu, of rillettes (pork paté), fish, and a desert (*tarte*). The total came to 132 fr., with wine and service and all. Mouse immediately made friends with a French family, and conned me into buying Plasticine ( 7fr.). We have also paid two péages, 6.50 and 7 fr. respectively.

*11.00 pm:* We decided to turn off at Versailles, after some debate. Drove into town, and found a little hotel in a side street, the Hotel Richaud (in the rue Richaud), which seemed all right. It cost 220 fr. for the night, though – almost Irish prices! – but we *are* in Versailles, after all. Tried to phone Peter and Elizabeth, but the phone doesn't seem to work. The air already feels much warmer, but I still have a stiff back from disrobing rather prematurely on the boat, where we had a good bit of sun.


## DAY 3, SATURDAY, AUGUST 9TH

*Versailles, 9. 15 am:* At a little café just off the Marché Notre Dame, having a café au lait and croissants – 33.25 fr. We spent a rather confused night – first all three in the bed, then Mummy on the floor, then Mouse on the floor, and Mummy back in the bed – this after Mouse flailed all over the bed, rooting me in the back, and ending up upside-down, sucking her thumb. Quite hot.

---

203    My brother-in-law Anthony Gore-Grimes, with whom I fairly regularly sailed, out of Howth. There would have been a major regatta this weekend.

Not much sleep got. Overcast when we got up, but still warm.

We went up to the Palace after breakfast, just to look around. In fact, there were enormous queues to get inside, so we just strolled around the gardens – a fantastic monstrosity, certainly, to which we must return. Queuing at one of the entrances, we came upon Charles Kannengiesser,[204] returning to Versailles after thirty years – a curious chance. He is on sabbatical in Paris for this semester.

Then we drove out to find the freeway, deciding to skirt Paris, and catch the A6 further down. We managed to achieve this by starting on the Autoroute to Chartres and diving off below Orsay. On the A6, we ran first into a traffic jam owing to roadworks, but once past that made very good time, averaging 80 mph to Lyons, which we reached about 5.30, after various stops. We phoned P and E, and told them to expect us late tonight.

*8.30 pm:* Sitting in the Restaurant Pigraillet, situated on a hill above Orange. This constitutes an *adventure* (which we may regret), which compensates for an otherwise rather boring day on the freeway (though a pleasant *picque-nique* at an *Aire*). We drove into Orange, found it totally crowded, and wandered up a steep hill, on the top of which we found this restaurant, down a lane. It has a swimming-pool, where Mouse and I disported ourselves, J drinking an *Amour Sunrise* by the poolside (Tequila and Cointreau), and we are sitting out under an awning in the warm Mediterranean night. I have declared this to be J's *birthday dinner* – where would one get such another in Ireland for 110 fr.?

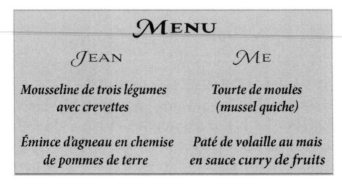

### MENU

| JEAN | ME |
|---|---|
| *Mousseline de trois légumes avec crevettes* | *Tourte de moules (mussel quiche)* |
| *Émince d'agneau en chemise de pommes de terre* | *Paté de volaille au mais en sauce curry de fruits* |

---

204    Charles Kannengiesser (1926-2018), of Austrian origin, was a professor of Patristics at the University of Notre Dame, and author of a number of important books on the subject. I had met him there on a number of occasions.

– but a bald description cannot do justice. What we have here is food as an art-form (e.g. a simple grilled tomato, but with slices of courgette inserted.)

We will have to leave the rest of Orange – the triumphal arch, the Roman theatre – for some other occasion. *Not* on a Saturday night, anyhow! Dinner lasted till almost 10.15, so we are pushing things to get to Aix before midnight.

We actually made the distance in about an hour, but the problem began when we got off the freeway. We couldn't make out where we were. Finally we found a street name, located it on the map, and drove through the centre of town, and found P and E's about midnight. The children had actually put up a Dillon-welcoming notice, which helped. Peter gallantly made a cup of tea, and then drove us in convoy over to our flat. The flat was in good shape, and we flopped into bed about 1.30 am, the Mouse continuing lively to the last. (She had eaten virtually no dinner, but involved herself, with another little boy, in a game of boules by the pool.)

## DAY 4, SUNDAY, AUGUST 10TH (MOUSEY BIRTHDAY)

Up not very early, found some tea, and ate our stale croissants. I went down the rue d'Italie, but failed to find a milk shop open – lots of others open, though. Our area is fairly grotty, in a rather French provincial way – the Cours Gambetta is hardly high-class, but very convenient for the centre of town, and the complex of apartment blocks is very pleasant. We are on a ground floor, which means things are cooler. There is a rather miaowy Siamese-type cat in the vicinity.

In the late morning, the Garnseys came down to collect us, and we all went up to visit the Jesuit Conference Centre that Peter had discovered, La Baume, on the south of the city, past the Cité Universitaire. There is a useful library, mainly patristic and theological, which is our pretext for being there, and an excellent swimming pool, which is our real reason for being there. Since the temperature must be in the 90s, this is a great boon. I found in the library the *Sources Chrétiennes* and various other useful items, and will have lots of things to do, if I get a chance.

*We mainly sat around the Garnseys' lovely garden in the afternoon and were entertained to a concert by all the children. Luckily we brought Ruth's violin, because Silvia is also learning Suzuki. Julian played the clarinet, Monica the piano, Ruth and Silvia violins, and Peter piano. It was lovely, and Ruth was quite proud of herself.*

(Elizabeth had got Mouse a cake, which we much enjoyed!).


## DAY 5, MONDAY, AUGUST 11<sup>TH</sup> (JULIAN'S BIRTHDAY)

It was decided to go to the seaside for Julian's birthday, if we could get ourselves organised. Peter was doubtful, as he had to renew the car, but in fact all was under way by about 11.20 (early for an *afternoon* expedition), and we headed off in convoy down the autoroute to Cassis, a little fishing port on the coast. It is lovely, but fashionable and crowded. We had a hamburger and chips on the seafront, and then decided to take a trip, with a cheerful bandit of a boatman, whom Elizabeth had met earlier, on a conference in May, to see the *calanques,* the remarkable series of fjords on the coast between Cassis and Marseilles, which is actually very precipitous, except for these inlets. He let us off at the Calanque d'En-Vau, where we had to scramble along a very narrow cliff path to get down to the beach, but managed it, and spent a couple of pleasant hours bathing and sunning ourselves (along, it must be said, with a load of others, many from yachts moored in the cove), before he came back for us. There was a stiff *mistral* blowing, which made the ride quite lively. Mouse enjoyed it all vastly, though she hid under a towel from the spray.

Back home by about 5.30, and then up to La Bencista (Garnseys' place) for dinner – not, however, before Mouse had almost electrocuted herself on an electrical connection to the hair dryer, with which she had been fiddling. So she now knows about electric shocks!

Back quite late to bed. We are having problems sleeping, with the heat – and problems with where to put the cot. There was quite a thunderstorm in the middle of the night, but it didn't wake the Mouse.

## DAY 6, TUESDAY, AUGUST 12<sup>TH</sup>

Breakfast on the terrace. Some washing – no washing machine in evidence – and then out to explore the town, and visit the Musée Granet, which houses the few Cézannes which survive in his home town of Aix. They are pretty miserable, it must be said, and badly framed to boot. There is nothing much else of note in the museum (though the finds from Roman and Gallic excavations around town are here), but there is a good exhibition of a Dutch artist, Van Velde.[205] (Léveau, by the way, is the Director of Archaeology for Provence, which is a rather nice job.)

We went down the Cours Mirabeau – the main drag of town – and bought some postcards and a map, and then a nice pair of shoes and matching top for Mousey – a present from Mar,[206] who had provided money for this before we left. They were on *solde*!

After lunch (back at the flat), we decided to go exploring up the mountains behind the town, to find a nice walk. We went up beyond Vauvenargues, trying to find a walk up Mont St. Victoire. (In Vauvenargues, we approached a fine château at the edge of town, to see what gave, and found a notice saying it was private, and that *the Museum was in Paris*. Only later, when I consulted the Blue Guide, did we find that it was where Picasso had lived during the latter part of his life, and where he died. We found a little path leading up through a wood along a ravine, and followed it up for a while, the Mouse in flying form,

---

205     Bram (Abraham Gerardus) van Velde (1895 – 1981) was a Dutch painter known for an intensely coloured and geometric semi-representational painting style related to Tachisme and Lyrical Abstraction. He is often seen as a member of the School of Paris, but his work resides somewhere between expressionism and surrealism, and evolved in the 1960s into an expressive abstract art. His paintings from the 1950s are similar to the contemporary work of Matisse, Picasso and the abstract expressionist Adolph Gottlieb. He was championed by a number of French-speaking writers, including Samuel Beckett and the poet André du Bouchet.

206     That is to say, her grandmother, my mother.

organising games and tyrannising generally. We found a bush full of butterflies (mainly reddish-brown with black spots, but one black and white one), but no other wildlife. Still, it was a delightful walk.

On the way back, we turned aside to visit a place called Les Écuries de l'Aube, which turned out to be a riding stables with restaurant and swimming pool, set very pleasantly around pines on a ridge. We had a swim, wherein Mouse suddenly began to *swim*, and swam ultimately the length of the pool. We must return to this place (though the dinner would be rather expensive, I think).

Dinner once again with Garnseys, who had gone over to visit some Canadians who were in a house they had been offered which has a pool. It apparently has some disadvantages, though – including a lot of watering to be done!

### DAY 7, WEDNESDAY, AUGUST 13^TH

This morning J and Elizabeth went off in search of a market, leaving me with Mouse and Sivley.[207] They messed about for a while, and then I brought them downtown for an ice-cream, then they messed about some more. I managed to do a *little* Dexippus;[208] *not* a very stimulating morning. The weather continues beautiful, of course, and there is an awful lot of Provence out there waiting to be viewed.

*Elizabeth, Monica, Julian and I went to shop in the town. We found a very picturesque market selling all sorts of fruits and vegetables, and especially herbs. I bought some lavender, which is one of the main herbs grown here. We also visited the cathedral, which had a wonderful dragon-like creature carved in stone. We had coffee at a nice café in the square opposite the main post office.*

In the afternoon, the ladies returned, and we went up to Garnseys' for a leisurely lunch. Then there was a *concert des enfants,* and then off to La Baume for a leisurely swim. First, though, Peter and I went to the library to do our token piece of

---

207     This is Mouse's version of the name of the Garnsey's daughter, Silvia.

208     I was currently engaged in a translation, with commentary, of Dexippus' *Commentary on Aristotle's Categories.*

work. I had barely read a page of Origen's *Commentary on St. John's Gospel*, XIX, when the door opened and in walked an ancient figure who turned out to be Édouard des Places.[209] He seemed delighted to come upon me – and upon Peter – and talked at us for almost an hour non-stop, expressing views on many matters – including a regret that French classical scholars do not write big general books any more (true?). Only at almost 6.00 pm did we get down to a bathe. But it was delightful to meet the old boy. He is here for a week or so, standing in for the librarian, Père Morel. Most of their books, he lamented, were taken off to Chantilly.

Then back to Garnseys' for dinner, this time for quite a good lamb stew. I provided a bottle of local rosé, *Les Bastides,* which was not bad. We are trying to work our way through the local wines.

## DAY 8, THURSDAY, AUGUST 14ᵀᴴ

Today we decided to visit the Camargue, after some debate. P and E were not equal to this excitement, so we took Monica and Julian overnight, and set out with them at 8.30 next morning. In fact it only took less than an hour to get to Arles, on the freeway (and near-freeway). We skirted Arles (which I intend to reserve for another day), and headed down into the Camargue. It is fairly dismal scenery in itself, but certainly a notable area. We stopped first at a Musée Camarguaise, which looked interesting, but would have involved a walk of a couple of miles in 100° heat through representative bits of Camargue landscape, so we passed it up, in favour of an ornithological musée down the road, which was more rewarding. Initially, all the birds were in cages, including some splendid owls (notably an Eagle Owl, of enormous dimensions), and there were birds loose in lagoons – ducks, gulls, cormorants, pelicans, storks,

---

209    Édouard des Places SJ (1900-2000) was a French classical philologist, and a distinguished authority on both late antique philosophy and patristics. He was by now fully 86 years of age.

and *flamingoes*! Again, there was more, but our smaller persons were giving up. It was certainly very hot.

We then drove on, stopping at one small herd of horses (grey, with the foals a dark brownish grey), towards Les Saintes Maries de la Mer. On the way, we passed innumerable riding stables, offering rides into the Camargue – something else we couldn't face in the heat, and with so many non-riders. The camarguais ranch is called a *mas,* whatever that means, and most of them seem to rely on giving rides to tourists, at least to some extent.

The Holy Maries-by-Sea were an appalling revelation – Blackpool, or Clacton-on-Sea, or Bray! Of course, this was the most awful time of year. In May it is given over to the gypsies, it seems, who have a pilgrimage there, in honour of the two Maries – Magdalene and the Mother of the Lord – who landed there some time after the Great Showdown. All the marks of mass proletarian relaxation – swings and roundabouts, ice-cream vendors, mums and dads sweating and bewildered, plodding from place to place, lots of music and loud-speakers – and, above all, *bodies*. So we had an ice-cream, and drove out of town, in search of a boat which would give us a view of the Camargue. We found a nice, not *too* crowded beach, had a pleasant bathe, and then found a little place for a snack – surrounded by horses, including one feisty little miniature stallion. We feel sorry for the ones left standing in the sun with their saddles on.

The boat trip on the *Tiki III* was a bit of a rip-off. All we did was cruise up the Petit Rhône for a mile or so, feed some rather bored horses and bulls with hay, view a good number of wild tourists (*dindons sauvages*), doing various exciting things like fishing or snoozing under umbrellas – and sail back again. And that cost 42 fr. a head (mice 21fr.).

After our boat ride we drove back to the Holy Maries to change some money, and so home *via* a Géant Casino outside Salou, where the prices are remarkable – Gordon's Gin for 60 fr., a three-pack of red wine (which turned out very passable) for 23 fr. The drink is actually cheaper than the duty-free, as has been said.

On the way home, we ran into very heavy traffic. Only when we got home did we realise that tomorrow is the Feast of the Assumption, a major public holiday here, as it is in the rest of the Mediterranean region.

Dinner at La Bencista, and so to bed.

## DAY 9, FRIDAY, AUGUST 15TH

We had a notion to go off to find the Cathedral, but just went to La Baume instead. Peter and I made a feeble effort to do something in the library, then joined the family at the pool. I am trying to translate some Dexippus, read Dover, *Greek Popular Morality, Scarlet and Black* by Stendhal, and *Germinal* by Zola.

After a *very* leisurely lunch (until about 4.00), and a *Concert des Enfants*, we set off to visit the Cusacks[210] in Grasse (I should say that last night I decided to phone them, found them at home, and they urged us to come over today for dinner, and stay the night). We set off down the Autoroute about 5.00, and reached the Adrets turn-off about 6.00 – a very expensive drive: 49 fr. from Aix to Fréjus, essentially. Up past a beautiful lake, which is swarming with French for the holiday, and onto the Draguignon-Grasse road, as far as the village of Spéracèdes, where we found a most idyllic situation. Roy and Jackie Cusack live down at the end of a little lane, in an old (re-built) stone house, looking over a valley – and indeed looking all the way down to Cannes, and on clear days all the way to Corsica, a truly splendid panorama!

They live in a sort of family group of six houses, all children or relatives of Ralph Cusack, who bought the place back in 1954, and lived there till he died in 1965. When he arrived, there were only ten houses to be seen in the whole valley. Now it is

---

210    This was Roy Cusack, who was the son of Ralph Cusack (1912-1965), a rather notable character in Irish society of the '40s and '50s (see his memoir, *Cadenza* [Hamish Hamilton: London, 1958]), who had been born and lived in our home, Drumnigh House, Portmarnock, before us. Roy had just driven up one day, a year or so previous to this, and introduced himself, and we kept in touch subsequently.

dotted with thousands of them, the result of a great population movement to the south of the well-to-do. Roy is a partner in an obviously successful building and decorating cooperative, and they are both active in the cooperative movement, Jackie having to make frequent visits to Marseilles as a delegate.

Before dinner, which did not take place till about 9.30, we had a swim in the pool of his brother's house (currently rented to some Americans, who are out), and then took a little tour of the estate, climbing up the hill a bit to pick some grapes for dinner (they have a problem with *badgers* eating the grapes!). Roy's sister and her husband have a house just behind them, which is now vacant, since they have had to move to Paris, so we have set our eye on that!

Supper was pleasant, consisting of a thick soup (*pistou*), and a mushroom omelette, with grapes and cheese to follow – almost all the produce of the place. It reminded me rather of the Sherrard household in Limni. The analogy became closer when we learned that Jackie has gone into publishing (like Denise), and has produced, first a history of Spéracèdes, and now a charming cookbook entitled *My Provençal Kitchen,* of which she presented J. a copy. It is delightfully chatty and easy to follow.

Mouse finally went to sleep on a sofa, and we retired to our comfortable loft beside the kitchen, the room of their son Patrick.


## DAY 10, SATURDAY, AUGUST 16<sup>TH</sup>

Very hot, but a more comfortable bed than in the flat, so we did not wake up with sore backs, as we have been doing. Had a pleasant, leisurely breakfast, during which Jackie produced an unfinished autobiography of Ralph Cusack, with a great deal in it about Drumnigh – a great description of a cook pouring a pot of starch over his mother in what was the Laundry (our woodshed). I think it must be published, and offered to introduce it to Michael Gill. She would actually like to publish it herself, and start a subscription. They know Sam Beckett – an old friend of Ralph's

– and he might help with a message or introduction. Then the Boydells[211] might write an introduction as well.

After breakfast, we said goodbye, with many expressions of thanks, and drove off to visit Grasse. Grasse is quite a charming old town, mainly devoted to the making of perfume and candied fruits. We began by visiting a famous perfumery, Fragonard, which was quite interesting, and J bought some gifts. Then we strolled around the streets of the old town, Mouse in buggy, until about 11.30. It was cool in the narrow streets, but fairly broiling on the road. We set off to drive the upland route back to Aix, *via* Draguignon. Stopped for lunch at a pleasant little restaurant just outside the little town of Lorgues, where we also bought a pottery garlic holder. Then we drove down to the Cistercian monastery of Le Thoronet, but when we got there we decided we weren't prepared to pay 16 fr. a head to get in, so we drove on till we found a lake, the Lac de Carcés, which seemed inviting. No one was swimming in it, though some were fishing, and when we climbed down it was somewhat green and cloudy, but we plunged in anyhow, and had a good time. We still don't know what, if any, the problem was, and we're not sure we want to.

We got back around 6.30, rather exhausted, and stayed in the flat.

## DAY 11, SUNDAY, AUGUST 17TH

This morning we decided to drive round and go to the Cathedral for Mass, if there happened to be one. We actually found one in progress at 10.30, and stayed for that. An elderly priest gave us a sermon about persecution and the Église de Silence – à propos of what I don't know. It is an interesting old church (from Roman times on – still a Roman baptistery), and a very charming cloister attached.

On the way back, we stopped in a Casino, using an Access card, since we were all out of money. Then over to La Baume

---

211    That is, Brian Boydell, Professor of Music in Trinity College, and his wife, later neighbours of ours in Howth. They had quite a number of Ralph Cusack's paintings, as I recall.

for a swim, and up to La Bencista for lunch. The ladies went off to another open-air market, and Peter and I sat around and read. Peter is trying to finish off his book for Duckworth.[212] I am mainly reading Stendhal, to the neglect of Dexippus. Stendhal entertains me, but he is not the equal of Saul Bellow.

Peter proposed that tomorrow we make an expedition to Marseilles, and go out to the Château d'If – and possibly take a bouillabaisse! That sounds a good idea.

### DAY 12, MONDAY, AUGUST 18TH

This morning we set out by 10.30 to drive to Marseilles – actually only about half-an-hour down the Autoroute. People are said to commute there from Aix. An unremarkable drive, but the freeway leaves one almost all the way into the Old Port, which is handy. We parked opposite the Hotel de Ville, and found the family Garnsey bearing down on us almost immediately. We checked out the boats, and found one leaving at 12.00, which we boarded.

The Château d'If is certainly impressive, in the style of Alcatraz,[213] but not exactly cosy. It commands a fine view of the Bay of Marseilles. Many distinguished people were imprisoned here in the 18th cent., including 'The Man in the Iron Mask', and a lot of Protestants, who are duly commemorated. There are two other islands adjacent, on one of which there is now an elaborate yacht harbour and hotel complex, as far as I could see.

Back in Marseilles, we decided to look for lunch, and were subjected to great hard sell by an old bandit of a woman – who had an *inside* restaurant, however, and we wanted to sit out. First, she claimed they were all shut, but then sent us round the

---

212    Not sure now what this was. Peter's only book for Duckworth that I know of was *The Roman Empire,* eventually published, with Richard Saller, in 1996.

213    The prison island which dominates San Francisco Bay, as one drives across the Bay Bridge.

corner, where there were rows upon rows of them. We picked one which *said* it took credit cards, and offered a menu of 79 fr. I chose their *special* bouillabaisse, at 73 fr. The whole thing was very second-rate. Bouillabaisse is a dangerous thing – it can mean *anything*. Mine had four mussels, a head of the ugliest-looking fish I have ever set eyes on, a large goldfish *in toto*, and a piece of some substantial fish (perhaps *lotte*). It was a 3-star rip-off. The wine was good, though – a white of Cassis (Domaine de Fontblanche, I think) – but we had asked for the house wine. J had a *loup*, but it was pretty tasteless. Our lunch cost 250 fr., and was not one of our prouder moments. Later I recalled that we had the names of two superb restaurants in my guide-book, though they might have been very expensive. At the end of all, they *wouldn't* take the credit card, so we had to pay cash.

After this distinguished meal, we went off, in the burning heat, to discover some antiquities. We got as far as the excavations of the old Greco-Roman port, which has now been laid out as quite a nice little park, with the tiny harbour in the centre. It is remarkable how small it appears to have been. The museum which contained a Roman boat was closed, and we were now exhausted by the heat, so we staggered along the north *quai* for a while to where we were parked, then stopped in a café for a drink, and then off home.

We managed a while at La Baume in the evening before dinner.


DAY 13, TUESDAY, AUGUST 19<sup>TH</sup>

Today very little was done. La Baume in the morning. Peter and I scouted out Entremont and the Atélier Cézanne in the afternoon, but found both shut (*Mardi,* of course!). In the late afternoon, we went off for a walk and a picnic in the foothills of Mt. Ste. Victoire, beyond Le Tholonet. A very pleasant nature walk, and a little stream (very cold) in which Sivley, Juligan,[214] and the Mouse plashed and played (mainly floating sticks under a bridge).

---

214    Mouse's version of 'Julian'.

Peter and I and Monica and Julian then walked across a meadow towards the rocks, and found ourselves in the middle of an army firing range (we hoped inactive), with bunkers and so on. Then we noticed what seemed to be lots of little white flowers on the plants in the meadow. When we investigated, we found that they were thousands of tiny snails – presumably in desperation at the drought – looking for dew on the plants. But they were all dead. Rather sad.

Afterwards we had a frugal supper, and went home. After dinner, we took a walk down to the Cours Mirabeau, and had a coffee and *pastis*.


## DAY 14, WEDNESDAY, AUGUST 20TH

We failed to rouse P and E, but decided nonetheless to do a tour of Arles and Les Baux, since they are not really very far away. J was very tired at first, so I drove. We parked in a parking very convenient to the Old Town, and visited the Theatre and the Amphitheatre, the Church of St. Trophime, and walked down to the Rhône. No museums or frills, because J was very exhausted. Arles is certainly very pleasant, though not more so than Aix, apart from the monuments and the river, but the Amphitheatre is much messed about by being used for shows – wooden erections over the old stone seats, and so on. The Theatre is also in use, but the surface of it is much better preserved – used by a better class of person, no doubt!

So we drove on to Les Baux, hoping not to be totally exhausted, and found the place completely enchanting. It is an old fortified village perched on a hill, under its (now ruined) castle, beautifully preserved, or rather restored, under the inspiration of such people as Frédéric Mistral[215] and Louis Jou, around the

---

215     Joseph Étienne Frédéric Mistral (1830 – 1914) was a French writer of *Occitan literature* and *lexicographer* of the *Provençal* form of the language. He received the *1904 Nobel Prize in Literature* in recognition of the fresh originality and true inspiration of his poetic production, which faithfully reflects the natural scenery and native spirit of his people, and, in addition, his significant work as a *Provençal* philologist». Mistral was

turn of the century. The Seigneurs de Baux were a rough and riotous lot, controlling at various points most of Provence, and even further afield, and finally had to be suppressed, but it was a great pity to demolish their splendid fortress, some of it built into the solid rock. The views of the surrounding countryside are magnificent. We had quite a pleasant lunch of crêpes and salad, and made our tour, much revived.

We set off home in mid-afternoon, and called into the Géant Casino in Salous along the way, where we bought, among other things, a dozen bottles of the local red plonk, at about 80p. a bottle. We had bought a three-pack of it earlier, and found it very drinkable. We had supper when we got back, and then Garnseys came down for coffee and ice-cream and a little walk around the town – down to the Dolphin Fountain and around.

## DAY 15, THURSDAY, AUGUST 21ST

This morning, P and E, perhaps feeling the need to do *something*, proposed another visit to the seaside, this time to Le Ciotat, or, if that proved too nasty, the next place, Les Lecques. We followed them at an interval of an hour, and found them on the beach at Le Ciotat. The sun was warm, and the beach not unpleasant, but the sea was extraordinarily *cold*, rather like Dublin.

They wanted to go on and try the next beach, but we felt we should take just so much sun, and stayed on where we were for a bit (buying the Mouse a rather superfluous bucket and spade), and then drove up into the mountains, where we found a lovely little village called Cayreste (originally the Greek settlement of Kitharistia), which indeed seemed strangely like a little Greek village. I was rather hoping to find a lovely little restaurant which I could not resist, serving *bouillabaisse,* but, perhaps fortunately,

---

a founding member of the *Félibrige* and member of the *Académie de Marseille.*

none such appeared. So we drove back home, by a pleasant mountain road, avoiding the Autoroute.

After lunch on the patio, we drove up to La Bencista, had a cup of tea, and then P and E and I drove down town to visit the University Bookstore. In fact, I bought a book on *Le Provence de Cézanne* and a honey dispenser (12 fr.). No Classical books worth a damn in the bookstore.

Meanwhile, J and the small ladies had gone up the road and found a rather lovely hotel with tennis and piscine, with rooms from 220 fr. a night (comparing favourably to most Irish hotels). We went up after dinner (of rolled breast of turkey – very good!), and had a lemonade by the pool.

J began the cleaning of the flat.


### DAY 16, FRIDAY, AUGUST 22<sup>ND</sup>

Today was a day of cleaning. I walked down to do some shopping, including a present (of teas and jams) for the Léveaus. Then off to La Baume for a last visit around 11.30. Peter and I did our bit in the library (I read three or four articles by Des Places), then took a final swim. There was amusement because Mouse jumped in by mistake without her water-wings, and survived, giggling (she is now swimming confidently, like a waterbug, *with* the wings).

I bought *Le Figaro* yesterday (to P and E's disapproval, as it is too right-wing), and it reported that the temperature in Dublin is 12°. What is happening to us?

Back to La Bencista for a copious lunch, and then down the hill for more cleaning. After much humming and hawing, P and E agreed to go out for a final dinner tonight. We agreed on a place where we could sit out, and the children could run about. We found the perfect place in the old Roman Forum – at the Restaurant du Forum, indeed! We ordered from the menu, not a fixed menu, which was a better idea, as we had a superb set of meals, which put everyone in excellent humour. I had a very good *confit de canard,* with pears and minced mushrooms, and a marvellous chocolate concoction to follow. Wine good, too. All came to a little over £12 a head.

Back to the flat, then, and said goodbye, since they are off to the airport at crack of dawn tomorrow. We undertook to get together, if possible, in California next year. Elizabeth was keen on Stanford, but we might actually need to be in Berkeley to oversee our transfer of house.[216]

## DAY 17, SATURDAY, AUGUST 23RD

Washed up, and J set about cleaning the kitchen. Mouse and I were banished down the town to buy a paper, and by 10.00 all was ready. We drove round to some Algerians in the Rue Jaubert to leave the key, and then out by the Rue d'Italie and Cours Gambetta to the Autoroute by 10.30.

Started off well, but various bits of congestion prevented us from getting to Lyons for lunch (must be another big weekend in the French holiday calendar!). We actually got off the freeway for a bit between Mâcon and Tournus, which was not bad, but we gave up rather than face Châlon.

Then I got the notion that we might dodge off, and connect up with the Loire, and proceed *via* Orléans and Chartres, rather than just head for Nemours, which was our alternative, This started off well, but disintegrated progressively. We turned off at Avallon, which is a lovely town, perched above the valley of the river Cousin, with old walls still in place. We drove down a little side-road in the direction of Vézelay, and suddenly found ourselves at an old inn by a mill, which we realised we had looked at before, on our way back from Italy. This was a great re-discovery, and we probably should have stopped right there – an excellent establishment, most romantic wooded walks by the river, and so on – but we felt it was too early, and pressed on. Vézelay was also beautiful, but after that we got into the valley of the Loire, and things became flatter and duller, and we became hungry and cranky. The ambition to get to Sully faded, and we ended up dining in a horrible little hotel in an

---

216     I no longer have any idea what this could refer to. We had sold our Berkeley house back in 1980, and I had no arrangements to return to California.

223

undistinguished town called Bonny sur Loire. They had no room (perhaps fortunately) and their dinner was a disgrace. I had a *coq au vin,* which may or may not have been an old rabbit (with some chicken skin thrown in?). It was mainly bone, in thick brown sauce, and I think may even have included the *head.* I really should have made a scene, but I'm not accustomed to that, and was so tired than I couldn't think in French anyhow. J's veal was less awful, but not good. Mouse's steak and chips was the best bet. We left *no* tip.

Anyhow, we drove on until we found a sort of motel, which was itself full, but kindly phoned on to its next incarnation, which was a Sanotel in Gien, on the Loire. This was rather expensive (260 fr.), but we were not in a mood to look further. It was very clean and efficient and American – on the river, looking across to the château. A curious feature of the evening was a vast plague of moths, which were besetting the lights at the front door.


## DAY 18, SUNDAY, AUGUST 24<sup>TH</sup>

There was a lot of ground to cover today, since we were a bit behindhand. The château at Gien has a hunting museum and looks interesting, but we decided to drive to Sully – not before J bought a nice piece of faience, though, which is a product of Gien.

Then we drove on to Sully, just on the south bank of the river, where two nice little inns had been recommended. We didn't actually find either of them, but looked at the fine old moated château. Then we drove on, past Orléans, to find the autoroute to Chartres. This we did, and followed it for about 20 miles, cutting off then at Janville for Chartres. We made very good time, but just missed a High Mass at the cathedral. There is plainly some sort of patriotic commemoration today, since there were lots of old gents to be seen bearing banners – probably war or resistance veterans.

Chartres Cathedral is surely one of the wonders of the world. One could plainly spend years studying the details of the stained glass alone. We could only get a superficial impression. I like the way they keep it *as a church,* and do not charge for anything, though their expenses must be vast. They just request offerings, which we gave. We then looked round the streets surrounding the Cathedral for a lunch place, and found a little Breton crêperie where we had some reasonable crêpes, to the accompaniment of Irish music.

From Chartres, on to Verneuil, a beautiful little town, where we had a cup of coffee, and then, *via* Argentan, to Falaise, birthplace of William the Conqueror, where we viewed his dad's castle (Robert le Diable). There is a curious double loyalty, historically, in all this area, because they were the Duchy of Normandy, and were under English rule for so long. At this point, J swore she would look at no more monuments, and we were no longer early, so we headed on to Cherbourg, *via* Caen.

(I should mention that just before Argentan, and after Nonant-le-Pin, we came upon a splendid château close by the road, which was also plainly a stables. It gave guided tours, but the next one was not till 6.00 pm, so we had to leave it. Its name was Le Pin au Haras. Perhaps the Aga Khan owns it?)

The weather actually cheered up as we approached Cherbourg, and we boarded in good time, and left, on the dot of 21.00, in bright sunshine. (The weather in Chartres had actually been rather grim – windy and cold, with showers.)


DAY 19, MONDAY, AUGUST 25<sup>TH</sup>

The day dawned grim and overcast, but still not windy. Mouse had made friends last night with a little girl called Joanne, whose parents, Des and Siobhan Moran, of Sligo, we then got to know. He is a very pleasant fellow, a doctor, with historical and political interests (he actually drove down to Uncle James' funeral),[217] and his wife is into disabled riding. He is a member of Sligo Chamber of Commerce, and was most interesting about recent visits there of C.J. Haughey and Garret Fitzgerald in turn, where he found CJ talking excellent sense, and Garret quite up in the

217    James Dillon had died, in Ballaghaderreen, on February 10<sup>th</sup>, 1986.

air, though he *likes* Garret. Garret promised them a hospital, which they don't need, instead of any really wealth-producing idea, like a fish-processing plant, for instance.

As we approached Ireland, a storm got up. We landed on time (2.00 pm), however, though in pouring rain, and the rain and the wind got steadily worse as we went on. We stopped for a snack at a nice little pub just beyond Wexford, and then pushed on, the weather getting wilder and wilder. We expected misery, but this was unbelievable. We finally reached Drumnigh, to find a large branch down across the avenue, and electricity gone. Fortunately, Peter[218] was home, so he and I used the crosscut on the branch, and got that clear.

And so the journey finally ended. We had in fact  got in just before the full force of Hurricane Charlie hit the country, leaving tremendous devastation.

---

218  My brother, Dom Christopher Dillon, O.S.B.

# 11: To Hawaii and Princeton

## NOVEMBER – DECEMBER, 1987

*The purpose of this trip was to attend a conference organised by the International Neoplatonic Society (of which I was a founder member) on the general theme of Neoplatonism and Jewish Studies. On the way back, I dropped into Princeton University, to visit an old friend, Michael Frede, and give a lecture.*

### DAY 1, FRIDAY, NOVEMBER 27<sup>TH</sup>

It is now about noon (GMT), and we are well out over the Atlantic on our way to Boston, on NW 49. Lunch is about to be served. The connections which Barbara of Atlas Travel fixed me up with are all a little tight, but all has gone well – so far! I am feeling more guilty than usual about departing now, both because of the emergency with Mum (though she was looking pretty good yesterday evening), since Jean is under stress, and because of leaving my charges for over a week when I am going to abandon them again next term. But as to that, I am in a rather rebarbative mood. There is a limit to what I am prepared to put up with in the way of increased work-loads and decreased facilities, and trying to put life into the department, all on my own. If I had a lively, dedicated team, we could do a lot, but, apart from Brian (and Karim, who is excellent),[219] nobody is really prepared (or, in Tom's case, able) to do a stroke extra. So I keep my options open, regretfully – and so these trips are *important*. I have various bits of reading to get through, in particular Lamberton's *Homer*, but I have started off by reading *The Irish Times* as it deserves to be

---

219    That is, Brian McGing, and Karim Arafat (who left us shortly after that, to take up a position in King's College, London).

read – which one does about twice a year, perhaps – and finding lots of interesting items.

*Now 3.00 pm (GMT).* I have just been watching a light-hearted, but rather crapulous, police film starring Richard Dreyfus and Robert De Niro, *Stakeout,* which for some reason has left me feeling rather sad and self-critical. I see myself now as a bad husband and a bad father, and a rather irresponsible head of department. This jaunt, and the coming expedition to Princeton,[220] are beginning to look like self-indulgence at the expense of everyone else. I hope I cheer up. All I can say is that these expeditions have a purpose, which at least benefits the rest of the family ultimately – to maintain my international standing, such as it is. What I would fear most is losing that, and degenerating simply into a general drudge, at the mercy of the local authorities, with no outside contacts any more. If I lose contact with the cutting edge of my subject, I will become just a hollow shell, going through the motions of teaching things I am not much interested in – perhaps dabbling a little more in politics and journalism, but only dabbling. I would have *liked* to be a writer, and I would be prepared to go into politics seriously if any opportunity arose, but that would mean letting go of the only thing I'm any good at, and perhaps coming up with *nothing.*

But let us change the subject. I have got to remember to collect my Swiss Army knife in Boston – they relieved me of it in Gatwick, at a new sort of check – designed, I gather, to catch plastic devices as well as metal.

Now 5.20 pm Detroit time, and I have just boarded a plane for San Francisco. I don't think I've lost anything yet, but I feel as if I have been travelling for days. I hope the conference people appreciate the money I've saved them by undergoing all this trouble. I wonder if Katy[221] managed to contact the lady in

---

220    I was due to spend the coming Winter Semester of 1988 at the Institute of Advanced Studies in Princeton.

221    That is, our old friend from Berkeley days, Katy Mulvany, who, with her mother, Mildred Osmer (Mrs. O), looked after us in various ways

Hawaiian Holidays. I'll be coming a day early, really, but they owe me something, I think. I got the penknife back in Boston, but it had to come out on the baggage carousel, in a little packet of its own. I have bought various pills – my only expense so far – including Sudafed, which I have just taken (I was getting terribly blocked in my ears – I hope this helps), Nytol, in the hope of snoozing a bit, and Excedrin. It came to over $12. The weather in Boston was 0° Celsius, but clear-ish. In Detroit the same, and drizzling. But things could be worse. I'm beginning to regret involving Katy and Mrs. O in my affairs now. All I will really want to do is sleep.

Getting away from it all should provoke some clarification of view on things. What am I unhappy about? Some bits of the course – e.g. my senior seminar – are pretty scrappy, and the Classical Civilisation programme I am sure is still the pits. Perhaps I should put out a circular? I must also institute *evaluations*. Some parties won't like that! I hope that Brian will rise to the challenge of the newsletter.

I arrived a quarter of an hour *early* in SF, in fact, and, after some confusion, met up with Katy and Tom,[222] who were a little *late*. We drove back to 793 San Diego Avenue, to find the Pesht[223] more or less the same as before, though a little stiff in consequence of a fall she had two months ago just at the bottom of the steps coming down into the garden. Lisa, Julie and Kathy[224] had taken her out to San Francisco for a jaunt, and this happened on the way back – mainly because she was *in high heels*! But we had a good gossip, until about 9.30, when (after just *one* Bourbon, to Katy's frustration) I had really had enough, and had to retire to bed. It is always nostalgic to be back in the old room (unchanged since 1966 – and long before!). Decided not

---

from our arrival in 1966 to our departure in 1980, and constituted our Berkeley family.

222    Katy's son, Tom Lawrence.

223    Our nickname for Mrs. O, who used to call up from time to time, introducing herself as 'that old pest again'!

224    Three of her grandchildren, children of her son Dick.

to phone anyone – except David Winston[225] tomorrow, perhaps – since it will cause more complications than it is worth. Perhaps that is foolish of me!

## DAY 2, SATURDAY, NOVEMBER 28<sup>TH</sup>

Woke up at 2.00 am, of course, being eight hours out. Read a bit – John Fowles' *Mantissa,* which I had brought with me on an impulse, and which is actually amusing. Perhaps I will try some others of his, though he is not the equal of Saul Bellow, I think. Then I took two Nytol, which more or less knocked me out till about 8.00, though they left me feeling a bit fuzzy.

Mrs. O flubbed about industriously making breakfast, waiting on me hand and foot, though she must be over 90 – moulded salad, muffins, and so on. I tried to phone Pleasant Hawaiian Holidays (!), but they're not there on Saturdays. Katy phoned the lady, who declared she had never heard of me, which wasn't very sensible, since the call was actually to inform her about me. But it sounds as though I will *not* be met in Honolulu, and there may not even be a place for me at their hotel. It was actually most remiss of me not to tell the man ages ago when I was arriving.

I phoned the Winstons, talked first to Irene, then to David – very sorry Jean was not coming. They thought we were in Princeton, actually. They are flying tomorrow, as is more proper. We can have a gossip then.

It is now 12.00 noon, and I'm waiting for NW 61 to Honolulu to board. I got Katy to leave me down to the Durant, to take the limousine, which was much more sensible than driving me all the way. A pleasant ride over – the weather beautiful, but a slight haze. I couldn't see the Golden Gate from the bedroom window, but San Francisco was shining like a jewel as we drove across the Bridge. Berkeley looking the same as ever. The coffee

---

225    David was Professor of Judaic Studies at the Graduate Theological Union, and an old friend. We had cooperated in an edition of some works of Philo Judaeus, among other things.

shops full at 10.00 in the morning. Some new shops at the top of Telegraph,[226] but Telegraph looking more shaded and pleasant, with trees having grown somewhat since our day. I felt strongly that this is where I *belonged,* that I should never have left. We just came to be Berkeley people in those fourteen years, and now I am condemned to nostalgia.

I note in the *Examiner* that Dessie O'Hare was caught after a shoot-out, apparently in Kilkenny (just a small paragraph). Good for the gárdai! Something interesting always happens when I get on an aeroplane.


*Now 6.45 pm Hawaian time.* I am seated in the Lanai Room at the Hilton Hawaian Village, waiting to have a shrimp *hula* and a *mai-tai* for dinner. I tried to get into the Bali, their most prestigious restaurant, but they couldn't take me till 9.00, so I prowled around, first to the Chinese one (Golden Dragon), full up till 8.30, and now here. I had a stroll on the beach first.

I have to say this is a rather splendid place – a totally self-contained environment of great luxury and variety. I am having to spend this night here at my own expense, though, and I dread to think what that will cost. To go back a bit, we had a pleasant flight from SF on a fairly full jumbo – an amusing movie, *Beverly Hills Cop II* – and then, to my joy, I was met by a girl from Pleasant Hawaian Holidays, who draped me with a *lei* (of tuberoses and orchids, very fragrant!), and put me into a limousine for the Hilton. The drive into town was pleasant, as the driver was most chatty and informative – but the outskirts of Honolulu are pretty dismal, in fact, very much like any American city: the used car area, industrial areas, and so on. Also, I was greeted by a rainstorm – no harm, since the temperature was 80°, and I was still in my tweed coat, clutching an *overcoat.* The rain soon passed over, but it is plainly around. The driver pointed out Diamond Head Mountain, Pearl Harbor, a mighty supermarket

---

226    That is to say, Telegraph Avenue, which leads away south from the campus, and contains a plethora of both bookstores and cafés which one tended to frequent.

and shopping centre, and an apartment block where every apartment cost $200,000 – he did his best! He announced proudly that Hawaii was unique in having *no snakes*. I had to tell him about St. Patrick, which shook him considerably. Strangely enough, as we flew in, the countryside looked rather Irish (green, small fields), as did the sky (sunny, but a variety of clouds about).

My room is actually rather splendid, with a balcony which gives a fine view of the sea and of the town, and otherwise very spacious. There is quite a brisk breeze, which makes things pleasantly cool. Altogether, a marvellous place. I hope we have *some* time to explore even this island, never mind some of the others.

The shrimp hula was good – shrimp stuffed with bananas, and deep fried, with coconut sauce. J would *not* like that! And the *mai-tai* went down well. I am now finishing off with a cup of coffee, which is also better than average for America.

DAY 3, SUNDAY, NOVEMBER 29TH

Woke up once again at about midnight, so watched some TV, read some more of *Mantissa* (can't decide whether it's crap or not, yet – *very* self-indulgent, certainly), then took two Nytol, and slept till 6.30. I fear that it is raining steadily as I wake up. I phoned to see if the Catamaran is running for breakfast cruises to Diamond Head, as advertised, but it is in dry-dock till Dec. 5th.

Am now sitting at breakfast in the Tapa café, watching the rain struggling with the sun over the pool. All the breakfasts come out at about $10.00, however you hack them, so I am having a 'pancake sandwich' – pancakes with eggs and bacon in the middle. I must then go to find Pleasant Hawaian Holidays in the lobby. We are surrounded by quail (or I *think* that's what they are), endlessly patrolling the tables. We are asked not to feed them.

I am now in bed, at 10.45 pm, after an eventful day. After breakfast, I went to the PHH desk and got a packet of vouchers, and

232

then brought this to the front desk, but it proved not to contain the most important voucher – that for the hotel itself. Instead of going straight back to them, however, I went up to Mass on the second floor of Tapa Towers – nice to catch the service, though the priest was rather poncey, I fear. Then I decided to have a swim in the ocean, rain or no rain, so I changed and marched down. In fact, in face of my determination, the rain stopped for a while, and, after a short swim (keeping a nervous eye on my trousers), I actually had a brief sunbathe, before the rain started again. Then back to my room and watched football, until it was time to go on my tour (which I also booked just after breakfast).

The tour was an American Express tour up to the north of the island, to a valley called Waimea, which was a sacred place to the Hawaiians, containing a fine waterfall, a marvellous botanical garden, and a number of archaeological remains. We got a grand view of the whole centre of the island, an upland plateau (about 800 ft.), situated between two mountain ranges – mainly given over to the growing of pineapples and sugar-cane, but with a number of pleasant little settlements. At one place we paused at the side of the road and admired, in a little garden, bougainvillea, poinsettia, frangipani, hibiscus, orchids – and a mango tree, a banana tree, a macadamia nut tree, and something else that I cannot recall. It is really a tropical paradise. The growing season never ends – like the land of the Phaeacians![227] Pineapple plants actually take up to two years to grow to maturity, but then they produce up to five pineapples in succession, of which the first is the biggest, but the third is said to be the best (all this courtesy of our guide!).

When we reached the north coast, we got a view of some splendid breakers. This is apparently where a lot of high-class surfing takes place. Waves of 15-20 feet are normal, and waves of up to 40 ft have been surfed in! It seems incredible.

All this time one shower after another was coming over and when we reached Waimea this continued, but we ignored them.

---

227    That is to say, the mythical people whom Odysseus is entertained by in the Odyssey.

There was a little open bus which ran up to the Falls, where there was an exhibition of high diving from the rocks – up to 60 ft above the pool, which is only 15 ft deep; so quite awesome. Then we took a stroll down through the botanical wonders to a meadow where some old-style hula was danced, which was very impressive – not at all like the sort of stuff one would normally see commercially. In this field traditional Hawaiian sports are also played. Of the botanical displays, I found the hibiscus the most impressive – a full array of both traditional species and modern hybrids. Otherwise, I was really too ignorant to appreciate the wonders, but flora of the whole Pacific basin are on display.

Then, at 3.30 pm, back to Honolulu, *via* the Dole Pavilion, where we had a pineapple ice-cream, and viewed *enormous* pineapples, but unfortunately I am not in a position to bring any home (one can buy a box, and collect it at the airport, but that would just be a nuisance in Princeton).

Ed, the driver, was full of interesting facts about the island. Military expenditure had been the main source of income till the Second World War. Now, of course, it is tourism. Five-and-a-half million people visited the islands last year, and spent about *$6 billion*. It keeps half of the population in work. He told us about Capt. Cook, and how the Hawaians eventually killed him, but did *not* eat him. He told us about the raid on Pearl Harbor, and the remarkable element of surprise that the Japanese achieved. As we drove back, we viewed Pearl Harbor, and reviewed the disaster. A number of battleships are still down there, most notably the *Arizona*, with about 1300 men *still on board*. The furthest bend of the bay is nowadays top security, and probably houses nuclear weapons.

Back in the hotel, I phoned up to see if David and Irene had arrived, and found them in, and that an invitation was issued to all of us to dinner at the Goodmans. Just as well I phoned! I had ten minutes to be down in the lobby. We assembled, and were driven over by van. The Goodmans were most hospitable. His wife Madeleine is actually Asst VP for Academic Affairs, which is helpful. A very pleasant woman. In view of the company, everything was *kosher,* but none the worse for that. No booze, though (I didn't

234

know *that* was forbidden!). I got closeted with Baine Harris,[228] who is desirous of divesting himself of the headship of the Society, but I am not going to take it on. We talked over the Vanderbilt project, which would be most interesting.[229] I also met Bernard McGinn,[230] theologian from Chicago, and his very pleasant wife; Richard Popkin;[231] Moshe Edel from Jerusalem, who had been at my talk to the Academy there; and various others – but they are really all mediaevalists and Judaic scholars, not Classicists. The party broke up fairly early, in view of universal jet-lag, and we were all taken back to the hotel.

I should mention that I had to pay for my first night in the hotel – $120, plus tax! I hope I can claim it back somehow!

## DAY 4, MONDAY, NOVEMBER 30TH

Woke up shortly after midnight, and took Nytol, which kept me asleep till about 6.30, which was not too bad. I decided to order breakfast in the room – just continental, fruit and rolls. Not

---

228    R. Baine Harris (1927-2013) was the founder of the International Society for Neoplatonic Studies, and the editor of many of the earlier publications of its proceedings. He never actually wrote anything on Neoplatonism himself that I ever saw, but had adopted the subject as a promising field of research. He was most amiable, but a bit of a cod.

229    Unfortunately I have forgotten what this was.

230    Bernard McGinn (b. 1937) is an American Catholic theologian, religious historian, and scholar of spirituality, based at the University of Chicago Divinity School. A specialist in Medieval mysticism, McGinn is widely regarded as the preeminent scholar of mysticism in the Western Christian tradition. He is best known for his comprehensive series on mysticism, *The Presence of God*.

231    Richard Henry Popkin (1923 – 2005) was an American academic philosopher who specialized in the history of enlightenment philosophy and early modern anti-dogmatism. His 1960 work The History of Scepticism from Erasmus to Descartes introduced one previously unrecognized influence on Western thought in the seventeenth century, the Pyrrhonian Scepticism of Sextus Empiricus. Popkin also was an internationally acclaimed scholar on Christian millenarianism and Jewish messianism. He would have been at UCLA at this time, I think.

really a great success. They forgot the rolls, and I had to phone down for them. I won't do that again.

We assembled down below for the bus at 8.10, and were driven over to the university. The weather has now thoroughly recovered, and is about 80°, though there is always a pleasant breeze. We gathered for a coffee, during which I met a jolly old lady, a Mrs. Altman (?), who turned out to have a daughter who had married Gerald Goldberg's son! Small world. I met also a rotund, jolly man called Carl Mathis, from LA, who is a most remarkable bibliographer, and had written an article on Ibn Gabirol and Iamblichus, coming to the same conclusions as I have.

The first session starred David Burrell of Notre Dame, Rabbi David Besich of Yeshiva University (very orthodox!), and David Winston (on Philo's Conception of God). We had an excellent *al fresco* lunch in the courtyard at Sakamaki Hall, and then returned for the afternoon session, led off by *me,* on Ibn Gabirol.[232] It had a good reception, with some useful information given – by Arthur Hyman,[233] in particular, about Isaac Israeli, whom I must investigate. Hyman has offered to lend me a book on the subject. Shalom Rosenberg and Bernard McGinn gave talks complementing mine very satisfactorily.

Back to the hotel towards 6.00, and I agreed to meet David and Irene for dinner in the Rainbow Lanai Room. The only trouble with this is that David is a very restricted eater, so no question of exotic foods. But I had some boiled *mahi mahi,* and it wasn't too bad. Then we walked on the beach, and chatted.

It looks as if we are to be worked pretty hard. No afternoon off – no excursions. Just as well I took a trip on Sunday. We all declined to go back and listen to the evening lecture by Popkin.

---

232    It was entitled 'Solomon Ibn Gabirol's Doctrine of Intelligible Matter'.

233    Arthur Hyman (1921–2017) was a professor of philosophy at Yeshiva University. He was a great authority on mediaeval Jewish and Arabic philosophy, and Maimonides in particular.

Down to breakfast in the Tapa café, joined by Bernard McGinn and his wife Pat. I just had a bowl of fruit salad. Then up to the university for the morning session. A good series of talks on Maimonides, by Alfred Ivry of Brandeis,[234] Menachem Kellner from Haifa, and Idit Dobbs-Weinstein, from Vanderbilt. She is a nice girl – Ph. D. from Toronto, but ultimately from Israel. Very lively.

For lunch, we walked about half-an-hour to a vegetarian health food store – thoroughly kosher, but actually very good. All the walking made the afternoon session rather late, though, and we didn't get back to the hotel till almost 6.00. The afternoon talks were all lively and good – Lenn Goodman himself on 'Angels and Emanation in Maimonides' (he is an authority on both Arabic and Hebrew philosophy); Seymour Feldman, of Rutgers, on Gersonides – another interesting character; Gersonides is a most impressive philosopher. Feldman tells me he is looking for Classics faculty – he is Dean of Humanities, and has been Chairman of Classics, which had to be placed in receivership. David Novak, of Baruch College, CUNY, and a practising rabbi, is a very lively fellow, with whom I had lunch. He has recently been in South Africa, and was very interesting on that subject. He is a *very* fast talker, but amiable.

Back at the hotel, I once again agreed to have dinner with David and Irene – in the Rainbow Lanai – though I was hankering after things like a *luau* or a Japanese meal (but a *luau* really needs a party of people, and I couldn't seem to stir that up). Anyhow, we had the buffet this time, and that was good.

---

234    Alfred L. Ivry (1935 - ) is professor emeritus in the Skirball Department of Hebrew and Judaic Studies and the Department of Middle Eastern and Islamic Studies at New York University. He is the author, editor, or translator of ten books. Most recently, he is the author of *Maimonides' Guide of the Perplexed: A Philosophical Guide;* and recently edited Averroes's Middle Commentary on Aristotle's "De Anima" in both Arabic and Hebrew critical editions, as well as supplying an English-language translation.

Then we went for our statutory stroll on the beach. And so to bed, where I watched a movie, *Dirty Dancing,* a pleasant piece of 1960s nostalgia. I am not getting much serious reading done, I fear. We are being kept hard at it, even without going back for the evening lectures, which we have generally declined to do.

## DAY 6, WEDNESDAY, DECEMBER 2^{ND}

Met for breakfast at the bottom of Tapa Tower: Al Ivry, Steven Katz, Seymour Feldman, David and Irene. Then up in the van to the university. The morning session was on the Kabbalah and the Renaissance, and again good. An entertaining talk by Richard Popkin on Spinoza and the idea of some contemporary critics of his that he was a secret Kabbalist. Moshe Idel (who had been at my talk in Jerusalem on 'Female Principles in Platonism') talked on the Kabbalah and its relationship to Neoplatonic ideas, and Hubert Dethier of Brussels discoursed on Leone Ebreo and his doctrine of Love and Intellection – he provided a text for his talk, which makes good reading!

Then lunch in the Student Union, since we want to break early today, to get to the beach. That was . The final session was more general. Steve Katz was very lively on Utterance and Ineffability. Arthur Hyman excellent on Isaac Israeli, but more generally on the principle that 'from one only one can come to be'. Finally, a rather silly talk, full or errors, by Robert McLaren, of Cal State Fullerton, on 'the Psycho-dynamics of Neoplatonic Ontology', but really an attack, from a Calvinist point of view, on the Neoplatonic view of the evil of the world, and what should be done about it.

However, all in all, a most enlightening few days!

Back in good time to get to the beach for a pleasant swim and sunbathe. Irene took our pictures, so I hope something comes out. I am very bad about cameras, but I'm afraid that in this case records of my journey will only annoy everybody else. I prefer, anyhow, to record in words. I must say that the water even off Waikiki is remarkably clear and (ostensibly) unpolluted, despite the enormous concentration of population. I joined David and

Irene on the beach, and then Seymour Feldman. Irene took all our photos, which we may see the results of in due course. Then most of us assembled in the bar area of Tapa Tower for a drink at 7.00, and following on that I once again accompanied D and I to dinner in the Lanai, this time joined also by the Popkins. Mrs. P especially is good fun, and he is entertaining also. He is an old friend of Tom Rosenmeyer's.[235] They started together in the University of Wyoming, or wherever. We reminisced about the 'troubles' of the 1960s, when he was head of the Philosophy Department in San Diego, and hired Herbert Marcuse and Angela Davis, to Reagan's rage.

After dinner, we took our usual promenade, and so to bed. We are being very unenterprising about evening entertainment, but it all seems so *bogus*.


## DAY 7, THURSDAY, DECEMBER 3<sup>RD</sup>

This morning, I signed up to go on a snorkelling expedition to Hanauma Bay, round the coast a bit, the other side of Diamond Head, since I am not concerned with the Jewish Studies meeting. First, however, I had to settle where I am to stay tonight. I phoned up Pleasant Hawaiian one more time, to see if they would extend me, since the hotel has no objection, but they were adamant, so I have decided to take refuge in the Travelodge across the road, for a mere $65 a night(!).

I had breakfast with D and I and Carl Mathis. Irene loaned me a beach towel and a mat, but I must have left the mat under the breakfast table in my haste. I was collected at 8.05 by a character called Lee, who was dressed like an old-time big game hunter, and had a personality to match. He was good fun, though. He collected all the customers from other hotels, and then we set off, round Diamond Head, past the very posh suburb of Old Kahala (real estate at $7 a square *foot*, I think he said – or was it $700?) – very beautiful homes, anyhow – one going for $25 million.

We arrived at the site, Hanauma Bay, which is most impressive – an old crater with the side blown out of it, I should

235     My former colleague from Berkeley.

say, to form a bay. A steep path down to the beach. It had been thoroughly fished out, but is now a nature preserve. Lee advised us to buy popcorn, as the fish love it. We were all issued with our flippers and masks. I declined to rent an underwater camera – partly to save money ($15), but also because (a) I wasn't sure if I could handle it, and (b) I would only be aggravating grievances and jealousies by showing off splendid underwater pictures of fish. I went out first without popcorn, and swam up and down the reef for about half-an-hour. It is certainly spectacular – a bit choppy where the waves break, but otherwise no trouble keeping the snorkel above water. Every conceivable colour and shape of fish, going about their business. Then I came in (worrying about my valuables), bought a coke and some popcorn, and lay and sunbathed and read *The Green Fool* for a while. I came to be surrounded by pigeons and sparrows, who had their eye on the popcorn, so I foolishly distributed some, and became besieged – indeed *walked over* – by pigeons. So I put the popcorn into a plastic bag, and headed back to the reef. This time I was the most popular guy around – clouds of fish fought for my attention as the Lord of the Popcorn. I became almost afraid that a moray eel might join them. I spent another twenty minutes or so, till the popcorn was all gone, and then came in.

A pleasant drive back, and then I went over to Travelodge to check in, but they told me to come back at 6.00. Back in the Village, I came upon David Burrell, who asked me to join him and Idit and Al Ivry for lunch, at a little Chinese place round the corner on Ala Moana, which serves espresso coffee. Idit is a funny girl, very hyper, doesn't eat much (just strong coffee), may well be divorced (as who isn't, these days?), has a small daughter, and is lean and wiry, like many Israeli girls. But she got a degree from the Mediaeval Institute in Toronto. I never learned how that came about. I had a plate of pork and pineapple – OK.

I had to leave the party, to go up to the university for a session of the ISNS, scheduled for 2.00. Got a taxi up, and walked up to the Korean Center, a delightful Korean temple, specially erected here by Korean craftsmen – again that characteristic of hyper-reality, the 'genuine imitation'. Well, Baine delivered his set spiel, and then we had two quite good papers, one by a John Cronquist, from Cal State Fullerton, on 'Plotinus on Civic Virtue', and another by a man whose name I didn't catch on 'Spenser's Neoplatonism'.

I agreed after that to ride back with Baine, Hubert Dethier, and Robert McLaren in McLaren's car, but that involved waiting till 5.00 for his wife to come back from a visit to a botanical garden. What with finding Baine's hotel and getting lost in the great shopping centre complex, we barely got back by 6.00, but no trouble in fact about checking in. Indeed, Travelodge gave me a luxury $85 room for $65! Very comfortable.

I installed the bags, then watched Reagan being interviewed by four top journalists. He actually did pretty well, except for rambling in a senile way when they got onto the Iran-Contra question. He plainly now wants this deal with Gorbachev to succeed.[236] The administration is a bit taken aback by the great popularity which Gorbachev has achieved over here. Various efforts are being made to be difficult about 'human rights' (i.e. Jews who want to leave for Israel) and Afghanistan, but not too much.

Then I went out and found a good Chinese restaurant (the Dynasty), full of *Chinese,* which seemed a good sign, and had an enormous plate of oysters (*vast* oysters), with ginger and green onions, which finished me. After that I staggered over to the

---

236    A series of meetings in August and September 1986 culminated in the Reykjavik Summit between Reagan and Gorbachev on 11 and 12 October 1986. Both agreed in principle to remove INF systems from Europe and to equal global limits of 100 INF missile warheads. Gorbachev also proposed deeper and more fundamental changes in the strategic relationship. More detailed negotiations extended throughout 1987, aided by the decision of West German Chancellor Helmut Kohl  in August to unilaterally remove the joint US-West German Pershing 1a systems. Initially, Kohl had opposed the total elimination of the Pershing missiles, claiming that such a move would increase his nation's vulnerability to an attack by Warsaw Pact Forces. The treaty text was finally agreed in September 1987. On 8 December 1987, the treaty was officially signed by Reagan and Gorbachev at a summit in Washington and ratified the following May in a 93–5 vote by the United States Senate.

Rainbow Bazaar, and splurged on presents – a netsuke for J, skirts for Mouse and J, and a lighter for Mum.

## DAY 8, FRIDAY, DECEMBER 4TH

I decided to spend my extra day lazily. My feet are sore, and I have no further desire to explore downtown Honolulu, beginning at 8.15 am or so, which is what I had been considering. Instead, I finished my book review of Lamberton's *Homer,*[237] read some Plotinus II 9, wrote some postcards, and then went off for a swim in the rooftop pool at 11.00 or so. I swam and lazed there for a while, until a rain shower passed over, when I returned to the room, and turned to correcting my paper, with the help of Schlanger, who did in fact discuss Israeli – I can't see how I missed it. Then down for a *mai tai* and hot-dog by the pool, checked out, and over to the Village for my 3.00 pm limousine.

It turned 3.15pm, and no limousine had appeared. On calling, I found that they had changed the time to 2.30, and had left a message for me at the Hilton, which of course I never got. But they decently sent a taxi, and that got me to the airport in good time.

There was a lovely view of the island as we departed, and then the clouds closed over, and the sun went down. I had an uneventful flight to San Francisco, where we were changed to a smaller plane, and flew to Minneapolis. I managed to snooze a bit on this leg, but had to sit for one-and-a-half hours in Minneapolis, where it was 17°, to get a flight to Newark –

## DAY 9, SATURDAY, DECEMBER 5TH

– which I boarded about 7.00pm, and flew uneventfully to Newark, arriving at 11.16 pm. I must say all has been very smooth so far, considering I am going about at the beginning of December. Michael[238] was there to collect me, looking rather

---

237    This was *Homer the Theologian,* by Robert Lamberton, which I was reviewing for the Journal of Hellenic Studies. It appeared the following year.

238    That is to say, my old friend from Berkeley days, Michael Frede, now a professor of ancient philosophy in Princeton.

relieved, as he feared I might have been caught in a snow-storm. He drove me back and lodged me in the university guest house, the Palmer House, which is a grand old place, given to Princeton by a Mrs. Palmer, obviously a rich old bird. He then drove me back to the house (they can't put me up, as Gisela Striker[239] is staying for the Colloquium) and Gabriella made me coffee. She is amiable, but really not a patch on Dorothea,[240] I would have thought. And she has landed him with twins (girls), which he can't relish. But there it is.

Michael spent a long time trying to phone Richard Sorabji,[241] unsuccessfully, and then we went up to start the colloquium, I still feeling quite lively. Many interesting people there – Mary Margaret McKenzie,[242] in very good form, Josiah Gould (rather elderly now), Charles Kahn, André Laks, Michael Erler, Gisela. David Furley is in England at a conference. No sign of Peter Brown, though this might have been of interest to him. Bob Lamberton's talk was interesting, if a bit unfocussed, and well replied to by David Blank. Then coffee and doughnuts. Then my talk, which seemed to go down well, and was well replied to by Steve Strange, who made a number of good points, which will much improve it.

Then over to the Faculty Club for drinks and dinner. I talked first with Gisela and MMM, but got stuck at dinner with the (still) egregious Paul van der Waerdt (whom I quite failed to recognise – I am quite hopeless in this regard – but it didn't faze him too much). He is completing a thesis on the Stoic Theory of Natural Law, and will be in Cambridge, studying with David Sedley, in the winter – which makes me rather glad, on the whole, that I will be in Princeton.

---

239 Gisela Striker was at this time Professor of Ancient Philosophy in Cambridge. She later transferred to Harvard.

240 Dorothea Frede, Michael's first wife, whom we had got to know when they were in Berkeley. They had divorced some years before this.

241 At that time Professor of Philosophy in King's College London, and a major authority on later Greek philosophy in particular, but on Plato and Aristotle as well.

242 Now Mary Margaret McCabe, Professor of Ancient Philosophy in King's College London.

After dinner, there was a party at Michael's, but I was beginning to fade. I talked with Laks and Erler and Christopher Callanan, an American who teaches in the Classics Department at Göttingen (as a Privatdozent), and is absurdly Germanic. He is talking tomorrow. He is in search of a topic for his Habilitation, and I suggested Syrianus. There was a fine spread of cheese and paté, but one couldn't eat any more. Steve Strange and Erler and myself grabbed a lift from an obliging graduate student, Manfred Mann, and retired about 11.00.

## DAY 10, SUNDAY, DECEMBER 6<sup>TH</sup>

I actually woke at 8.30, though feeling rather groggy. I had a bath, and went down to breakfast, finding coffee and croissants laid out in the dining-room (the drawing-room was full, absurdly, of Santa Clauses and a toy train set). I brought down my bags, having failed to get hold of a Salem limousine, and walked over to the colloquium with André Laks and David Blank. I'm afraid that Callanan's paper on Hermeias was entirely inappropriate. Instead of dealing with his exegetical method, he gave us a sort of encyclopedia entry on Hermeias, mainly biographical. I'm afraid he is less impressive than he looks. Certainly he had no clear notion of what the colloquium was about (he is at the Centre for Hellenic Studies in Washington this year, as are Erler and Laks). After this rather dismal performance, Manfred Mann kindly drove me to Palmer House, where I collected the bags, and then to the Nassau Inn – which is a well-appointed place, I must say!

Then I took my leave of all, and walked over to the Nassau Inn, where I caught the bus for JFK. No problem with flights, and I am now (at 3.00 am GMT) on the flight to Gatwick, about to have dinner.

*And there the account ends. We presume there were no further mishaps.*

# 12: TRIP TO KATOUNIA, GREECE

## AUGUST – SEPTEMBER, 1988

*This was mainly a return to Katounia, the home of the Sherrards in Northern Euboea, this time with the family – the first of many such visits over subsequent years.*

### PROEM: AUGUST 27<sup>TH</sup>–28<sup>TH</sup>

PROEM: AUGUST 27TH–28TH

We started the holiday period in style last night with a dinner-party for Tom and Jean Flanagan,[243] with Heaneys and Deanes, and a friend of the Heaneys, a Greek-American sculptor from Boston, Dimitri Hadji – and Ivor,[244] who popped up just that day. An excellent dinner, with everyone in good form. Tom's new novel is to be launched on Wednesday next, which we will miss, but it is in the shops already, and I bought a copy for him to sign.[245] I have read the first two chapters, and find it excellent. He has concocted Kilpeder on the basis of a number of notable incidents from the Fenian Rising, but situates it on the road from Macroom to Killarney. Seamus H. was in great form. He was most amusing about a game he invented with Robert Pinsky, a charade called 'Death of Poets' – one mimes the

---

243 This was the distinguished Irish-American academic and author Thomas Flanagan (1923-2002), whom we had got to know in Berkeley, where he was in the English Department. In 1978, however, he had moved to the East Coast, to the State University of New York at Stony Brook. He and his wife Jean came to Ireland more or less every summer.

244 That is to say, Ivor McIlveen, who had been married to my cousin Kate (Sweetman), and continued to stay in touch with us.

245 This was *The Tenants of Time*, which still reposes on my shelves.

way they died. Rather macabre! Seamus D. in reasonable form, looking forward to going off to Minnesota for a semester. The household is just about holding together, it seems. Ivor's job in Sri Lanka seems to be over, so he is back here for a while. He is thinner, but in good form. He stayed on gossiping for an hour or so. We only got to bed at 3.00 am.

This morning I went into town to get notes and summaries of Plotinus off to Penguin.[246] Madeleine had failed to do one page, so I had to leave off the end. Most annoying, But I got *most* of it off. Also wrote to Abraham Bos, apologising for not replying earlier on the *Kronology*. It is quite an interesting book, in fact.

David Ellsworth duly arrived at midday, having missed a number of connections, but in good form. At least the weather has started off quite pleasant for him.

Tennis in the afternoon with the Kinsmans and Jamie Hely-Hutchinson – very much Eton and Cambridge, but pleasant enough. He is about to take up a position in a merchant bank in the City.

Back to chat to David around 5.00. A quiet evening in front of the telly. Mouse is in dire excitement about Greece. She has packed and re-packed many times a day for the last week. This morning we searched the coin-pots and found some drachmae (sadly devalued, I may say, since they were first collected), and she is bringing these. We got £420 sterling in cheques, and £100 in drachmae (at about 220 to the £). That *should* do us, along with the plastic. Car rental should be the main expense. I hope it is not prohibitive.


DAY 1, SUNDAY, AUGUST 28TH

Rose early, and went off to Mass with Mouse and David (Mouse now in an unbearable state of excitement – she actually thought that Fr. Gaynor invoked a special blessing at the end of Mass for those who were going to *Greece!*). We spent the day largely

---

246    I was just at this time completing an edition of Stephen MacKenna's translation of Plotinus' *Enneads* for Penguin, which ultimately appeared in 1991.

*Aegina - the temple*

*Pic: Athanasios K. Vionis*                    *The bay, Paros.*

*Jean and Mouse, Katounia*

*Philip and Denise Sherrard,
our hosts in Katounia, Evia.
Captivated by this corner
of the world, we ultimately
called the house we bought
in Howth, 'Katounia'.*

*View from near the villa, Katounia*

*John looks seaward, Pylos*

*The medieval town of Semproniano, Tuscany*

*The town of Pisa, Italy*

messing about, tidying – but off for a visit to Malahide Gardens to show David in mid-afternoon, mainly to divert Mouse.

Finally, after dinner, we piled into Katharine's car, and were conveyed to the airport. Once arrived, we checked in, resisted the Duty Free, and boarded without incident – except that I left my briefcase, with tickets and traveller's cheques, on the pavement outside, and had to rush back to retrieve it!

*Now* (1.25 am, Athens time) we are well on our way to the Promised Land – though surrounded, I fear, by a gang of the most ghastly yobbos, who should be out snagging turnips, but instead are going off to disgrace Ireland abroad, and who seem mainly to be going on to Paros – alas for that pleasant isle! But first we may have to endure them for a while in the hotel.

We arrived just on time in Athens, piled onto a bus (the taxi-men are on strike!), and drove first to the port of Piraeus to deliver the 'lads' to their respective boats (Mykonos, Paros or Ios – which used to be a quite remote destination!), and then us to Athens, to our hotel, where we arrived towards 5.00 in the morning. The *Kerameikos* is actually a nice little hotel in the centre of town, not far from Omonia Square, and quiet (except for traffic) and cheap (2658 dr. a room in high season).

## DAY 2, MONDAY, AUGUST 29TH

We slept happily till almost 10.00 am, and then I staggered down to the foyer to see if there was any chance of breakfast (which had officially ended at 9.30). In the foyer were actually the manager, Mr. Tsimbalis, and a lady. Breakfast, they confirmed, was over, but if we just wanted coffee and croissants, they could oblige. Very civil! So I was loaded with a tray, and served breakfast in the room.

I had a chat with Mr. Tsimbalis, who noted that I was learning Modern Greek, and that I was a professor of Ancient Greek. He revealed that he knew Kevin O'Nolan and his brother Fergus, and produced a copy of *The Best of Myles*,[247] which Kevin

---

247    This, of course, by Kevin's brother, Brian O'Nolan (aka Myles na Gopaleen).

251

had presented to him. I had to tell him the sad news of Kevin's death.[248] He says he has been entertaining the Irish for 20 years now.

Mouse woke up with difficulty to face her first day in Greece, and now, at 11.00, we are almost ready to face Athens...

*Now, at 4.45 pm,* we are back in the room, after a walk round the neighbourhood and a siesta. We walked down to the Kerameikos, through rather seedy streets – lots of spare parts shops – across Piraeus St., a grim thoroughfare, and down through little streets to the Agora. I couldn't interest the family in going in, and Mouse is a bit dim still, until we found some curio shops, and bought her a bracelet and a necklace (480 dr.). Then we had a little lunch – gyro, chips, beer, 300 dr.

We walked back – no taxis, since they are on strike – and had a siesta. At least I slept, but the Mouse was unsleepy, and involved Mummy in various ghastly projects, which I dimly overheard. Then we rose again, about 4.30, and tried to phone both the School and Janet.[249] I got through to The Fowdens' house, but they are away. Then we went walking again. And decided to go on the train, down to Phaleron, to see if we could swim, the heat and smog being dire. The train only costs 30 dr. (as do buses), and we got to Neo Phaleron in no time. We found ourselves opposite a fine new stadium, at the other side of which was a beach. Unfortunately the water, when we inspected it, was the dirtiest I have ever seen – a dark brown soup, with *things* floating in it, a minestrone of pollution! And yet I think when

---

248     He had died in 1987.

249     This was Janet Coggin (1936-2010), an English novelist and all round interesting lady (she had found herself married to a KGB spy in South Africa, and left him to come to Ireland), whom I had met back in Ireland in circumstances I can no longer now recall. She now lived in Greece. She had recently published a novel, *The Leaving*, which I had helped her with the publishing of. She later published a number of others, including one about discovering that her husband was a spy.

Grimes[250] and I were here in 1960, this was a popular beach. Anyhow, I went in and *sat* in it, and Mouse approached the edge of it. Then we retired to an adjacent playground, where Mouse found swings and slides, and even a little friend. Then back to Omonia and the hotel. Still no taxis, so we set out to find a local café, which we did at the corner of Kerameikou and Zenonos. It was OK, and not expensive.

By the end of the evening, we had decided that we must get out of Athens at all costs, and we are tempted by a tour of Poros, Hydra and Aigina which is advertised. I have been unable to get hold of the School or the Fowdens or Janet, and am discouraged. We did get Paul Kalligas,[251] however, who has invited us round to lunch on Wednesday. This may interfere with our plans for escape, but I would like to meet him.

In fact, when we got back to the hotel, there was a message from Janet. It turns out that she was up in Katounia for the weekend, and had only just got back. We had decided to go on this tour, so we fixed up to go out to dinner tomorrow night.


DAY 3, TUESDAY, AUGUST 30<sup>TH</sup>

Up at 6.30 am, for breakfast at 7.00, and departure on the bus at 7.20. All very efficient, and we were aboard the good ship *Aegean Glory* by 8.30am. I was interested to see that we were all frisked pretty thoroughly at the beginning of the voyage, but not at later embarkations, so some dastardly terrorist could have smuggled something aboard, say, at Hydra. There was, indeed, a rather grim-looking fellow, with a shaved head, sitting near us on the sun-deck, who looked capable of anything, but he was

---

250    My old school friend (and subsequently brother-in-law – married to my sister Katharine), with whom I had travelled to Greece  back when we were both in College.

251    Paul (Pavlos) was, and is, a Greek scholar and gentleman, to whom I had been introduced on a previous visit to Athens by a mutual friend, Alexander Nehamas. Paul devoted his life to a fine translation of the *Enneads* of Plotinus into Modern Greek, with copious commentary, which has since been published (and the commentary translated into English).

actually quite harmless, and remained somnolent throughout the voyage.

The basic charge for this voyage was 4500 dr. per person (half-price for Mouse), which was not at all bad, but once one was on board, an atmosphere of rip-off manifested itself, with drinks at very inflated prices being thrust under one's nose. Still, once we got the idea, one could resist.

Poros was a bit pointless, though a charming little town, since we were only there for half-an-hour. Hydra we visited for one-and-a-half hours, which was better, and we could get a swim, though only off rocks, which didn't suit Mouse, though a nice Greek girl and her boyfriend did entice her *most* of the way in. Hydra is interesting as having been a place of refuge for Greeks fleeing from Turkish domination, and a centre of piracy in consequence. It has some fine old houses, of rich local families, and a well-protected harbour. Lunch was served between Poros and Hydra, again with a drink being served under false pretences.

After Hydra, we set off for Aigina – the real point of the expedition, as far as I was concerned. Good views of the adjacent Peloponnese, and little nameless (or at least uninhabited) islets. Aigina is apparently quite difficult to approach, which was part of its strength in ancient times. It is now well-inhabited and prosperous, being particularly famous for its pistachios. We had signed on for an optional tour, to visit the Temple of Aphaia. This involved a drive through the island, which was very pleasant – past Old Aigina, up on a hill, now ruinous, but where the Aeginetans retired in the Middle Ages, to protect themselves from Saracens and others. Also a splendid new church to the latest Orthodox saint, a St. Nectarios, who sounds thoroughly mediaeval, but was only canonised in 1960!

The temple itself is very fine, in Doric style, put up just after the Battle of Salamis, but on the site of an earlier temple. Aphaia is an old mother-goddess, assimilated in Classical times to Athena. It is in a very good state of preservation – all things considered – with even a bit of the second storey still visible. The views in all directions were spectacular, not least over to Salamis and Attica. All these old enemies were in full sight of each other, at least in the old days – now largely obscured by *nephos!*[252]

There was a good beach at Aigina, but we had no time to get onto it. We came home pleasantly in the evening, helped by *bouzouki* music and native dancing in the lounge, and got back to the hotel by 8.00, giving time to rest and wash, before Janet appeared shortly after 8.30.

She was in good form. The taxis were back since the morning, so we decided to go up to the Square at Kaisariani, a little above the smog, and dine there. There then began a fearful struggle to catch a taxi, which led us all the way past Omonia onto Stadiou before we ran one down. Mouse joined in with a will, and I became enraged and hurled abuse at ones that wouldn't stop. Janet is of the opinion that this is a symptom of the collapse of Greek society: but why should these people not want to earn money? It remains quite strange. Still, we had an excellent dinner for about £9. Janet revealed that she was hopelessly broke, since her pupils have stood her up in the last month, and she has of course not yet received any royalties – and may never do so, unless Robert Hale[253] get their finger out. I was urging her to come over at all costs if she was invited on the Late Late Show, or even Gay's morning show. It would make all the difference.

We finally broke up well after 11.00 – Mouse virtually stocious by this time – caught a taxi without difficulty, and so back to the hotel, dropping Janet on the way. I had an interesting conversation with the taxi-man, whose English was excellent, when I asked him how the strike had gone. Had they won?

"Win? No, one never wins in Greece!"

He seemed to indicate that the strike was about the quality of diesel which is supplied to them, which is very bad – it causes the engine to seize up in any sort of cold weather. He feels that the government is in cahoots with the oil companies. I could actually find nothing about the strike in the local paper I bought.

---

252    That is to say, smog. The word means, literally, 'cloud' or 'mist'.

253    The publishers of her novel.

Andreas Papandreou, as it happens, is in London undergoing treatment for a blocked aorta, and the country is on tenterhooks. There are rumours of a power struggle breaking out in Pasok in anticipation of his not being able to carry on. Very open comments, I must say, in the papers. There is speculation as to whether his wife Margaret, now estranged from him, will visit his bedside. Probably not!

### DAY 4, WEDNESDAY, AUGUST 31ST

Very hot last night. Indeed, the papers remarked yesterday on the dire quality of the *nephos* over the last few days, and it is pretty foul this morning. The Mouse is quite flaked out, and we are letting her sleep. J went down and brought up breakfast to the room. I went out to explore, and to change more money. I walked to Omonia, found a bank, signed cheques, but then found I had forgotten my passport. A slightly sneaky young fellow actually approached me in the bank, and said he would be prepared to change money, at 240 dr. to the £, but I declined. I walked as far as the Museum, but then turned back, and rooted out the family to go to lunch. Since we had to change money, we were a bit late, but got out to Kephissia by 12.20, to find Paul Kalligas waiting for us.

He is actually quite young – not above 40, I would say[254] (I had envisaged him as an elderly, eccentric millionaire!), and very pleasant. He has a beautiful house, with fine garden, in the best part of Kephissia, which is now inevitably becoming rather over-populated with middle-class commuters. Herodes Atticus'[255] villa has not yet been identified, but Paul feels it is not far away, as antiquities keep turning up in the area. We first went back to his house for a drink – his family (wife and two children) are in Spetsai for the summer, and he has been commuting back and forth the whole time. He is actually going back this evening to bring them back to Athens at the weekend. School begins on September 12th.

254    This was right on the button. Paul was actually born in 1948.

255    He was a notable millionaire patron of the arts and philosophy in the early second century A.D.

We had drinks in the garden, then, and gossip about Plotinus (he has finished a first draft of his translation, and plans notes and an introduction), and then he drove us off to a very pleasant taverna in the country, at Tatoi (where the summer royal palace was, and which is the Classical Decelea – one can see why the Spartans chose it; there is an excellent view of Athens below), the Taverna Leonidas. We just had something simple – excellent mixed hors d'oeuvres and a kebab. Some plain spaghetti was found for Mouse. More gossip. We agree about the curious quality of Porphyry's *Life of Plotinus* – he is even more sceptical than me about Porphyry's portrait of his master.

Then he took us back to the train, since his car has an *even* number-plate, and he can't enter the city on an uneven day – he can't even drive to the Piraeus to catch his boat! We got back to the hotel just after 4.30pm, to be collected by a very prompt taxi-man and driven to Treis Gephyras, to catch the bus to Limni. Alas, we should have checked Janet's information. The bus was not at 5.30, as we thought, but at 4.45, and it had just left – on time! However, there was a bus to Chalcis at 5.00, so we just caught that, determined above all to get out of Athens.

We had a pleasant one-and-a-half hour's drive to Chalcis, costing only 840 dr. (Mouse free). Chalcis is rather big and ugly, so, after a brief stop at a café for beer and coke floats (which I think we introduced to Chalcis – great incomprehension when we ordered it; I finally said 'Bring two cokes and one ice-cream', and we made the mixture ourselves, to the great astonishment of the waiter), we decided to take a taxi to Limni, if we could get one. The first taxi I stopped, a cheerful young man, was willing to drive us to Limni, and we engaged him.

It was a long drive, and expensive (4500 dr., including tip), but we had to reckon that against a possibly expensive, and surely very unpleasant, night somewhere in Chalcis. As it was, we arrived at the taverna in Katounia around 8.30pm, just after dark, after a delightful drive through the hills and pines of Northern Euboea (except for the last stretch of road into Limni, which is being 'improved', and is currently a dirt surface). We were booked into a room, which cost 2100 dr. –

OK, but rather cramped quarters for any lengthy stay!), and had a pleasant dinner in the taverna. This went on till about 11.30, because Mouse found many little friends – there seem to be lots of children – and finally could hardly be parted from them, after a slow start. Lots of activity – many cars drove out, and this is just a Wednesday. Things seem to have developed somewhat in the last five years – I hope not too much!

## DAY 5, THURSDAY, SEPTEMBER 1<sup>ST</sup>

A pretty hot night, and we woke fairly early. Not much activity in the taverna before about 10.00 am. We had a pre-breakfast swim at 8.30, to start us off, on the little beach in front of the taverna, and finally rustled up some breakfast around 10.00.

After breakfast, we decided to walk up and visit the Sherrards. We were joined on the journey by a stout little boy, who followed us like a stray dog. He was most voluble, bilingual in English and Greek, since his parents are Greek and live in England, and he turned out to have a little sister. His name is Alex and his sister's is Carolina, and Mouse took to Carolina at once. We were received very warmly by Philip and Denise, and after a drink of grapefruit juice, Philip came to collect our bags from the taverna in the van, and we hauled them up to the house, which was still being cleaned by Liadain, her friend Rhonnda, and an old cleaning lady.

It is a villa of surpassing magnificence, even more so than I remember it, and actually sleeps *seven* (four bedrooms), so we will be rather rattling around in it. Two large bathrooms, which I approve of. The only mild drawback is a lack of electricity, but even that I think one could come to appreciate.[256] The cleaning only really finished about 2.00 (the old lady was being *very* thorough). I delivered Mouse to her new friends (whose names I have still not grasped), and J went into town with Denise to shop. By 2:00 pm we were all reassembled, and able to move in.

---

256    Philip Sherrard just did not approve of electricity – his argument was that it was unreliable – so until his death in 1995 there was no electricity on the estate. We survived on candles and oil lamps, but, as I suggest, we got used to that. We cooked with gas.

*List of vegetation on the estate: delicious figs, which are ripe now; grapes; olives (not ripe till November); long green peppers (sweet); rosemary; bougainvillea on pillars in patio, which has a pond with water-lilies, frogs and goldfish; lemon trees, oranges; pines; magnolias; something which looks like a rowan, but I'm not sure about it; palms, jasmine.*

*Animals: lizards; crickets, frogs; various finches; enormous butterflies.*

After a rest, we went down to our beach and had another swim. It is very like the Fallen Leaf situation,[257] a path down to the water just across the road from our front gate – a stony beach, of course, but with quite smooth stones, and a fig tree for shade – though not much shade in the afternoon, as we face west. Then up to the house, to start up some dinner, after which we strolled over to Philip and Denise, meeting Rhonnda on the way, with her dogs and her *goat*. Philip and Denise were just setting out to visit *us*, so we brought them back, and sat out on the patio, in the turret, watching the sun go down,[258] and drinking retsina and beer, and eating olives.

We discovered that the vegetable stew that J had begun had largely burned, so we had the remains of that and some sausage for dinner, before retiring early. It is quite a wrench to get used to the oil and kerosene lamps, but once one does, it is sort of pleasant. Philip was saying that they were feeling quite pleased with themselves just recently when there was a total power cut throughout Greece – it didn't affect them at all. The taverna has its own generator, so it is independent too.

## DAY 6, FRIDAY, SEPTEMBER 2ND

Up quite early – still difficult to sleep from the heat, though much better than Athens – partly woken by sounds of Rhonnda

---

257    A reference to Fallen Leaf Lake in the Sierras in California, south of Lake Tahoe, which we used to retreat to for periods of the summer, when we lived in Berkeley.

258    From the turret which formed the far edge of the patio, one gazed across a narrow stretch of sea, to watch the sun go down over the mountains of Boeotia.

watering on the patio. We had breakfast on the front patio. We had used the big torch as a night-light last night – foolishly, but we didn't trust the kerosene lamps – and it is exhausted by this morning, so we need another battery. Then down with Mouse to meet the little friend for a morning swim, and then I agreed to go into town with Rhonnda to do a little shopping.

She collected me at 12.30 – she has an old Ami-8 jalopy – and we went in to Roussos' supermarket on the seafront, where I got some cheese, wine, ouzo, beer and so on. Then, since Rhonnda was not yet back, I settled down to an ouzo in the nearby *ouzeri*. She appeared, and joined me in a beer, waiting for her wine merchant to unload his wine. We had a bit of a chat. She has had an interesting life – in Greece for 14 years (I think), mainly as a copy-editor for the Greek Information Service, but also as a fisherman in Samos for three years, and now as – what? She has been living here for 18 months, watering the plants, and doing some interior decorating (!). Like Janet, living from hand to mouth. Indeed, I am provoked to wonder a bit about Liadain. She would seem to be someone of rather high potential (a university graduate, I think!), but she seems just to be living here with a British composer called Tavener, who is rather pompous and preposterous.[259] But what does *she* do?

Back to Katounia, to find Alex and Carolina installed in the house, having lunch and rioting about. Alex is a great trencherman, and threatened to finish off the chocolate spread, if not gently prevented. Finally we packed them off, and prepared for a siesta. Mouse actually went down to sleep, and we dozed.

---

259    This was in fact John Kenneth Tavener (1944 – 2013), an English composer, known for his extensive output of choral religious works. Among his best known works are *The Lamb* (1982), *The Protecting Veil* (1988), and *Song for Athene* (1993). He was actually knighted in 2000 for his services to music. He would have been there, I assume, to consult Philip about Greek Orthodox liturgy, something they were both interested in, and had taken up with Liadain. I am being rather uncharitable about him here, I regret to say, but we found him, initially, distinctly off-hand and snooty. I suppose now that he felt we should have known who he was, and been suitably respectful.

Another swim, and then Philip and Denise came to collect us, at 8.30, to take us down to dinner in the taverna. I remember them not being too keen on the taverna the last time I was here, but it would seem to have improved a bit. David Ioannou, the owner, is obviously quite enterprising. He is now an *exokhikon kentron*,[260] and obviously an attraction for the neighbourhood.

We had a medium-sized fish, called a *sargos* (we think) – a sort of disk-shaped fellow – grilled, which was good. The Sherrards were full of interesting conversation. They know Paddy Leigh Fermor well (as I would expect), whose *Mani* I am reading with great pleasure. Fermor actually stayed at the villa, and is responsible for installing the great millstone in the turret, where we enjoy the sunset, and have dinner.

Dinner never ends much before 11.30 – Mouse rampant to the end; we hardly saw her. Some friends of the Sherrards appeared just at the end, who live the other side of Limni, having retired from South Africa.

And so to bed.

## DAY 7, SATURDAY, SEPTEMBER 3^RD

This morning we rose early (8.00), to walk into Limni, a journey said to take half-an-hour. Actually, with Mouse, it took an hour, though it was a pleasant stroll, and we got there about 9.30. The first problem was to find some breakfast, as we had a longing for *loukoumades*. No sign of them, though some people seemed to think they could be found somewhere else. We settled finally for Nescafé and cake – very good chocolate cake, in fact – and nibbled some bread we had bought. We also got a battery for the torch, a chicken for dinner (600 dr.), some good postcards, of Katounia as well as Limni, and took a taxi back (200 dr.). The post office is closed on Saturdays, so the postcards continue to pile up.

Back for a swim, and then lunch. Then Rhonnda came round for a chat, to fix up about watering the patio (a lot of time is taken up watering the estate - there is an elaborate complex

---

260    That is to say, a 'rustic centre'.

of gardens).[261] We had had a good lunch of roast chicken and ratatouille (since Mouse was invited for a birthday party in the evening, and she thought she wouldn't eat then), and we all felt slightly queasy as a result – just the oil and the sun, probably, but we took pills.

The little friends came round and fed the fish, but then Mouse felt poorly, and by the time the party came round, she was not prepared to go. Carolina seemed to have gone on, so she got to keep the present we had bought that morning! She cheered up rather horribly later, though, when we came down to the taverna for a drink after dinner, and all the little friends came back from the party.

I have arranged with Philip and Denise to go up to the convent to Mass tomorrow at 6.45am, so we need to get to bed!

## DAY 8, SUNDAY, SEPTEMBER 4TH

Up just in time to catch P & D as they passed the gate, and we drove up to the monastery. Preliminaries were going on when we arrived, but we didn't get to the Mass proper till about 8.00. Denise lent me an Orthodox prayer book, which was a great help. The service is a diffuse form of Mass, following the same format – not surprisingly, I suppose. They follow the liturgy of St John Chrysostom, which supplanted that of St. Basil.

The monastery of St. Nicholas goes back to the 8th cent., though the present church is 12th/13th cent. The murals are much defaced, unfortunately, perhaps by the Turks, perhaps not. Previously, there was a temple of Poseidon here, one pillar of which is visible in the nave of the church.

To P & D's disgust, the Bishop was visiting, and gave a rambling sermon, just after communion. After Mass, there was the usual coffee and sweetmeats in the visitors' room, and we greeted the Abbess, but *not* the Bishop.

Philip was interesting about the history of Limni. There was

---

261     In fact, the estate was more or less self-sufficient in vegetables and fruit, and Philip and Denise subsisted on a largely vegetarian diet.

an ancient town here, Elymnion, but nothing has been found of it, except a large 4th/5th cent. basilica, which must have serviced a considerable community. In the 8th cent. or so, a settlement of people from Patmos arrived, fleeing from the Saracens, and they contributed to the place's culture. It was really cut off from the rest of Euboea. There is no road along the coast between the monastery and Chalcis – just cliffs. In more recent times they have made their money from shipping and trading, and most recently from the mining of magnesite, which is still going on, though very unsuccessfully – it has been taken over by the government!

I returned about 10.00, to find Mouse and Mummy up and tidying. We went down for a swim, as usual, before lunch. We are now beginning to get a bit restless, and wondering if we can't arrange an expedition somewhere next week. We are also wondering if we want to go back to Athens in this great heat. It was 102° (35° C) on Saturday – bearable here, but not there. We made some Knorr's *avgolimeno* soup for lunch, which actually came out very well. Had quite a long sleep in the afternoon, having got up so early. Mouse's little friends had paid a last visit before lunch, and then we said goodbye to them, but forgot even to ask them their surname, or address, so Mouse can't write. But perhaps we can ask her brother, who seems to be still here.

I am reading Fermor's *Mani,* Philip Sherrard's *The Wound of Greece,* Browning's *Survey of the Greek Language*, and am on ch. 17 of *Demotic Greek.* I had brought Eyfi's Plotinus book[262] and some Heidegger, but haven't opened them yet.

We had supper at home, out on the turret, while Mouse built a House – this rather to the detriment of the cushions, so we may have to restrict this activity. The fish also will have to be protected from 'catching'. Feeding them bread is OK, though, and they seem to love it. After dinner, we went down to the taverna for a beer, and fixed up a trip for Tuesday, though with misgivings, round the north circuit of Euboea – it would cost

---

262    That is, my friend Eyjolfur Emilsson's *Plotinus on Sense Perception* (Cambridge, 1988), which had recently appeared.

10,000 dr. for the day by taxi, with is IR£50. We may just settle for a ride to Oreoi.


## DAY 9, MONDAY, SEPTEMBER 5TH

*Got up about 8.00. Had a light breakfast of toast, coffee and juice, lit the hot water furnace, and set off to walk to Limni, which we did in just over half-an-hour this time. It was pleasantly cool, and we wandered about the town for a while, going to the Post Office, and then up the town to get a view from the top of the hill, which was lovely. We went down then to our favourite café for a slice of their delicious chocolate cake and some Nescafé. Then back up to a little shop and bought a little vase and some hairbands for Toot.[263] Then to the bus depot, to find out about buses to Oreoi on Tuesday, and the times of buses to Athens on Saturday.*

*Back to the house in a taxi about noon, to find that Rhonnda's dogs had found the chicken carcass in our rubbish, and had dragged it into the hall. The dogs' names are Lucy, Amy (who is our constant companion), and Leila. We had a swim, and then lunch. We didn't take a nap, but Mouse had a long bath, singing heartily away, while John and I read Philip's article, 'A Greek View of Life'. Then I washed my hair and brushed it in the sun to keep away the frizzies. Then John had a short rest and then a bath, after which, after another gap with Mouse practising her hula-hoop (bought in Limni because it is the rage with all the children here), J and R went for another swim, while I washed dishes. At about 6.45 we set off up the hill behind us for a walk, which was quite spectacular, and reminded us very much of the hills around Fallen Leaf. It was really quiet, and the colours were lovely, as the sun was setting across the bay.*

*We went down to the taverna at 8.40 for dinner, and met an English couple to whom we delivered Philip's article and whom we invited for a drink tomorrow before dinner. They are Sara and Phil (didn't get surname!). She used to work with Denise. Mouse was so tired that she sat on our knees all evening. She is missing her little Greek/English friend Carolina, who left yesterday.*


## DAY 10, TUESDAY, SEPTEMBER 6TH

*We were still eating breakfast when we were surprised by the taxi-driver*

---

263     Another name for the Mouse.

*who was to take us to Oreoi (it was only 9 am) —it seems he hadn't got the message from David to come instead at 11.00. So he went off in disgust. We didn't expect to see him again, but he did return at 11.00, and was very pleasant. He had spent six years in Germany, so John and he conversed in German most of the journey. We drove through really lovely country, mostly along the coast, and past some pretty little villages, the two most interesting being Ilia (between Limni and Aidepsos) and Pyrgos (near Oreoi). The road from Limni to Aidepsos is quite new, and is opening up quite remote areas (such as Ilia) to development.*

The journey came ultimately to 2500 dr., not bad for the distance – about 60 km. Oreoi itself, however, is a grotty little seaside resort – most disappointing, since I was hoping for antiquities, it being the ancient Athenian colony of Oreus, which displaced Histiaea (until itself displaced!). But all that is to be seen is a very fine marble bull of the 4th cent. B.C., installed on the seafront. There is an *arkhaiologikos khôros somewhere,* it seems, but it can only be approached in company with the museum director, and the 'museum' (a one-room affair) is closed today. Otherwise, the town is just a seafront, and very little else. Mouse and I bathed, J wouldn't. It was a gritty sand, studded with cigarette butts. A man near us was cruising about with a snorkel, and caught a few *kalamari.*

I went off and found out that a bus left in the Histiaea direction at 2.30, so at 1.45 we moved off to find some lunch. We passed a large group of yacht flotilla people, whose yachts were in the harbour, being lectured to by an Australian. It seems quite fun! We found a little café, which gave us a lunch of beer, peppers, feta and bread (with yoghurt and sugar for the Mouse). The Mouse gave an exhibition of hula-hoop dancing for the two old ladies who ran it, which pleased them greatly.

The bus turned up finally at 3.00, but at Histiaea it stopped. No further buses that day! So we took the same bus back to Loutros Aidepsou, and then had to take an extortionate taxi (actually a rented car – i.e. no meter!) back to Limni for *3000 dr.* We arrived at 4.15 or so, in the midst of the siesta, so had to wait for the shops to open to do some shopping, and had a coffee and cake in our favourite café, the Neon. Then we shopped at Roussos', and came home in a taxi. The taxi-man had heard my 'discussion' with the bandit from Aidepsos, and was dying to hear what I paid him. He was disgusted to hear 3000 dr. "*Klephtês!*",[264] he exclaimed, "The real price is 1600. You were robbed."

Back in Katounia, we went down to the beach as fast as we could for a swim, and reflected that we were really were in the best place, and were now sadder but wiser travellers. On the beach we communed with Rhonnda, and then with John Tavener and Liadain, and invited all to come over for a drink. So a long party began, when Sara and Phil came over at 7.20, and others followed later. Phil is interesting – he is in marketing, and is now going back to school. Tavener is also interesting, and not really as pompous as he seems.

We finally broke up the party at 9.15, and tottered down to the taverna for dinner, where Mouse found little friends (Yiota, Katy), and consequently ate nothing. J had lamb cutlets, I liver – both very good.

### DAY 11, WEDNESDAY, SEPTEMBER 7<sup>TH</sup>

*I was woken about 7.45 by the sound of planes. I went out to the balcony and saw that there was apparently a large fire in the hills behind us. These planes (seven in all) were landing in the bay, where they sucked up water to spray on the fire. We later heard that the fire had started the night before, at 6 or 7 pm. I decided that Mouse and Daddy would be annoyed to miss all the excitement, so I went and got them out of bed. We sat out and had breakfast and watched the planes for a while, and then walked up the road behind us to take a picture of the villa from above.*

*Then we came down and went for a swim. By now quite a lot of cloud was gathering, but we managed to get in our swim before it clouded over. We went back, had lunch, did a bit of washing, and then had a long siesta until about 5.30 – Mouse perched between the two chairs in our bedroom; she was difficult to rouse at 6.15. We went for a walk up Philip's valley, stopping to look at the hens and goat – they had a cock also. We passed a babbling brook with lots of wild flowers and blackberries. Oleander is*

---

264     That is, 'Robber!'.

*plentiful round here, as is plumbago. We called in at Denise and Philip's on the way back, to find that she had called round to our house to invite us for a drink around 8.00. We said we would come back at 8.00, not realising that it was already about ten minutes to 8. When we got to the house, we realised the time and had to go back almost immediately. We had stopped to talk to Rhonnda on the way, so we were further delayed. Before going back, Mouse played a couple of tunes on the violin. On our way back we met Phil and Sara, who were also on their way to Sherrards.*

We had a pleasant drink and gossip on their verandah. Phil had managed to lose *two* keys to their room, but Denise had found one in the car. He was in great embarrassment. There is a festival in Limni at the moment,[265] beginning this evening with the taking of the wonder-working icon of the Virgin in procession from her church in the middle of the town to the chapel of her mother St. Anna half way up the hill, pausing on the way to auction the privilege of carrying the image up to the chapel. Then tomorrow there is a service at the chapel, and then a communal feast – like the feeding of the 5000, free food for all! Originally there was an all-night vigil at the chapel, but no longer. Sara and Phil are going in this evening, but we are all promised a ride in tomorrow morning by Denise, if we can get up by 8.45.

Down then to the taverna for dinner, and to tell David that we won't be needing a room in the taverna for Thursday/ Friday. I spoke to Liadain, and we agreed on half price for the two following days, since the next people are not arriving till Sunday. That is much better. Then we will take the evening (4.00 pm) bus to Athens on Saturday. I will pay her in sterling (£50) when I get home.

I have at last finished off *Mani* and Browning's book on the language. Tsakonian does at least seem to be based on ancient Doric – too many distinctively Laconian features to be accidental. Fermor has apparently built a house in the Mani, which was intended to be inaccessible, but the Greek Minister

---

265    This is the annual *panegyri*, as in so many Greek towns of a certain size. This one interested me particularly because it seemed to be a Christian-ization of the reuniting of Persephone with her mother, the earth-goddess Demeter, which marked the start of the ancient Greek New Year.

of Agriculture built a house just beyond his, and drove a road through to it, so Fermor is exposed, to his great annoyance.

## DAY 12, THURSDAY, SEPTEMBER 8<sup>TH</sup>

We got up early, to join Denise for an expedition to the *Panegyri*. She had actually brought a picnic, to our embarrassment. Philip had decided to come, but, to keep himself honest, *walked* all the way. He went up to the top of the valley, and walked along a forestry road at the top of the ridge – a pleasant two-hour walk in the early morning, when the day is not too hot.

We arrived just as the liturgy was beginning at the little church of St. Anna. The idea is that the Virgin is brought back to her mother on the occasion of her birthday – very much like Persephone being returned to her mother Demeter. I suspect this whole thing as being yet another instance of Christian highjacking of an ancient ceremony! The whole community turns out. There are family groups everywhere, and hucksters hoping to get rid of every kind of assorted junk. Mouse was unfortunately feeling sick when she got up – may have a tummy bug – but gallantly kept going, though vomiting twice, and eating nothing. We queued up – or at least Denise and I did – to light a candle and kiss the icon, and slowly processed into and out of the little church, which was packed. A choir of six stout citizens was belting out the liturgy – unfortunately *amplified,* which was ear-splitting. Philip and Denise say that this is now characteristic of the music of the festival in the evenings, and is hardly bearable.

Philip duly arrived, having lurked on the hillside until the end of the sermon, which he heard just as he was arriving, over the loudspeakers. We then watched the main event, the blessing of the food, and then the mad scramble, led by fierce old grannies and little boys, to partake of it – a tasty stew of goat and noodles, with a hunk of bread to mop it up. Finally, Denise, J and Mouse went down, and came back with plates of pasta – the goat was all gone – but that was good, and we had tomatoes and home-made white wine to go with it. We communed with their former gardener, Yannis (now retired with bad eyesight) and his wife Voula, who were most hospitable. Voula's little grandson had had the tummy bug, and she had medicine left over, so she offered to give it to Mouse, if we couldn't find a *farmakeio* open. So we collected it from her house (in Limni, just behind the Communist taverna), but then found a chemist open, so we can return it to her. We came back around 1.00, and all retired for a siesta.

We slept for about three hours, and when Mouse arose she was much restored, and began to bounce again almost immediately. We went down for an evening swim, and then had an early dinner in the turret – mainly vegetable stew and eggs. After dinner, we all played cards in the sitting-room (it had got quite cloudy and cool outside), both pelmanism and poker, which Mouse is very keen on.

## DAY 13, FRIDAY, SEPTEMBER 9TH

We rose early again today, to walk into Limni and take care of a few messages. Started off after breakfast, at 8.45 – Mouse fully recovered, it seems – and made good progress. When most of the way there, we were given a lift by a friendly old couple, the husband of which had fought against the Germans in Crete. We shopped at Roussos', then walked around some little back streets for a while, and went into the post office to change some money. We changed £50 at 247 dr. to the £, but then realised that each transaction, of whatever size, attracts a fee of 200 dr., so I would have been much better changing everything at once. We have lost 600 dr., really, on this messing. I am keeping £100 in reserve, hoping we may get away with not spending it.

We had our usual coffee and cake, and then got Yannis's taxi back. We got stuck in a traffic jam resulting from the erection of all the booths for the fair, and it cost us 250 dr. We had a swim and then lunch, trying to use up what we have. We tried a siesta afterwards, but we couldn't sleep, so we finally went for a walk up the monastery road for a mile or so, which was pleasant. The coast gets steeper and steeper, until after the monastery there is almost continuous cliff until a little north of Chalcis – nothing marked on the map.

In spite of this, I gather that there is very little wildlife left in Euboea – no boar, no deer, just a few hares and foxes; not even many birds – some finches and tits (a few in the fig tree beside the back verandah as I write), but nothing much else – so that after a while one senses a certain bareness. There are not even many fish left in the sea, as the Euboean Gulf has been grossly over-fished. The Greeks had better look out. This particular corner is kept blooming by a most elaborate system of irrigation in the valley – largely administered by Rhonnda at the moment – all dependent on a little stream which runs all the year round – a great boon!

After the walk, Mouse was exhausted, and actually slept for two hours. Philip and Denise came along at about 8.15, and we had a few drinks before setting off for dinner. J is determined to hear music, with P & D demurring that it will be too loud. We stopped at a little waterside tavern of Philip's acquaintance and had a reasonable dinner – good caper pesto salad, but Philip and I had salted cod in batter (*bakalarios*), which is really just salty fish and chips. Still, we *chose* it.

Then Philip was prevailed upon to drive over to the Communist taverna, where in fact there was a most interesting gipsy band sending out a good solid beat, with weird, oriental singing, and a number of aficionados were dancing. We listened for a while, but Philip wouldn't get out of the car. He didn't approve of the sound level, or the corrupt 'modernity' of the music, so after half-an-hour or so we left.[266] I suppose if one has lived in Greece as long as he has, and has experienced the old ways, these developments would be profoundly depressing, but we were too ignorant to be other than enthralled. Anyhow, we experienced a sample of it.

And so to bed, at a quarter to one.


## DAY 14, SATURDAY, SEPTEMBER 10TH

Up early – Mouse slept well, fortunately – to clean up and have breakfast. Now (9.10 am) sitting on the verandah,

---

266    In truth, Philip didn't like Communists (including the poet Yannis Ritsos), even as he didn't trust electricity.

contemplating the view – the broad sweep of the Euboean Gulf, a solitary fishing boat, someone sitting on the pier, a solitary gull drifting by – otherwise, sea, mountains, pine-trees, and *sunlight;* all marvellously peaceful and serene. We do not at all want to leave – though we could not live here permanently, I think. The sea began calm, but now little waves have arisen for no reason – hardly a breath of wind, though pleasantly cool; perhaps a small earthquake offshore? The fishing boat has just started its engine, breaking the calm. Only then does one realise how *quiet* it is. Before the taverna starts its generator in the evenings, there is a great silence if one walks up the mountain road. The cicadas seem to stop for a while before evening. I think I will go and feed the fish with the remains of our breakfast bread.

Eleni arrived at 10.20 to begin her cleaning, and we departed for a swim, having moved everything out onto the verandah. From the beach, we proceeded to the taverna for lunch, about 12.30, and fell for David's suggestion of *red mullet,* which was good, but resulted in by far our most expensive meal yet – 2900 dr.! Avoid large fish in Greece! I urged him to tell Yiota to write to me when she is settled in Cambridge.

Then back up to the verandah at 2.00, where Eleni was just finishing up, being waited for by Liadain, so we chatted a while. Then Philip and Denise came by to collect us very promptly at 3.30 pm – though I was already getting fussed – and took us to the bus. No fuss on the bus – went first to Chalcis, arriving about 6.00, and then we got another bus to Athens at 6.30, arriving about 8.00. Then a taxi to the *Kerameikos,* where we found most of the tour already assembled, including yobbos, slightly subdued. Out to a 'dinner' at the *Taka-Taka-Mani,* and so to bed.

I thought of calling the Fowdens again, or Denise, or even George Huxley – but we really have nothing to propose, since we only have a few thousand drachmae to live on till tomorrow night.

## DAY 15, SUNDAY, SEPTEMBER 11TH

Up fairly early, breakfasted, and decided to go down on the Metro to the Agora and Plaka. We got out at Thissiou, and found a

Sunday morning flea market in full swing. Just bought a Greek coffee-maker and some more skewers, then wandered into the Agora, to muse about. We went through the Museum in the Stoa of Attalus, very well laid out. I appreciated it all more this time, somehow, thinking of it as Homer and Dorothy's[267] 'life's work'. Now it is a very pleasant archaeological park. As for the Acropolis, I really don't want to return there till they have cleaned it up.

Then out into the Plaka, had coffee and cake at a very expensive café instead of lunch, and then walked up to Syntagma, where we decided to take a trolley-bus to the end of its route, to see where it would go. We took the No. 11, and ended up in the suburb of Vironas (Byron), on the slopes of Mt. Hymettus, where Mouse found a park with swings and slides, so we pottered there for a bit, and came back down to Omonia on the next trolley. Not a bad idea.

### DAY 16, MONDAY, SEPTEMBER 12TH

Back to the hotel, then, and slept till 8.00 am, then bought tickets for the bus, and with our remaining money set off on the Metro, on J's proposal, to Piraeus, to find a cheap restaurant there. In fact we found an excellent proletarian restaurant on the front, very Turkish in influence, where we had, respectively, *stifado* of goat and eggplant, and *stifado* of pork and onions, both excellent. Mouse had chips and yoghurt with burger. All came, with beer, to 1200 dr.

And so back on the Metro to the hotel, where we snoozed till 1.00, and then got on the bus for the airport. We boarded the plane duly at 4.40, reached Dublin on time, and headed by taxi for Drumnigh, arriving exhausted at 7.10, to find David Ellsworth there cheerfully to meet us. The house and garden look good. He did a great job. A most successful expedition, really – as we will appreciate when we recover!

---

267    That is to say, the distinguished Greek archaeologist, Homer Thompson (1906-2000), and his wife, also an archaeologist, whom I had met previously at the Institute of Advanced Studies at Princeton.

# 13: JOURNEY TO FRANCE & ITALY

## AUGUST — SEPTEMBER, 1989

*This was a rather complex expedition, having the ultimate purpose of attending a conference of the Fédération Internationale des Études Classiques (FIEC) in Pisa, at the end of August, but taking in also a number of venues in France, and a holiday home owned by my old friend, the distinguished Classical scholar, John Rist, in Semproniano, in the depths of Southern Tuscany. The middle of August is a crazy time to venture on a holiday in France and Italy, without forward planning of hotels, but that is what we did, and just abovut got away with it, as will be seen.*

### DAY 1, SATURDAY, AUGUST 12TH

We had a leisurely drive down to Rosslare yesterday, leaving about 1.30 pm, and got to Bray for lunch – in a pizza parlour near the station called *Peaches n' Cream,* in a nice little passageway. Very good, but too much. Then to Frank and Olive's[268] to leave off something for Sara-Jane. Then down to inspect the dive at Killoughter.[269] Unfortunately, nothing of much significance has been found – nothing to identify the boat, even. But really, ten days for an underwater excavation is not nearly enough. I'm afraid this is the end of the road.

---

268    Jean's brother, Frank Montgomery, and his wife Olive. Sara-Jane is their daughter.

269    This, as I recall, involved  an attempt to salvage a ship that has been coming from Rome in the early 19th cent. with, among things, Classical treasures from Roman noble houses, in which project our archaeological colleagues in Classics were interested; but nothing much came of it, sadly.

The weather was excellent, and we arrived at our B&B in Kilrane, beside Rosslare, at about 6.45 pm. A very pleasant young English couple (the Whiteheads) have just taken over an old guest-house, and are doing it up. Excellent plasterwork in the drawing-room, and even the dining-room. Then down to the hotel for a drink, but we found it expensive and vulgar (a large wedding was in session), so we then went back to have supper in a pub across the road, which was friendly.

We slept well, and the boat is said to be a bit late, so we rose at about 7.15 am, had an excellent breakfast (rescued the smoked salmon from the fridge, where I had lodged it – we are trying to bring smoked salmon both to the Pillet-Wills and the Violas,[270] which may not work!). Down to the boat, found a long queue, and then found out we were in the *Fishguard* queue, and the *Pembroke* boat was almost ready to leave. It wasn't really very late at all. But we got on all right, and are now (10.40 am) established in the lounge. The weather is still pleasant, pretty calm, and it's bowling along. We should be in Pembroke about 12.30. I am working away on the Italian, but I'm not sure how much is sticking.

Now, at 4.35 pm, we have just crossed the Severn Bridge, out of Wales into England, and stopped at Aust, at a service stop, to let Mouse go to the loo. We forgot at lunch. Our lunch was OK, but I am ashamed of having eaten it, as I swore I would eat no lunch, and then my eye fell on a piece of pork pie, which I had with salad. But I didn't need it. Perhaps I'll skip dinner. I had better clamp down, or the advances of the last few weeks will be nullified in a few days.[271] *And* it was expensive. We always start this way, before we develop a sort of road-wisdom – start

---

270    That is to say, my cousin Elizabeth (née Mathew) and her husband, Jacques, Comte de Pillet-Will, a delightful French nobleman, who, as I recalled, owned the Banque de Picardie, and lived in a rather fine castle, the Château d'Offemont, some way north of Paris, to which we were headed; and my colleague in the CNRS, Coloman Viola, and his wife, who had a holiday home south of Paris, in the Auvergne.

271    This would be a reference to my perennial efforts at dieting.

picnicking instead of Trust House Forte-ing, and avoiding dinner in luxury hotels.

Earlier, we had had hopes of leaving the road at Bath to go down to visit Downside, but now that would seem a recipe for disaster. It has taken three-an-a-half hours (with lunch) to get from Pembroke to the Severn, and we are only half way. It is a long slog from the far end of Wales. We still have hopes, though, that we might be able to drive past Stonehenge.

*10.50:* Now safely on the Le Havre boat. We having got to Portsmouth quite early – about 7.30, in fact. We *did* get to Stonehenge, after a pleasant drive through the countryside, turning off the M4 at Chippenham (Exit 17), and driving through Devises and the Salisbury Plain to Stonehenge. It seemed somehow smaller than one imagined it would be, but when one examines it, it is indeed a massive structure – though only 1500 B.C., as against about 3000 B.C. for Newgrange! There is the same mystery about how the vast stones were transported, but the usual suggestions are made – hundreds of men, and wooden rollers. The alignment with the summer solstice is indeed impressive. There was a ceremonial avenue, up which one doubtless processed on mid-summer's morning – as the hippies would love to do nowadays, if they were let! But no one is now allowed near the monument, as constant tramping was causing deterioration.

We drove past Salisbury, and thought of visiting the Cathedral (which was swathed in scaffolding), but decided we had no time. As it turned out, we would have had, as we were left cooling our heels at the port of Portsmouth at a rather unattractive pub – though we *could* sit out, away from the jukebox. But there seems to be *no* old Portsmouth, despite advertisements to that effect.

We boarded the boat without difficulty, and found our Pullman seats. We actually had a chance to get a cabin, but decided against it. We had something of a snack in the cafeteria, and then settled down to sleep.

The boat got in to Le Havre about 6.00, after a smooth enough crossing, though the captain talked about force 6 wind. J did not sleep very well. I did, after I made my coat into a pillow, and so did Mouse. No chance to have breakfast before we disembarked, so we headed off straight for Rouen, in pleasant early morning sunshine. The roads were very empty, and we got to Rouen about 7.30, and parked beside the Cathedral. Had coffee and croissants (hot chocolate for Mouse) in a little bar across the street, and then headed for what we *thought* was 8.00 Mass. Only later did we realise that we had forgotten to turn the clock on an hour! Anyhow, it was pleasant – the sermon preached very clearly – a smallish congregation. We admired the Cathedral once again (we had been here in 1981, on our way to Agello), and then took a stroll around the environs, admiring the Horloge, and many lovely old buildings – including the hotel we stayed in last time, Hotel de la Cathedral, still going strong, and *not* expensive.[272]

Then we drove out of town, towards Compiègne, not hurrying because we thought we were early. We actually stopped off at an old château, now a museum of Normandy furniture, the Chateau de Martainville, built by a prosperous Rouen merchant, Jacques le Pelletier, sometime in the 15<sup>th</sup> century. It was delightful – and there were also excellent apples in the grounds! Then we realised that we were an hour on, and that we were *late* for lunch! We steamed through Beauvais to Compiègne, and then off the N 31, through ever more rustic side-roads, past the place where the Armistice was signed, to St. Crépin, and then Offemont, where we found the château, standing imposingly over its little village and valley.

We were intercepted half-way up the avenue by a reception committee, consisting, as it turned out, of Nadir Hoceimi, the

---

272     Unfortunately, no diary survives of this expedition.

Shah 's former finance minister,[273] and Theo[274] (who has been here for the past ten days), who led us for lunch to a farmhouse on the estate, St. Croix, where the huntsmen in the winter have their celebration dinners. Here a spread was laid out for a large company straight out of a modern Italian surrealist comedy. I never quite worked out who everyone was, as they mostly vanished very shortly after lunch, but I was seated beside the wife of Nadir, Heidi, who is herself the descendant of former shahs of Iran (before the Pahlevis), and an interesting and lively person.

Lunch continued for a few hours (we *were* rather late for it, but it didn't seem to matter) – couscous salad, macaroni pie, chicken and new potatoes, strawberry fool, lots of excellent red wine. Then we loaded everything into the back of Jacques' car, and it was driven up to the château. Theo and I walked up, and he filled me in on a few things. There is an old riory on the estate just opposite the farmhouse, which Jacques informed me about – originally 15th cent., but added to (17th cent. cloisters), dispossessed in the Revolution – run by an order I hadn't heard of (an offshoot of the Benedictines), built to house a fragment of the True Cross that someone had brought back from a Crusade. He is thinking of cleaning the site up a bit; it is quite overgrown.

The château itself is a splendid pile, again originally 15th cent. – the towers and original donjon – but developed further in the 17th cent. A fine moat, and it is perched on something of a cliff above the valley. After a short siesta, shave and wash, we went for a walk around *some* of the woods with Elizabeth and her dog (a gift from poor Theobald who died).[275] We hoped to see some deer – there are also wild boar – but it was too early in the evening.

---

273    As I recall, Jacques and Elizabeth were quite close to various members of the Iranian aristocracy, who had recently been driven from their homeland by the Ayatollah.

274    Elizabeth's first cousin, and my second cousin, Theo Mathew, at that time the Rouge Dragon Pursuivant in the College of Arms in London.

275    Her brother Theobald Mathew, who had been at school with me in Downside, but had had rather an unfortunate life.

We dressed for dinner – Jacques and Theo resplendent in dinner jackets, cummerbunds, etc. I managed at least a coat and tie, and J her nice outfit. Mouse mocked Theo by saying he looked like a waiter, and he made a variety of faces at her. Theo seems to be restored to favour at the château. We drank some pleasant pink champagne (from a firm which Jacques patronises) before dinner, and then sat down to a pleasant supper of soup, bean soufflé, cheese and raspberry fool, with a good red wine.

The old comte, who is 90 and quite gaga, presided, making impassioned speeches at intervals, and having to be fed by Elizabeth. There is a mad butler called Georges, who thinks he is an opera singer, and is otherwise quite incompetent. After dinner, Jacques was prevailed upon to play his electronic organ, which is a marvellous instrument, and Mouse was allowed to play as well.

And so to bed – Mouse and J in double bed, me in Mouse's room.

## DAY 3, MONDAY, AUGUST 14<sup>TH</sup>

We rose *not* early, and trickled down to breakfast towards 9.30 am. Mouse had kicked Mummy out of bed, and was sleeping soundly with Peter,[276] Mummy spending the night in an eiderdown on the floor. Breakfast was set on the patio, with an assortment of brioches, croissants and jam, but Theo insisted on serving me boiled eggs – which emerged rather *unboiled,* but I ate them. A glorious morning. We were much tempted to stay where we were, but packed up and were on the road by 11.30 – *not* very early, again!

Our first problem was to find petrol, but we did so on the outskirts of Compiègne, and then headed for the A1 into Paris. No great problem with traffic, though fairly thick around Paris itself. We decided (or I did, after consultation with Jacques) that we could see no reason for Coloman Viola's instruction to go via Orléans, and headed down the Autoroute du Sud as far as

---

276    Her favourite doll, called after one of her cousins.

Nemours, where we branched off to Nevers. Again, no trouble with traffic, but the going was slower off the Autoroute.

We had a picnic lunch (provided by Elizabeth) in an *aire*, found Mouse her Magic Markers in a Mammouth, and were within striking distance of Clermont-Ferrand by about 5.30 pm, when we saw a sign for an Autoroute over to the west a bit – Clermont-Ferrand being 105 km. further on. We decided to head for this, and found we were driving about 30 km across country to link up with the Autoroute from Montluçon, which was not on the map I had, but was the real reason why Coloman recommended Orléans – when I read his instructions more carefully, I found that he had specified that.

Anyhow, we got there, found more petrol, and phoned up his local café to say we would be arriving about 8.00, but would eat first, so not to keep dinner for us. It in fact took us another hour and a half to get to Brioude, at about 8.30, and we cruised around there, trying to find somewhere to eat, but there was nowhere suitable, so we set off in the direction of La Chaise-Dieu, hoping to find an auberge.

In fact we were almost at Cistrières, over half-an-hour later, when we saw a notice for an auberge at St. Didier-sur-Donlon, just off the road. It was in fact very pleasant, and we had a nice steak and chips and escalope de veau (I think ) and chips, while Mouse had chips, and played at a futbol machine, which other teenagers were using. This cost 114 fr in all, which is more than we should have spent, but still... Then a short further drive to Cistrières, where, to our confusion, we found Coloman and his children at the turn of the road waiting for us (How long for? We didn't ask!), and a supper laid out on the kitchen table. The farmhouse is still in process of reconstruction, but quite delightful.

*We saw an owl and a red squirrel on the way. The Violas are very hospitable. They waited till we arrived (9.45!) to have a 'colazione' with us – wild raspberries and myrtle-berries from the forest, cheese, bread and salad, with beer, which Coloman said would help us to sleep (as if we needed it!). His house is delightful, and he is renovating it himself (or was, until he tore a cartilage in his knee two weeks ago). He discovered a stone on the outside in the shape of a head, very reminiscent of a Celtic one. We have photographed it, and will show it to P. Hab.[277]*

*Rita (Coleman's wife) is very brave to have us, as she has been very ill, but has been treating herself with natural foods and seems to be winning the battle. The children, Bernard (14) and Marie-Genevieve (10) have taken to Ruth, and she is having a wonderful time.*

## DAY 4, TUESDAY, AUGUST 15TH (FEAST OF THE ASSUMPTION)

We rose late-ish, and, after a leisurely breakfast of bread and honey, yoghurt, and coffee, we went off to mass with Coleman to the Abbey Church of Chaise-Dieu (Rita and the children went locally in Cistrières). The mass was very well attended, so we were standing outside the inner area. Afterwards, we viewed the Danse Macabre fresco, and the fine tapestries of the life of Christ, as well as the carving of the choir stalls. A remarkable Gothic church (11th cent.), it seems more massive than it is because the roof is quite low. An important foundation in the history of European monasticism, it was founded by Robert de Turlande in the Benedictine tradition. Dissolved at the Revolution, but recently revived – after La Chaise-Dieu had been picked by the Hungarian pianist Cziffra to be the site of a music festival! Coleman is very proud of this, being Hungarian himself! – by the Canons of St. John (a conservative outfit set up after Vatican II!).

Then back for an excellent lunch of cutlets and potato salad, after which Coleman proposed a tour of interesting churches in the vicinity. Since he has wrecked his knee, Jean drove, and we had a most interesting tour, first to Auzon, where there is a delightful old 12th cent. church with good frescoes, recently rediscovered. The whole town is delightful, walled, with narrow streets on a hill. Then on to the corresponding nunnery to La Chaise-Dieu, also founded by (St.) Robert, at Lavaudieu. The nunnery is long since abandoned, but is now a museum, and fine frescoes have once again been recently rediscovered and restored – very Byzantine,

---

277     That is, my old friend Peter Harbison, a noted Celtic archaeologist.

really, not least a Christ looking down in triumph from the nave (*not* the narthex). Also a fine early head of Christ (original now in the Louvre, and the body in the Metropolitan Museum in New York – where the notice states proudly that several miracles have been attributed to it, which seems unlikely!).

Mouse had fun all afternoon, cycling and playing games with little friends, including the son of a neighbouring couple, Nicki and Domenique – the mother (Nicki) being English.

We got back some time after 7.00, and after supper decided to go to a concert of sacred music back at Chaise-Dieu, Mouse and all. We didn't think that organ music would be that interesting, but in fact it was splendid – a great organ, well played, Bach, Mozart, Vivaldi and an unknown (to us) French composer – and a good soprano. Mouse lasted through it well, and even drew a picture of a crucifix.

And so to bed, after a beer or so back at the farm, at 11.30.

## DAY 5, WEDNESDAY, AUGUST 16$^{TH}$

We had planned to move on today, but were persuaded to stay on for another day – and indeed we are in no hurry at all. I can't really see why we chose to go *eight* days before the house was ready! It only takes three days at the most to get to Italy from Le Havre – two and a bit, really,

*I got up early (7.15) and found Rita in the kitchen, and we went off for a glorious walk in the woods. We chatted all the way (she in French, I in English) until we got somewhat lost. After many wrong turns, we managed at last to find a track that took us back to the meadow where we started. On the way, we found lots of wild raspberries, strawberries and myrtle-berries. The silence was wonderful, and the smell of pines so refreshing.*

I arose much later, and we had a leisurely breakfast with Coloman, eating too much as usual. Then we all (adults) went into La Chaise-Dieu to shop, and bought two chickens for dinner and two bottles of wine. Also a curious 'comb' for picking currants, which we hope will work! We tried to visit the Echo Room (for hearing the confessions of lepers! You could sit in one corner, and hear a whisper in the other corner), but it was closed.

Back to the house for lunch, before which Coloman introduced me to the wonders of his Mackintosh SE, and Word 3, and Macromaker. He is by way of being a bit of a computer nerd, and it was hard to get him away from it even for lunch, but it is certainly fascinating what one can do with the editorial capacities of Macromaker – doing the publisher's work for him, though, for which he then still collects the money. I prefer to let the publisher *publish;* I'll do the writing.

After lunch, we took the children for a swim at a *plan d'eau* about half-an-hour away – an artificial lake, rather like Lake Anza,[278] and about as dirty! We all swam except J, and played with a ball and a rubber mattress. A storm seemed to be brewing, but the weather remained good till we got back, around 6.00. Bernard and Marie-Geneviève are good to Mouse, though she is bumptious. They seem to like her.

The storm broke about half-an-hour after we got home, and proved very persistent. Coloman turned off the lights, and we sat watching and discussing the storm. A bolt of lightning actually crashed just outside the house, so close that I felt a tingling in my hand. Rita is mortally afraid of thunderstorms, so she was quite uncomfortable. Eventually it settled down just to rain, but that went on most of the night. We had a good dinner of smoked Auvergne ham – lovingly sliced by Coloman, who was reminded of real Hungarian ham – and local cheese.

Coloman is really in a sad state, what with the Communists, and the Socialists, and the Jews, and the atheists. He feels embattled. He doesn't at all trust poor Mr. Gorbachev, but feels he is plotting an even harsher tyranny, having flushed out his enemies, and fooled the Western world! I suppose having suffered under Stalinist tyranny, he is not inclined to trust the good intentions of any Communist leader, but it makes life difficult.

We thought of playing RISK with Bernard, but in the end just went to bed. When I came down later to go to the bathroom, Coloman and Rita were still sitting on the couch, plotting, they

---

278    An artificial lake in Tilden Park, just above Berkeley, where we lived in California.

said, how to get us to stay another day! But we really must move on, though we're certainly not in any hurry.

## DAY 6, THURSDAY, AUGUAT 17<sup>TH</sup>

The day dawned wet and very foggy, the land reacting to the previous night's rain. Despite protests, we packed up, and, after another leisurely breakfast, left finally at 10.10 am, amid urgings to use the house on the way back if we wished. In fact, we met Nicki and her husband in the village, and said we might well be back on Sept. 4<sup>th</sup> or so. It would in fact work out quite well.

We set off *via* La Chaise-Dieu to St. Étienne, in a drizzle. We had thoughts of heading to Le Puy, to see it, but there was no sense in the weather there was, and we wanted to make some time. We got onto the Autoroute at St. Étienne in the direction of Lyon, but broke off at Vienne to get across country, heading for the Mont Blanc Tunnel (Coloman pointed out that it was much shorter than going along the coast).

We looked into Le Tour du Pin, to see if the Marquis had a château there,[279] but no luck. We found a château, but it belonged to someone else, and they didn't think there was a château of the Marquis. I explained that it was all a rather long time ago. I must finish reading my ancestor's memoirs. It might throw some light on things.

Then we dropped off at Annécy, to see if we could find Mouse a shop at which to spend her money, but no luck. We weren't prepared to drive into the centre of town, since we'd been there before, and it was getting late.

In fact, we reached the tunnel about 6.00 with no great delay, and got through it in ten minutes (costing about £11 – 10,000 fr.). No trouble with customs or passports, but we got into a very tedious procession to the freeway in Aosta. We made

---

279    The Marquise de la Tour du Pin, who wrote her memoirs in the early part of the 19<sup>th</sup> cent., was Henrietta Lucy Dillon, of the family of the Viscounts Dillon, to whom we used to think we were related. In fact, though, we now know that we are descended rather from the Earls of Roscommon.

various efforts to find a hotel, but had absolutely no luck. The Ferragosto in Italy is a time of maximum mobility.

*We took a turn off the highway into the mountains of Aosta, and found ourselves (to my horror) in a street so narrow that I couldn't make a left turn – I was afraid of barrelling into a house on the bend, and had to hand over the driving to John. Ruth and I got out of the car, while John manoeuvred a bit, and got the car going down another precipitous bit of road. Not a hotel in sight, so we got out of there as fast as we could. We reached a town called Ivrea, and found a nice little trattoria (we spent £25), and the owner was very kind when I explained that we needed a bed for the night. He telephoned around and found us a nice clean 2-Star hotel, called the Hotel Fontina. We had a good bath and a comfortable night, with the occasional interruptions of a barking dog, quacking geese, and at dawn a cock crowing. We couldn't see sight nor sign of them in the morning. In the morning, we observed their swimming pool green with algae, and were not tempted!*

### DAY 7, FRIDAY, AUGUST 18<sup>TH</sup>

The room cost us 65,000 lira (and extra 15,000 for Mouse) – not so bad, but a bit suspicious that we got no receipt! I learn that receipts for both hotels and restaurants are *compulsory* in Italy for some odd reason – one could be pounced upon and asked for one at any moment! Anyhow, the proprietor directed us to a bank at a place called Viverone, and we headed out in that direction, without breakfast. We found both the bank (changed £150) and a nice café for breakfast in Viverone, which is on a lovely lake, and is plainly rather a select resort. We viewed the lake, but saw no pedalos for rent, so we headed out on the autoroute for Alessandria.

We stayed on the autostrada first until Genova, through coastal mountains, and then on to La Spezia, through endless tunnels. I had forgotten how much of one's time one spends on the coastal highway *under* the mountains instead of over them. It is a marvellous feat of engineering, but one sees only glimpses of the scenery. And of course it *costs*. The toll to La Spezia was 20,700 lire.

La Spezia was rather grim – a big town, and a naval base,

but somebody had recommended Cinque Terre as a very pleasant area to visit, so we headed there (north of the town) by a spectacular coast road. However, it was a disaster! The place was absolutely awash with turkeys – primarily Italian, in fact.[280] The first little town we came to (all are nestled in breaks in the cliffs – no real beaches) actually said *Parking Completo*. We couldn't believe this, but it was so. Cars were parked all the way up the cliff road, and what the scene was when one reached the town one never found out, because we managed to turn round before that.

We headed back to a nice hotel perched on the cliff (*completo* – otherwise we could have stayed there), and had a picnic lunch in the pine woods near it, making use of the Violas' bread, cheese, ham and fruit. The Cinque Terre is famous for wine, but we didn't get a chance to sample it. We bought a beer from the hotel.

This theme of *completo* was to haunt us for the rest of the day. Our hope of finding an early hotel was fatuously optimistic on a Friday in late August. The seaside resorts we saw were unbelievable (e.g. Massa Maritima – or Marina di Massa). The beach was wall to wall umbrellas – people pullulating everywhere – more cars pouring in all the time, coming from their towering apartment-blocks in their little Fiats, with a boat or bicycle on top, to this incredible crowding on the beach.

But at least they were booked in somewhere, even if they were sitting in traffic jams miles long. *We* were not! After an excursion to a little town on a hill above Sarzana (near La Spezia), Castelnuovo Magra, which was pleasant, but hopeless from the point of view of accommodation, we headed, on the advice of a man in the Agipmotel at Sarzana (who laughed at the idea of our getting a room in his hotel, or *any* Agipmotel) for Livorno, as offering some hope.

Livorno was *awful*. We drove into the centre of town, which *should* be mediaeval/ Renaissance, but was flattened in the War

---

280    This a rather arrogant remark, I'm afraid. *We* were the turkeys, after all!

(by the Americans? They don't say!), found parking (paying), and walked around, but became more and more depressed by the company hanging round the streets. Fortunately, such hotels as there were were *completi,* so we drove out thankfully, to find an enormous queue of cars and RVs driving in, for what reason we could not imagine, unless they were coming home!

We got first to Cecina, where we decided to have some dinner, and stopped at a little bar, where we had a good lasagne. J tried the same appeal for a hotel to the proprietor as we had tried last night, but he was a grumpy old fellow, and not forthcoming. So there was nothing for it but to drive up the inland road towards Volterra, and find a place to sleep in the car.

This we did opposite the little town of Riparbella, in the driveway of what *seemed* to be an installation of the phone company. We rang the bell, as there was a car and a light there, but got no answer, so we first pulled in beside an outhouse. We took sleeping pills, lodged Mouse on the back seat, and settled down as best we could. Mouse slept the sleep of the just, snoring lustily, but we had a pretty bad time, pills notwithstanding. J found a rat in the middle of the night trying to climb in her window. A few mosquitos got in, but didn't do much damage. Frogs and crickets clamoured. At about 1.00 am, another car drove up, alarming us, but either it didn't see us or it ignored us. We got a bit of a sleep between about 2.00 and 6.00 am, and then woke blearily to face the day.

## DAY 8, SATURDAY, AUGUST 19<sup>TH</sup>

That was an experience one would not want to repeat too often, though Mouse survived in great shape. We shook ourselves, and took stock of our surroundings. The moon was still up, but it was light. We were in someone's farmyard – washing on the line, vines, vegetables. We drove out as fast as we could, in the direction of Volterra, where we arrived about 8.00, after an impressive climb up its mountain. It is an old Etruscan town (Velathri), then Roman, then mediaeval, and so on. A good time to arrive, the early morning. We had an excellent coffee and doughnuts in a little café off the Piazza del Duomo, and then went exploring. I bought a *Corriere della Sera,* which gave the news that Solidarity appears to be in effect forming a government in Poland, despite their declared reservations.

We visited the Duomo, then walked to the Parc Archaeologico, which covers the old citadel, where excavations took place back in the '20s (the Castillo is now a prison, so one can't visit that!), the Etruscan Museum, which has an excellent collection of funerary caskets. It is remarkable how the Etruscans took to Greek mythical themes to put on their funerary monuments – many scenes from the *Iliad, Odyssey,* and heroic cycle, and other myths, such as Perseus, and Meleager's Boar Hunt. A mysterious people!

The Mouse provided a counterpoint to all this by looking for junk in souvenir shops, which we managed to steer her off. It is in fact wall-to-wall boutiques, souvenir shops, and eating places, which is not surprising, I suppose. We left finally just as it was filling up, having got the best of the day in Volterra.

We headed off then for Siena, but on the way J saw a sign for San Gimignano, and this stirred our curiosity. No road to it is marked on the map, but there was a perfectly good road nonetheless, so we followed it, and arrived at our second remarkable town of the day. San Gimignano is noted for its *towers,* the mad result of a power struggle between the town's chief families, who aligned themselves with the Guelphs and the Ghibellines respectively, and built ever higher towers round the town to outdo each other. Finally, the town council declared that *it* would build the highest tower, and no tower might be higher than that. Thirteen of these absurdities still survive, and the town is otherwise charming and unspoiled. Not in fact as crowded as Volterra when we left it.

We had a beer in the main piazza, and then decided to move on to our destination, bypassing Siena for today. We made good progress, and reached a hotel on the Siena-Grosseto road for lunch and a wash. J and I had a good risotto, and Mouse had chips. Then on to Paganico, Arcidosso, and Semproniano. A long drive from Paganico, in fact, but through very pleasant rolling hills, with one little town after another perched on them, and finally got to Semproniano, also perched on its hill, shortly after 5.30. Some little difficulty finding the turn to the unmade road, but not serious, and there was John Rist[281] waiting for us at the top of the driveway. Pian Rocchetto is a charming old farmhouse on top of a hill, facing across to Semproniano itself, surrounded by oaks, and with fine views in all directions. The road up to it is *very* rough, and we might leave the car half way up most of the time.

John took us for a tour of the village, and to the bathing place, showing us all the best places to shop. It is very fortunate that we arrived in time to be introduced, as there are many details and hints that would have taken long to work out. His account of the history of the place is fascinating. Until 1945, the country between here and Siena was essentially in the hands of three families, the Piccolomini being one, and the Orsini and the Aldobrandeschi the others, and after 1945 the Communists proposed to the peasants that they just take possession of the land, so they did – the De Gasperi government did not venture to oppose this – and the countryside has faithfully voted Communist ever since.

We bought provisions, and came back to the house. There is a town festival tomorrow, which we are just in time for, and must attend. We had an aperitif of Cynar, an artichoke liqueur – not bad, in fact – and then went out to dinner at the local *albergo,* which was very pleasant. We had a first course of asparagus-flavoured pasta, and then pork. All very good. Local wine. The proprietor entertained us to a liqueur afterwards. John and

---

281     John Michael Rist (born 1936) is a British scholar of ancient philosophy, classics, and early Christian philosophy and theology, known mainly for his contributions to the history of metaphysics and ethics. He is the author of monographs on Plato, Aristotle, the Stoics, Epicurus, Plotinus, the dating of the Gospels, and Augustine. Rist is Professor of Classics Emeritus at the University of Toronto and part-time Visiting Professor at the Institutum Patristicum Augustinianum in Rome. During his lengthy academic career he has also been Regius Professor of Classics at the University of Aberdeen (1983–1996), and the Lady David Visiting Professor in Philosophy at the Hebrew University of Jerusalem (1995). I got to know him first back in 1970s, when he was at Toronto.

I split the bill, which wasn't bad – about 85,000 lire for the five of us. John continued to regale us with the gossip of the village. The present owners of the *albergo* were very low on the town totem-pole. Their daughter married a fellow from Naples when only fifteen, but now serves in the restaurant – indeed, she served us. All in all, a pleasant evening.

## DAY 9, SUNDAY, AUGUST 20<sup>TH</sup>

We all piled into the main bedroom, and slept very well. John and Tom[282] got up in good time, and left punctually just before 9.00. The day started with a heat haze, and was plainly going to be hot. We forgot to buy coffee, so breakfast consisted of hot chocolate and rolls, and then we went down to the village, about 10.00, to explore, and to attend the 11.00 Mass and Procession. We walked right up to the citadel, or Rocca, through the old town, which is quite charming – tiny little streets and passage-ways, thoroughly mediaeval. We noted a concert to be offered this evening, up at the Rocca, and decided to buy three tickets for it, at a store which was open. Then back to Mass, which was only moderately well attended, by Irish standards, even on the town feast-day. After Mass, the portrait of the Virgin was brought out, and the band led a solemn procession through the town. At this point we retired to the *latteria* for a coffee.

Then we decided to explore the bathing place in the river, before lunch. We avoided John's tough place, and took the path lower down, where we found a number of cars already parked. A tough drive for the car even so, and a tough walk down, but we made it, and it was very pleasant. Just a small pool in the river, but deep enough to submerge in, and great fun for Mouse. She actually floated as well as swam. She also met another little girl, who had been stung on the bottom by a horsefly or something, and whom J rescued with our cream for bites. Some Italians were down there, and some Germans, but it was not too crowded.

---

282    I can no longer remember who Tom was, but I presume that he was John's son.

Back then for lunch, and a bit of a siesta. Then we took a walk in the vicinity, finding wild flowers and blackberries, and after that a fine concert by Mouse on the verandah. After dinner (of excellent roast chicken), we went down to the concert at 9.30 (though it began late), at the citadel, in the open air. It was a beautiful setting, and the menu was Haydn, Mozart, Poulenc and von Weber – for a trio of flute, piano and cello, or duo of flute and piano. Two different girls, both excellent, played the flute, and the whole thing was delightful. We were not back till 11.30 or so, when we were kept awake further by a dementedly barking dog. It sounded as if the owner came out and kicked it every quarter of an hour, since it yelped at those intervals between frenzied barking – a mystery! But we got to sleep eventually. Mouse was really very good at the concert – and of course at her own concert as well!

### DAY 10, MONDAY, AUGUST 21ST

J was up early, doing washing. There is no washing machine, nor even any iron, which is most inconvenient. We may buy our own iron, and donate it to the household. After breakfast, Mouse and I went down to the village while J washed her hair, to shop and get money. We found a market in progress, and I bought a grill for a cook-out, for 10,000 lire, and Mouse a beach ball for 3,500 – in both cases no doubt swindled! Then we changed £150 at the bank, and bought some provisions.

Then back to the house, and we headed off to Albinia, on the coast, to check it out. After about one-and-a-quarter hour's drive (as described by John), first through hills and then through the Maremma (very hot), we got there. We stopped in town, and J got film, and then decided to buy an iron, and donate it to the household. (Only later did we realise that she must have left the camera in one shop or another there. We must now go back for it.) We found a pleasant beach for bathing, fringed by pine trees, with beach umbrellas apparently available. There was quite a breeze, though, and it was very salty, so I didn't find it so pleasant as the river – but very warm, so Mouse and J had a very good time. We broke for lunch at about 1.30, and went to a pleasant restaurant across the road – but it was *expensive*. We only had spaghetti (chips for Mouse), beer, and an excellent dessert (tiramisu for me, chocolate pudding for J), but it came to 50,000 lire (6000 *coperta*, and 15% tip added – a bad shock!)

We swam again after lunch. I am now starting Vasari's *Lives of the Artists* – a delightful book – in the Penguin edition. He has an interestingly Platonist view of art. We drove back without incident to Semproniano. It looked like there might be a storm, but it didn't materialise. We had another excellent concert from Mouse. Good risotto for dinner, eaten outdoors at the table, and we retired early to bed. The barking dog seems to have largely subsided.


## DAY 11, TUESDAY, AUGUST 22ND

We rose rather early. It was very pleasant in the early morning. J repaired my shorts, and took up legs of new trousers. Mouse slept on till after 9.00. I am preparing for the conference by reading over Charles Kahn's and Margherita Isnardi Parente's papers,[283] writing some introductory comments. I also read over the official bumf of the conference, and saw that we really should have booked the hotel from the 23rd, since things start at 9.00 on the 24th, with a reception on the 23rd. Stupid! We'll have to leave very early on the 24th, and hope not to miss too much. Also, I am in the middle of various books – my usual situation – and will finish *none* of them; but they are stimulating: Cobban's *History of France*, Vol.

---

283    I was chairing the section in which they would be delivering them. Charles H. Kahn was a distinguished authority on ancient philosophy, who passed his career as Professor of Philosophy in the University of Pennsylvania; Margherita Isnardi Parente (1928-2008), of the Università di Roma 'La Sapienza', was also a major authority on ancient philosophy, particularly on Plato and the Old Academy. Back in the mid-1970s, Charles had engaged me to complete the translation on Proclus' *Commentary on the Parmenides* begun by Glenn Morrow, who had died; it was ultimately published in 1987.

III; *Napoleon and Hitler* (for the Sunday Indo.)[284]; Vasari; Nadine Gordimer, *Something Out There* – excellent!

Down to the village to buy stamps and post postcards, then to do some shopping at the *alimentari* at the top of the main street Then down to the bathing place at the river. We had a good bathe. One Italian pair who had been there on Sunday were there again, with their dog, Axel. We walked up river and found the Rists' preferred bathing holes. Rather better, but not easily reachable from our path down.

Then back to a lunch of cold chicken sandwiches, after which a siesta. Then, about 4.30, we decided that a small expedition was in order, and went off to Santa Fiora, in the foothills of Mt. Amiata. This was a charming town, and we explored it for a while. We saw some Della Robbia terracottas in the Pieve – very fine. Lots of lovely little old streets – the usual! A wonder of Tuscany, indeed, is the plethora of small, obscure towns, after one has run through all the obvious landmarks, which are remarkable and delightful. A thunderstorm began on Mt. Amiata as we left, and accompanied us half-way back to Semproniano, but then faded out.

Back home, we decided to have a cook-out, since I had bought a grill at the market on Monday, and some charcoal today. Mouse collected wood, and we made a fire with very little charcoal, and cooked hamburgers, which were rather smoky and not very crisp on the outside, but still good. Perhaps a little more charcoal next time! Then a few games of poker and snap, before going to bed.


DAY 12, WEDNESDAY, AUGUST 23RD

We realised yesterday, finally, at Santa Fiora that J had left the camera in the shop at Albinia. Nothing for it but to mount a rescue expedition there, so J packed a picnic lunch, and we set off quite early. We arrived in Albinia about 10.00, went to the camera shop, and, happily, the lady in the shop recognised J

---

284    I was doing fairly regular book reviews for the *Sunday Independent* at this time.

immediately and produced the camera and film, with profuse apologies for not having caught her in time. We were much cheered by this, since a fruitless expedition would have been very depressing. We drove on past our bathing place, to visit Porto Santo Stefano on the Monte Argentario peninsula. A pleasantly situated town – beautiful panorama of coastline – but *very* crowded. So back to our bathing beach, which we found a bit crowded also. Not lunch-time yet, but we found an umbrella to borrow, and Mouse rushed to the sea, accompanied first by me, then by J. We still find it unpleasant after the river, but Mouse enjoys everything. Then the man who owned the umbrella arrived – a very nice fellow – we apologised, and went off to a picnic lunch on the back of the car – the pine forest just one big jax and garbage dump; such a pity! Mouse disgraced herself by not eating her sandwich, so *no* tiramisu at the restaurant nearby – probably just as well, as they would have charged us an arm and a leg again!

Then we drove off home, but decided on the way to look at another of John Rist's recommendations, the little town of Sovana, not far from Saturnia. To do that, we continued on a bit further on the road to Orvieto, to Pitigliano, which is a beautiful and fascinating town, worth exploring as well. The country all around is riddled with caves, since the rock is soft tufa, and there are lots of Etruscan tombs around Sovana. The town is just a long main street, really, leading down to the Duomo, a very fine Romanesque building – a most unusual structure for a small Italian town, but it may be because it is on a ridge. There is a nice old Lombardic altar also in the Church of S. Maria in the main square. It was too hot to start visiting Etruscan tombs, so we had a beer and coffee, and Mouse an ice-cream, and Mouse found a gaming machine, which was a much greater attraction than the Duomo.

We got home about 5.00, and Mouse and I went for a swim in the river, though there was a thunderstorm rumbling about (like yesterday, over Mt. Amiata). It never arrived, though, and we had a very pleasant swim (no one else there), and then back to a dinner of eggs and delicious potato and onion casserole which J had prepared. We played some cards in the evening, and packed for Pisa.

## DAY 12, THURSDAY, AUGUST 24TH

We started off reasonably punctually, at 8.30am. Took an hour to reach Paganico, as expected, then rather slow traffic to Siena (lots of trucks as well as cars), but it only took half-an-hour or so. The freeway to Florence was only another half-hour – but then we missed the turn to Pisa (A 11), and headed off for Bologna. We corrected our mistake after about ten miles or so, and got back on the Pisa road, after which it was only another 40 minutes or so.

We arrived at the conference, at the Palazzo dei Congressi, around noon, just as the reception was ending – but there were still lots of lovely hors d'oeuvres and lots of wine, so we started with a bang. We met George Huxley and Gerry Watson[285] on their way to lunch, and I also met Geoffrey Kirk,[286] whom I'd first met when he visited Berkeley in 1968, as Sather Professor of Classics. I was then only a graduate student, but he was always hospitable in later years, when I chanced to visit Cambridge.

We checked in, and they paid without delay all my travel money – very prompt and efficient! It looks like an excellently organised event. We met David Traill[287] and had coffee and a sandwich with him, and then drove down to Tirrenia to check into our hotel.

---

285    George Huxley (1932-2022) was a distinguished British Classicist, who was a great lover of Ireland, and taught at this time in Queen's University, Belfast. Gerard Watson (1934-1998) was Professor of Classics in Maynooth, and a noted authority on Greek Philosophy.

286    Geoffrey Stephen Kirk, DSC, FBA (1921-2003) was a British classicist who served as the 35th Regius Professor of Greek at the University of Cambridge. He published widely on pre-Socratic philosophy and Homer, culminating in a six-volume philological commentary on the *Iliad* published between 1985 and 1993.

287    David had been a fellow graduate student with me in Berkeley, back in the late 1960s, who subsequently went to teach in the University of California at Davis.

The Hotel Grand Continental is on the seafront of Tirrenia and very splendid, though its surroundings are somewhat tatty, and the beach is *not* an attractive prospect – a forest of umbrellas! But it has an excellent Olympic swimming pool, which is not at all crowded, and the Mouse headed for that straight away. I had a swim as well, and then drove back to Pisa to hear the afternoon session.

*We were all invited to an evening reception at the Giardino Scotto, where a tremendous spread (a Tuscan Feast) was put on for the Congress. There were endless courses: soups (2), pasta, ravioli and lasagne (of which Ruth ate three helpings!) and another choice of two things for the next course, one being a fish course, I think, but I'd had so much of the first courses that I couldn't eat any more. It was all really delicious, but a bit of a bear-garden. We gossiped to Tom and Lilo Rosenmeyer,[288] Martin Ostwald,[289] Fred Brenk,[290] Ruth Scodel[291] and others, but were exhausted by about 10.15, when we drove Tom and Lilo part of the way back to their hotel. It's hard to believe they're both almost 70.*

Before that, however, I went up to the afternoon session of the conference. It was presided over by Geoffrey Kirk (that is, the Mondo Greco section), and consisted of talks by Francisco Adrados and Ruth Scodel. Adrados gave a rather ridiculous talk, which was a survey of the position of the poet in archaic and classical Greek society, with copious references to his own works, after which there was absolutely nothing to be said, and

---

288    My former (senior) colleague from Berkeley, and his wife.

289    Martin Ostwald (1922 – 2010) was a German-American classical scholar, who taught until 1992 at Swarthmore College and the University of Pennsylvania. His main field of study was the political structures of Ancient Greece. I would have met him when he visited Berkeley in the 1970s.

290    Frederick Brenk, S.J., an American Classical scholar based in Rome, was a stalwart of the International Plutarch Society, and an old friend.

291    Ruth Scodel is an American Classics scholar, and the D.R. Shackleton-Bailey Collegiate Professor of Greek and Latin at the University of Michigan. She specialises in ancient Greek literature, with particular interests in Homer, Hesiod and Greek Tragedy. She graduated from Berkeley in Classics in 1973, so had been a student of mine in my earlier years.

nothing *was* said. Ruth (who must be about the most junior participant – a great honour for her), spoke on Greek funerary inscriptions as an art form, not entirely convincingly, but in a stimulating way, and *that* provoked discussion. Old Adrados was quite miffed, I think, but it serves him right. After the talk, I went up to Ruth to congratulate her, and it seemed to me she greeted me very coolly, but I think it is just her odd manner, because she chatted very affably at the Tuscan feast.

*Ruth swam in the pool all afternoon. I made friends with a Welsh woman named Wendy whose daughter Francesca was very nice to Ruth, and swam with her, Wendy and I had a gin and tonic at the bar at 5.30 pm, and the odd cigarette.*


## DAY 13, FRIDAY, AUGUST 25TH

I rose early-ish, but then decided not to take the 8.30 am bus to the Palazzo. Had an excellent breakfast, and then repaired to the swimming pool, where I read Margherita I-P's enlarged text. It really is a most useful paper, though it may be difficult to find commentators for it. I went up around noon to meet my *relatori* for lunch. Found Charles Kahn, but M. I-P escaped us until 1.00, when she appeared with a lunch ticket already bought. We had none, so I proposed we all meet for a drink after the evening session, and Charles and I drove back to Tirrenia, where we had lunch and a swim. The hotel buffet lunch is actually very good. We discussed many Platonic matters, and then drove back to the Palazzo.

A good pair of papers by Walter Burkert[292] (whom we had

---

292    Walter Burkert (1931 – 2015) was a German scholar of Greek Mythology and cult. A professor of classics at the University of Zurich, Switzerland, he taught in the UK and the US. He has influenced generations of students of religion since the 1960s, combining in the modern way the findings of archaeology and epigraphy with the work of poets, historians, and philosophers. He published books on the balance between lore and science among the followers of Pythagoras, and more extensively on ritual and archaic cult survival, on the ritual killing at the heart of religion, on mystery religions, and on the reception in the Hellenic world of Near Eastern and Persian culture, which sets Greek religion in its wider Aegean and Near Eastern context.

chatted with earlier), on 'Religion in the Archaic Polis', and Jasper Griffin[293] – most amusing, though Tom Rosenmeyer was rather disdainful – on bucolic and epic, or the bucolic *in* epic. I greeted him and Miriam afterwards. She is quite pleased, in the end of it, with Declan Lyons. Then I had a talk with my speakers – agreed on strategy, urged them to distribute copies of the papers to anyone interested. M I-P is a funny, rather anxious little woman, but plainly very competent. Back then to the hotel, and decided to dine in, since we thought we were on half-board. We found out that we are only bed and breakfast, but then felt stuck. The waiters were rather haughty, and the food rather mediocre, but we got out in time to catch the bus to the concert. This was a Brahms recital in the Campo Santo, the old burial ground beside the Piazza del Duomo. It was a beautiful setting.

*We viewed the partially restored frescoes (bombed during the War) in the interval. Mouse was very tired, and fell asleep during the second half. The bus was due to leave at 11.30, so we had a few minutes to have a beer and a coffee at a little bar before boarding – we also offered the driver a drink, and he had a coffee. He was inscrutable at first, and then became quite chatty. Ruth made friends with one of the Congress assistants called Katy – a lovely blonde girl – and she invited Ruth to meet her next morning at the conference centre.*


## DAY 14, SATURDAY, AUGUST 26TH

*We had a large, leisurely breakfast, and then went to do a tour of the old city. We saw the Leaning Tower, the Duomo and the Baptistry, where we were treated to a demonstration of the acoustics. One of the guides asked for silence, and then sang a series of notes. It sounded absolutely wonderful. I think we were very privileged, because when I mentioned this to Lilo Rosenmeyer, she*

---

293     Jasper Griffin (1937 – 2019) was a British classicist and academic. He was Public Orator  and Professor of Classical Literature in the University of Oxford from 1992 until 2004. His wife Miriam was also a distinguished classical scholar. She must have been tutoring a former Classics student of ours from Trinity.

*said they had not had this treat. We were all rather tired (it was very hot, so we didn't feel like doing any more. We drove back to the conference centre for a coffee and a bun (our lunch), where Ruth sought out, and found, Katy. She had a lovely time helping her to staple together some papers.*

I missed a session on the Greek polis, chaired by Emily Vermeule, but I can't say it was of vast interest to me. Back to the hotel for a swim, where we found Lilo Rosenmeyer, who had come all the way down on the bus to visit, and had fortunately been able to get into the pool. We had a beer, and I left her with J and R, and drove off to preside over my section. I tried to follow a more *direct* route to the Palazzo, derived from a superficial study of Charles Kahn's map, and ended up *in the airport*. I thought I would be in total disgrace, but about    five minutes later I found myself on the bridge across the Arno, just opposite the Palazzo, so I actually got there just in time. The session was well attended (not enough handouts!), and went off well, I think, though everyone spoke a little too long. There were questions after both talks. MIP especially alarmed me, as she started speaking very volubly *to* her paper, and after 50 minutes or so had only reached p. 6. I had visions of being there till 8.30 or beyond, still trying tactfully to shut her up. But she ended more or less on the hour, and we broke up just after 7.00. I didn't follow a word she said, nor, I suspect, did most non-Italian speakers, but I presumed that it resembled the typed text, so I spoke to that. I met Matthias Baltes[294] at the talk, and agreed to meet for lunch tomorrow in Lucca. After the talk, I had a beer with Fred Brenk – and Richard Talbert,[295]

---

294    Matthias Baltes (1940-2003) was Professor of Classical Philology in the University of Münster, and an old friend.

295    Richard John Alexander Talbert (b. 1947) is a British-American contemporary ancient historian and classicist on the faculty of the University of North Carolina at Chapel Hill, where he is William Rand Kenan, Jr., Professor of Ancient History and Classics. Talbert is a leading scholar of ancient geography and the idea of space in the ancient Mediterranean world. Before heading for the U.S., Richard had been on the faculty of Queen's University, Belfast, where I had got to know him.

who is looking very well and authoritative. He is here to launch his large Classical Atlas project, among other things. He is obviously flourishing in America.

Then back to the hotel, and we went out to find a place to eat. The first place I had my eye on – out in the pine woods – was full, but a little place on the Arno had room, and was pleasant – though it ended up costing us 68,000 lire for the three of us, despite the fact that we really only had the equivalent of one meal. Dining out is *not* cheap, we fear. Good seafood, though – J had large grilled shrimps, I had a frittata of octopus and small shrimps.

## DAY 15, SUNDAY, AUGUST 27<sup>TH</sup>

Today we decided to take a trip to Lucca for the middle of the day, since the whole conference was off on excursions. It is only about half-an-hour from Tirrenia on the freeway, in fact. It is a delightful town – not large, not too touristical, surrounded by its walls, and very quiet on a Sunday morning. We parked in the Piazza Napoleon (so called because Napoleon gave the town to his sister), and walked up to the Duomo (which is very fine, with a richly decorated portico, and, inside, the Volto Santo, a miraculous statue of Christ), and then through ancient streets to the Amphitheatre (late 1<sup>st</sup>. cent A.D.), *via* the Palace of the Guinigi, who were lords of this place. The Amfiteatro is actually built on the site of the Roman amphitheatre, but is very charming. Then back, *via* the church of San Michele (fine façade, but too big for the present church!), to the Duomo, to meet the Balteses, at 1.00. We found them strolling through the town, and they announced that they had *had* lunch, but came with us as we had a pizza and beer back near the amfiteatro, since the little café in the amfiteatro had just closed. We had a pleasant chat – Matthias is just recovering from throat cancer, but seems well enough, and cheerful. He has a pleasant wife, and teenage daughter, and is making good progress with Dörrie's great work – Vol. II just about to appear.

After lunch we left them to wander, since they had seen nothing yet, and headed back to the car, via a museum which was closed, and drove back to Tirrenia in time for a swim. I was so addled that I dived in at the deep end with my glasses on, and then couldn't find them when I got out, until Mouse saw them at the bottom of the pool, and I had to dive down to get them.

We had had an arrangement to go out to dinner with the Rosenmeyers if they got back in time, but they didn't in fact get back till 9.00 pm (which was just as well, since *we* were rather tired), so we just went across the street and had a tourist menu at a little place, which wasn't bad. Just after we ordered, the Spoerris asked us to join them in their restaurant, but it was too late. He's a pleasant fellow, working on Proclus' *Opuscula*.

After dinner we walked up to a fun fair, where Mouse had fun on the bumping cars, at a horse race machine, and on a caterpillar. Then home to bed.

### DAY 16, MONDAY, AUGUST 28^TH

We had decided to leave today, to get back to our farmhouse, and were confirmed in this by the weather, which has turned quite stormy (there had been quite a bit of rain here yesterday, which we missed – just a sprinkle in Lucca). Sunny today, but a high wind. We packed up, packed a lunch from the copious breakfast, paid the bill (only extras, but still 137,000 lire!), and set off for the Palazzo, to say goodbye to people, and to hear Tom Rosenmeyer's paper on Apollonius. That turned out excellently sophisticated and ingenious, as I would expect, and then we had coffee with Gerry Watson, and then Tom himself (I had taken photographs of him in full flight, at Lilo's request). He is a bit tired, though generally in good form. I greeted Gian Biaggio Conti before we left, and also Robert Renehan, who looked very cheerful.

The conference was pleasant, though I'm not sure how much value I got out of it. At least I performed my duties, so I don't think I short-changed them too badly. They certainly treated us very well and efficiently. They are much subsidized, it seems, by big banks and other firms, who are required by the government to direct a certain proportion of their profits in the direction of culture. An excellent idea, which we should adopt in Ireland!

We drove as far as Siena for lunch, which we had in the car, parked at a sports stadium below the Church of San Domenico. The weather had been rainy most of the way down, but cleared up for our arrival. We saw the Balteses standing by San Domenico, but just waved to them this time, as we didn't want to be delayed.

We plunged down tiny streets into a ravine, and up again to the Duomo. Siena is an extraordinary town, situated on three spurs, with deep valleys in between, and all covered with a maze of little streets. We just got to the Cathedral before the storm broke again, so we had lots of time to appreciate it – and it certainly is a place of many marvels. Mouse even had time to count the 171 popes round the top of the nave! The chief splendours are the façade (by Giovanni Pisano), the floors, the pulpit (by his dad, Nicola Pisano), and the Piccolomini Library, with frescoes by Pinturicchio and his pupils, celebrating the life of Aeneas Silvius Piccolomini (Pope Pius II). As one enters, the first figure that greets one in the pavement is *Hermes Trismegistus,* which greatly impressed me (Socrates, Crates (!),[296] and others are to be found further up).

We had to sit in the Cathedral for almost an hour, while the thunder rumbled and rain pelted down, and when it finally slackened off and we emerged, it was *autumn* – a distinct nip in the air, and leaves blowing off the trees. We hurried back to the car, ignoring the rest of Siena (a pity, but...), and started for home, stopping only at a co-op in Pagania for some shopping. It was almost 8.00 when we got to Semproniano, so we decided to try the pizzeria for a pizza. It is actually a very pleasant restaurant, run by a young couple, and worth going back to – not *cheap,* though, certainly, but what is?

The Mouse is not too well – bothered by an outbreak of boils, owing to a surfeit of chocolate, etc. She thought that chocolate taken on holiday *wouldn't count.* Alas, it does! J is determined to phone Martin O'Flynn[297] tomorrow for the right medicine.

---

296    The 4th cent. B.C. founder of the Cynic school of philosophers – a very strange figure to find in a cathedral – as, indeed, is Hermers Trismegistus!

297    Our family doctor, back in Portmarnock.

## DAY 17, TUESDAY, AUGUST 29<sup>TH</sup>

Down to the village for the great project of phoning home to the doctor. At the post office, they sent us to the Communist bar Sport, as the place to phone from. This proved to be the case, and after many attempts, and then the help of the operator, J got through, found Martin at his desk, and got the prescription. It only cost about 7000 lire in the event. Then down to the *farmacia,* to see if the stuff existed in Semproniano. It turned out not to be available in Italy, so the pleasant middle-aged proprietress chose something *equivalent* – which we hope is! We walked home and administered the first dose. Poor Mouse is very brave and optimistic.

After lunch, we decided on a small expedition to find pine-nuts, but were having no luck along the road to Santa Fiore, when we came to a notice we had seen before, saying *Parco Faunistico,* and J felt we must explore this. At the end of a long dirt road, we found the Parco, which only opened earlier this month, and is still mostly a gleam in somebody's eye, I think, but is claimed to contain deer and mouflon sheep and suchlike – and eventually, it would seem, wolves and bears! But of course in the middle of the afternoon, without binoculars, not a whole lot of any fauna was to be seen. Still, it was a pleasant walk, and we found a little farm which is being developed as a centre, which had ducks and geese and turkeys and horses, so we viewed those. On the way back to the main gate, we saw a series of waterholes where the fauna *might* come in the evenings, if they were desperate, so it might be worth being in the vicinity towards dusk. Anyhow, it was a pleasant idea, rather like Tilden or another of the California parks.

Back home, then, and had pork chops on the grill, which is working well with twigs and just a minimum of charcoal. The weather is still comparatively cool.

## DAY 18, WEDNESDAY, AUGUST 30<sup>TH</sup>

The conference will just be breaking up today. I feel slightly bad about deserting it, but various people were certainly leaving early. We got off to a slow start, deliberately. Mouse slept late. J has taken to making bread, very successfully, since the local bread is really pretty dire. It involves leaving it on the front seat of the car to *rise*. Nothing else will do, so the car must be brought up to the house. It must rise for an hour, and then for another while, divided into buns. Waiting for breakfast is now a new pretext for inaction.

Sometime after noon, we set out for Grosseto, just to check it out, and to the ruins (Etruscan-Roman) of Roselle (Rusellae) near it. It was a *long* drive through the mountains, *via* Scansano (calling into Saturnia, which is a nice little town, but not remarkable, though not without archaeological remains), and on the whole hardly worth it. We had a picnic on the way, in somebody's field, where there were splendid blackberries, and reached Rusellae about 4.00. It is an interesting site, but anything visible is almost entirely Roman – forum, amphitheatre, the main roads of the town. No visible temples. Some remains of Etruscan houses below the forum. It is still being worked on. There is no indication on the site of what may have been found.

We drove into Grosseto for a coffee. It is a quite unremarkable town, having been heavily bombed in the War, it seems. It still has its walls, but not much inside them. Lots of gypsies wandering about. We drove home, rather disgruntled, *via* Paganico.

We played cards in the evening . Mouse is getting quite good at poker and blackjack.


DAY 19, THURSDAY AUGUST 31ST

We did not do much today. Only down for a swim in the afternoon, where we found the river much reduced, despite Monday's rain. The pool was hardly worth getting into. Rather surprising and disappointing.

In the midday, we had walked round the village, and then down to a grove of pine-trees, which we hoped were public, and were, and harvested over a pound of pine-nuts, which we are going to bring home.

Hamburgers on the grill for dinner, and then down to town for a coffee.


## DAY 20, FRIDAY, SEPTEMBER 1ST

Today we decided to make a little tour to Pitigliano, Sorano and Sovana (again), since I thought I might write an article about them, as representatives of the hidden Tuscany.[298] Pitigliano has a very spectacular situation, and is a lovely town to stroll around, though it has no specific monument worth seeing, except perhaps the Castello of the Orsini (who controlled the town). We drove on from there to Sorano – similarly spectacular on its crag – where we had a picnic lunch in a little park outside the old town. However, rain, which had been threatening, began to fall at the end of lunch, and by the time we set out to view the town it was definitely *raining*. Three under one umbrella will not go, so we gave up, and drove off to Sovana for a coffee, thinking the café in the piazza had an awning. It didn't, and there wasn't much room. Also, we couldn't visit any Etruscan tombs – last time it was too hot, now it was too wet. We looked round the little museum, but really there is nothing in it except photographs and plans of the tombs – no contents.

So home in the rain, and the rain continued for the rest of the night. J cooked an excellent risotto, and we played cards for the evening. Mouse learned whist!


## DAY 21, SATURDAY, SEPTEMBER 2ND

The rain continued all night, and right through the day, until about 3.00, when it sort of gave up in exhaustion. Plainly, the weather has broken, and we are as well to get out of here. Finally, we decided to take a drive in the direction of Manciano, on the pretext of getting some petrol, but really to see if we could find the sun. In fact, we found both, in some measure. It is not a bad little town. We had an excellent coffee and tiramisu, and drove back via the *Terme* ('Baths') at Saturnia, where we looked in on

---

298    This project came to nothing, I'm afraid.

the hotel – a very splendid place, but the sulphurous waters smell foul.

Back amid threatening clouds, but the rain held off, and even allowed snatches of sun. We did some packing, and then went off at 8.00 pm to the new restaurant, *Il Molino* – leaving in the keys to the Bianchis on the way, The dinner was excellent. We didn't ask for the tourist menu, but the whole thing came to 40,000 lire in the end. I had *spaghetti al forno,* which contained ham and pine-nuts; J had *gnocchi al cinghiale* (wild boar!), which was rich but excellent. Then J had *scaloppini alla marsala,* and I had the same *alla milanese* – both excellent – coffee, and a grappa for me on the house. The German family reappeared, and this time Mouse was much more forthcoming, and they got on fine. Just a pity they all didn't meet the first time we went to the river to bathe, for example!

## DAY 21, SUNDAY, SEPTEMBER 3<sup>RD</sup>

*Got up at 7 am to start packing. I had cleaned the kitchen the day before. Mouse slept on while I dismantled our bed. John made coffee, etc. I finally roused her with the tape recorder at about 8.15 am. We left the house at about 8.50, turning off the water as we went, and putting some bottles in the bottle bank – every village has one now!*

Along the road to Arcidosso, we were stopped by the Carabinieri, who were obviously just curious. They assured us we had done nothing wrong (though we had passed them, as they were going at about 20 mph), but they examined our papers, and grooved over the licence plate. Perhaps distracted by that, we took the wrong turn to Arcidosso, and headed for Siena, over the mountains to the Rome-Siena road – good views, though, and not *much* out of our way. We passed Siena, Florence, Pisa, etc. without incident, and into the fantastic succession of tunnels that is the coastal *autostrada.*

Around Genoa, we ran into a ferocious storm (having had lunch earlier at an Autogrill – rather overpriced for Mouse's hamburger: 7500 lire!), and this continued to the

French border. Many cars were abandoned on the road, but the Honda soldiered through. One tunnel had actually become a river.

We crossed the border at 5.00 pm without trouble – glad we hadn't gone through the tunnel – and turned off what we *thought* was the Grasse exit – actually, the exit to Digne, considerably before it – and found a pleasant 2-star hotel, Servitel, which takes cards, and had a room for 380 fr. – rather a lot, but it boasted a bath, and a *swimming pool*. Mouse and I got in directly, though rain was threatening.

After settling in, we declined to take on the restaurant's 120 fr. menu, which was its cheapest offering, and drove up the road till we found a little village called Plan de Var (we are in the valley of the Var), surrounded by cliffs, in which there was a Snack-Grill, where we had each an omelette and an excellent dessert (myself a *marron glacé*, J a chocolate mousse); the Mouse had a crêpe.

The Mouse met a lady, who was dining by herself, and invited her over to give her a little frond from her dessert. They got talking, and then *we* got talking, and then invited her back to the hotel for a nightcap. She was great value – name of Stephanie Soper – her husband and herself run a franchise for staging conferences, and a group of chalets here, which she is administering till the end of the season. She says it hasn't been good for the Riviera, because of the excellence of the summer at home. Otherwise, she was full of chat of all sorts.

We tried to phone the Cusacks,[299] but the phone just gives a weird sound. We phoned Denis O'Brien at the château, but no reply.

DAY 23, MONDAY, SEPTEMBER 4TH

We have been waking up for the last week or so more or less punctually at 3.30 – the result, I suspect, of constant coffee and wine (though I haven't reacted to it as badly as I feared in other ways). This morning was no different, though we got to sleep again fairly promptly.

---

299    For the Cusacks, see p. 215 above.

Breakfast was served in our room at 8.00, but then J. felt a pain, and this got worse, and she became very ill. This continued through the morning, so we couldn't leave. We signed on for another day, and waited to see if a doctor would be needed. I drove up and got some money in a bank in a little town up the road (cashed the last £100 stg. – just got 995 fr., which is not great). Mouse had a swim, and then Mouse and I set off to see if we could make contact with the Cusacks – still no luck on the phone. I had to go back to the autoroute, and get out at a later exit, and it still took nearly an hour to get to Grasse, and some further time to get to Spéracedes. We actually found them at lunch – Roy just having a siesta before going back to work, Jackie and her mother, and daughter Kira and grandson Pierre just finishing lunch. We were welcomed warmly, and sat down to lunch.

Roy appeared and excused himself, and we stayed and chatted to Jackie and her mother for a few hours. Mouse got on well with Kira this time. Kira plays the clarinet, and actually marched up the Champs Elysées with the Provence delegation in the Bicentennial Parade! The autobiography of Ralph Cusack is apparently in train, and may be available by Christmas. Jackie had trouble with her printers, who went bust, but she bought her own press now. She was hoping for a preface by Sam Beckett, but he excused himself as being too old and blind. She intends a deluxe edition for £30, and a general edition of about 1000 for under £10.

We drove back in a nightmare of traffic and storm, Mouse in the front helping with the tolls on the autoroute, I fearing that we might never find the hotel again, but we did so without difficulty, and found J much better. Mouse and I had a swim, and she came out to read. For dinner we went out, first to a MacDonalds, which fortunately hadn't opened yet, and then to Relais Bleu, which had a good 65 fr. menu, with an excellent *crudités* board.

I called Alan Pugh at Denis' château, and learned that Denis would be glad to receive us, so our itinerary is now fixed. I phoned ahead to Cistrières to M. Mollin to warn Nicki Vigier.

## DAY 24, TUESDAY, SEPTEMBER 5<sup>TH</sup>

We packed up this morning efficiently, and set off about 9.20 am for Aix, having paid the bill of 1043 fr. – not *too* bad for two days at a 2-star hotel – 380 fr a night.

*I felt better, after lots of pills. The drive up to Chaise-Dieu, starting at Aubenas, was rather tedious, though spectacular. We drove up roads through narrow gorges which had no passing lanes to get rid of the awful lorries. We arrived at Chaise-Dieu at about 5.00 pm, where we bought milk and a couple of groceries. Then on to Nicki at Cistrières. They were waiting for us, and were going out to dinner later, so it was just as well we weren't delayed. Nicki and the children (Jonathan and Sara) accompanied us to the Violas' house, and showed us the ropes. She recommended a restaurant for our dinner a few miles up the road. Before we left, we lit a large fire in the stove with some wood we found in a shed.*

*We found the restaurant in a tiny, charming village, La Chapelle Geneste, and the restaurant was called L'Oustaou (a Provençal name, we believe!). Its speciality, recommended by Nicki, was a kind of potato cake called a crique. They were delicious. We then all ordered a spaghetti (me: carbonade, John: fruits de mer, Ruth: plain). They brought a large bowl of spaghetti, our sauces separately. Delicious! The family were lovely. The father greeted us first, looking like an explorer of the Gold Rush days – long beard, khaki trousers, with large pockets at the sides, and boots. The mother was a gentle little soul, the daughter who served us was very jolly, and delighted to try out her English. She insisted that we not pay for Ruth's spaghetti. She was in front of the fire, weaving pot-holders with old sheets, and let Ruth do one. We were admiring some lovely bird prints, which it turned out were by Nicki's husband, Dominique. We bought two.*

## DAY 25, WEDNESDAY, SEPTEMBER 6<sup>TH</sup>

We spent a reasonably comfortable night, and got under way about 9.30 am, having sent Mouse ahead to the Vigiers to play for a bit. Then we called in and greeted Nicki, who was up (Dominique was not), and we commented on the excellence of the bird paintings, so she showed us round his whole collection, which is remarkable. He is excellent, but quite un-commercial, and nobody seems to want bird paintings, so he sells no originals, and very few prints. Some day he must be discovered, as the Audubon of the Auvergne! We got him to sign the two prints from his bed, and moved on.

We hit the autoroute at about Issoire, and kept on to Montluçon or so, where it gave out for 50 km (it is to open next year!), and picked up again around Brioude, and then went on on this till between Orléans and Chartres, where we turned off to Chartres.

We had a snack of quiches (and a *croque monsieur* for Mouse) in a little town on the way to Chartres. Made good progress – not too many bee lollies[300] – and arrived in Courtomer shortly before 6.00 pm, as pre-arranged. I phoned Denis from the public phone in the village, and he drove down to meet us, and lead us back to the château. His little dog Futy was in the car, and while he and I went to the supermarket to buy some whiskey, Mouse approached the car to greet Futy, but he barked ferociously (of course!), and then when Denis tried to introduce them, he snapped at her. So Mouse was in hysterics, and the visit started unfortunately.

However, things were smoothed over when we got to La Perriere, where Alan Pugh was there to greet us with an excellent dinner of spinach quiche (with spinach sauce), salmon, and peaches and cream. I had hoped to take them out to dinner in Courtomer, so this embarrassed us. But I donated two of our bottles of Chianti, one of which we drank with cheese.

Before dinner, we had sat on the front steps, drinking excellent pop, and watching the sun go down. They are much persecuted by moles in the lawn, as is Jacques (there is a considerable symmetry about our holiday in this respect). A mole man has been coming for the last number of weeks, and has caught *86* of the little buggers, which he presents to them in bags. We sat out under a large chestnut tree until well after 10.00 pm, and then Mouse and J went to bed, so we went into the study and had a good Scotch malt and looked at some antique books, including a first edition of Plotinus. And so to bed, around midnight.

The château is actually very impressive. It is said to have belonged originally to Napoleon's personal doctor, whose last

---

300    The Mousey version of 'big lorries'.

descendant only died (here) ten years ago, after which it was bought by a retired naval officer, who sold it to Denis. There is lots of room – three floors and an attic. They keep rabbits, ducks and geese – no hens. Alan seems to live here now all the time, and gives English and piano lessons in Courtomer.

## DAY 26, THURSDAY, SEPTEMBER 7<sup>TH</sup>

We rose around 9.00, to find Alan up since 6.00 or so, having fed the geese and the rabbits and so on, and now getting breakfast. Denis rises late. What Alan finds to do all day is not clear, though when he has lessons to give that takes up the day, I suppose. Denis joined us for breakfast, initially in dressing-gown, but then dressed, and we tried to take some photographs. Their camera wouldn't work, as the battery was dead, and we had no film, so we drove into Courtomer to buy both. We took pictures of everything, including Mouse being given a ride on the tractor-trailer, and then headed off, on Denis's recommendation, in the direction of Sées, around 11.30.

Sées is indeed a pleasant little town, with a very fine 13th cent. cathedral, and we had a modest lunch there – a 39fr. menu, washed down by cider. Then up by degrees through Normandy to Rouen, where I sat in the car by the Cathedral, while Mouse and Mummy went off to find some baby-present for Helen's projected baby – really an excuse to go round the lovely shops around the Cathedral once again. Eventually they returned, and we headed off for Le Havre.

We arrived in good time, and found a snack in a rather grotty little restaurant on a large boulevard, and then joined the queue early to board the boat, which we did about 9.00 pm. This time we had a (tiny) cabin, so we got some sleep, with J on the floor, and Mouse in the upper bunk.

## DAY 27, FRIDAY, SEPTEMBER 8<sup>TH</sup>

*Here the diary ends, but we presumably passed uneventfully across Britain, back onto the Pembroke-Rosslare boat, and so home.*

# AFTERWORD

As one looks back at these various adventures, touristical or scholarly, from around forty years ago, one is moved to a certain degree of nostalgia – so many of these venues will have altered very much for the worse, and many are the victims of the sort of hyper-tourism that we discuss and deplore in the volume, edited by Prof. Lise Zovko of Zagreb and myself, on the philosophy of tourism, mentioned at the outset.

Our travels did not, it must be said, by any means end here, and another volume or two may follow, if there proves to be any interest in this. In later years, we added such venues as Moscow, Novosibirsk, Prague, Hvar and Zagreb (in Croatia), Sydney (and New South Wales generally), Tokyo and Beijing to the list, as well as visits to Morocco and South Africa. A feature of the later 1990s and 2000s, also, was a series of cruises along the coast of Turkey, and to many Greek islands, with an outfit called Westminster Tours, who have unfortunately since gone out of business, but offered delightful service while they were around. The only part of the world I regret never getting to, despite a number of opportunities declined, is South America – conferences in Buenos Aires and Brazilia chickened out of – and I very much doubt that we will get there now.

We have never quite got all the way round the world, to prove that it is round, but we have got round most of it, and are now largely content to stay where we are, on the Hill of Howth, and watch the rest of the world tramp past our front gate. Of all the places that we have spent time in – apart from Berkeley, and the Bay Area of California, which remains one of our favourite parts of the world – I think that our most cherished

311

venue would be Katounia, which I am glad to say has changed much less than most of Greece; Limni and Northern Euboea not, happily, being much of a tourist attraction. In general, however, this collection of diaries constitutes something of an elegy for more moderate times, such as we will not see again, unless the current succession of climate emergencies succeed in bringing the citizens of the 'developed world' to a more realistic state of mind.

- *FIN* -

KATOUNIA
PRESS